FUNNY BLIND STORIES

PERCEIVING THE HUMOR WHILE LOSING MY SIGHT

FUNNY BLIND STORIES

PERCEIVING THE HUMOR WHILE LOSING MY SIGHT

RAYMOND WHITEHEAD

© 2025 by Raymond Whitehead
All Rights Reserved
No part of this book may be reproduced in any form or by any electronic or mechanical means including information storage and retrieval systems without permission in writing from the publisher, except by a reviewer who may quote brief passages in a review.

Sunstone books may be purchased for educational, business, or sales promotional use. For information please write: Special Markets Department, Sunstone Press, P.O. Box 2321, Santa Fe, New Mexico 87504-2321.
Printed on acid-free paper
∞
eBook: 978-1-61139-740-6

LIBRARY OF CONGRESS CATALOGING IN PUBLICATION DATA
(ON FILE)

WWW.SUNSTONEPRESS.COM
SUNSTONE PRESS / POST OFFICE BOX 2321 / SANTA FE, NM 87504-2321 /USA
(505) 988-4418

I dedicate this book to the LORD Jesus Christ, to my mother, Barbara Basso, to my wife Jovanna and to my children Anthony, Elizabeth and Joshua.

To the LORD Jesus Christ because without Him I can do nothing but, through Him I am able to do all things.

To my mother because she gave me birth and kept me alive even when the doctors told her to give up. She supported me, encouraged me and gave me the tenacity to try, even when things looked impossible.

To my wife Jovanna who taught me how to be soft and gentle because I was hard and rough. Though I was able to smile and laugh, she taught me that it was not shameful to be sad or to cry because the greatest man in the world was able to do all of the above and His Father was well pleased with Him. Through her I have learned to communicate my feelings in a constructive way and to resolve issues so that we have been able to remain best friends as well as lovers.

To my children because they love to hear stories about my life and it is my hope that they can learn from them.

CONTENTS

Introduction ~ 13

1. Summer in the City ~ 15
2. Don't Eat Those ~ 17
3. Where Did It Go? ~ 19
4. The Diagnosis ~ 22
5. Tic, Toc, Crash, Bang, Boom! ~ 26
6. Salt and Pepper Please ~ 28
7. Beep, Beep, Five Degrees Left ~ 30
8. We Are Going to Die ~ 32
9. What Acting Career? ~ 34
10. All You Can Eat ~ 36
11. That Was Disgusting ~ 39
12. Up In Smoke ~ 42
13. Cliff Hanger ~ 44
14. Six Wheeled Bike ~ 48
15. Common Sense ~ 50
16. Science Project ~ 52
17. What Can You See? ~ 54
18. The Mayfair ~ 56
19. Feel This ~ 58
20. Gymnastics by Strobe Light ~ 60
21. Can I Get a Lift? ~ 62
22. Twilight Zone ~ 64
23. Look What I Caught ~ 67
24. You're Where? ~ 70
25. Safe! ~ 73

26. Tackled by a Bee ~ 75
27. You Eat Too Much ~ 78
28. Forest Fire ~ 81
29. Take Her Off My Hands Please ~ 83
30. Honkeys ~ 85
31. Over the Top ~ 87
32. I Cannot Bear This ~ 90
33. Where Are My Pants? ~ 92
34. Dueling Blind Men ~ 94
35. Have a Nice Trip ~ 96
36. Queer Cue ~ 98
37. Catch Her ~ 99
38. Watch Out for the Pitch ~ 101
39. Sticky Situation ~ 103
40. I Don't Want to Get a Shot ~ 105
41. Volleyball or Basketball? ~ 107
42. Manhole Cover ~ 109
43. Pain In the Neck ~ 111
44. Whoops, I Did Not Mean to Grab That ~ 113
45. Follow Me ~ 115
46. Can You Dig It? ~ 117
47. Wrong Accent ~ 119
48. No Time for Swimming ~ 121
49. Scared Straight ~ 124
50. Learning the Hard Way ~ 126
51. Bank Robber? ~ 129
52. Bumper Pool Champion ~ 131
53. Catch This ~ 134
54. What A View ~ 136
55. How Many Times Do I Have to Save You? ~ 138
56. Animals Communicate ~ 142
57. Professor Whitehead ~ 145
58. Watch Out, Coming Through ~ 147
59. I See, You Hear ~ 150
60. Look Both Ways ~ 153
61. Diplomacy ~ 155
62. Richard Goes on Vacation ~ 157
63. Unicorns ~ 159

64. Do Cats Have ESP? ~ 161
65. What Color Were They? ~163
66. Motorcycle Crash Number Two ~ 165
67. Bill and the Praying Mantis ~ 168
68. Bill and the Locust ~ 171
69. A Little Tipsy ~ 173
70. What Color is This? ~ 176
71. Stop Looking at My Girlfriend ~ 178
72. Will There Be Animals in Heaven? ~ 180
73. Who Was Driving? ~ 182
74. Water Fight ~ 184
75. Just Weight ~ 186
76. Did You Lose Something? ~ 189
77. The Blind Leading the Blind ~ 191
78. Fatal Attraction ~ 193
79. Pennsylvania State Fair ~ 196
80. Lights Out ~ 198
81. The Blind Leading the Blind, Again? ~ 201
82. Organization ~ 204
83. Oh No You Don't! ~ 206
84. Stand Back ~ 208
85. Usher ~ 210
86. How to Make People Cold ~ 212
87. To McDonald's, and Fast ~ 215
88. Take My Money, Please! ~ 217
89. Your License Please ~ 220
90. The Surveyor ~ 223
91. Confounding the Mime ~ 225
92. Who's Blind, Anyway? ~ 227
93. Heart Attack ~ 229
94. Everybody Limbo ~ 231
95. Speak Up, I Can't See You! ~ 233
96. The Wolf Spider ~ 235
97. Taxi Please ~ 238
98. Sheer Stupidity ~ 240
99. The Body Slide ~ 244
100. Totally Tubular ~247
101. T Bar ~ 249

102. Raymond the Junior Whitehead ~ 251
103. Guard Rail ~ 253
104. Against the Law ~ 256
105. Late for Lifting ~ 258
106. How Jovanna and I Met ~ 260
107. This Is My Sweetheart ~ 265
108. That Rings a Bell ~ 267
109. Some Friends! ~ 269
110. Nice Teeth ~ 271
111. Do the FDA and DOA Care? ~ 273
112. So You Would See Me ~ 276
113. Wrong Shoulder! ~ 278
114. Elizabeth's Birth ~ 281
115. That'll Learn Ya Dern Ya ~ 286
116. Joshua's Birth ~ 288
117. Five Loaves and Two Fish ~ 292
118. Is Anyone Awake? ~ 296
119. Blind As a Bat ~ 299
120. When Let Go Does Not Mean, "Let Go!" ~ 301
121. Be That Way ~ 304
122. Catch Me If You Can ~ 307
123. That Last Step Was a Doozy ~ 309
124. Sorry Is Not Enough ~ 312
125. Flushing the Manual ~ 314
126. To See or Not to See, That Is the Question ~ 316
127. Does Prayer Really Work? ~ 321
128. Whoops, That's Not My Daughter ~ 325
129. My Most Embarrassing Moment ~ 327
130. Go to Hell and Fry ~ 329
131. I Lost Jesus ~ 331
132. Who Was That Other Woman? ~ 333
133. A Wing or a Thigh? ~ 335
134. The Blind Burglar ~ 337
135. Looking for a Hand Out ~ 341
136. Why Isn't He Driving? ~ 343
137. Blow Me Down ~ 346
138. She Is Not There ~ 348
139. What is That Stick Anyway? ~ 350

140. Pay Attention, I Am Blind! ~ 353
141. The Blind Leading the Blind ~ 356
142. Are These Your Bullets, Sir? ~ 359
143. Flipped Out ~ 364
144. Surprise! ~ 367
145. Daddy's Little Gardener ~ 370
146. In Conclusion ~ 373

INTRODUCTION

I wrote this book for several reasons. The first of which is the fact that my children love to hear stories about me. Whenever we are around other people and are in story mode, my children will ask me to tell the people one of the stories.

It all started because since before each of my children was born, I have been writing stories for them. Every once in a while, I will go through the stories I have written for them and listen to the ones that I cannot remember by the title. Most of the stories have to do with the lessons I have learned through them and how much I love them.

Another reason is to help those who can see to better understand the things that happen to the visually impaired. As I have written in at least one of these stories, most people do not understand that there is a lot of variation between 20/20 and completely blind. Many people are uncomfortable dealing with those who have vision difficulties and I hope that by reading these stories they will become less apprehensive about interacting with the blind.

The visually impaired are no different from anyone else on the face of the planet. Everyone on earth has some difficulty they are trying to overcome or learn to live with. Whether it is physical, mental or emotional, we all are weak in some area and can use help once in a while. Sometimes that help is nothing more than understanding. Sometimes that help is to not put obstacles in our path. And yes, sometimes that help is pro-active.

My mother was a great encouragement to me as I was going through the adjustment of living with less vision. She never pushed me or my sisters to do anything but she did encourage us to try new things. Whenever we expressed an interest in something she would somehow find a way to afford us the opportunity. I now know that she had to make great sacrifices in order to allow us to accomplish our goals.

I know that not everyone has a mommy like mine but, what we do have is a Father in heaven who is there for us. If we surrender our lives to his Son, The Lord Jesus Christ, He has promised that we can do all things through Him.

The last and most important reason I wrote this book is to show others that, if God can help me to live with my limitations and cause me to be a productive child of His, he can do the same for you.

I hope this book causes you to laugh a lot, cry a little and to think about what comes next.

1
SUMMER IN THE CITY
AUGUST OF 1964

I was four, my sister Donna was two and my sister Lisa had just been born two months prior. My mother had a wading pool in the front of the building inside the chain link fence. Donna and I were enjoying the water on this hot day while mom took care of Lisa.

The baby needed a diaper change so our mother took her upstairs. Before leaving, she told me to watch out for Donna. A few minutes later, a man drove up and got out of his car. He was staring at my sister and came over to the fence.

As he leaned over the fence with his hands stretched out toward Donna, I screamed, "Mommy, some man is trying to take Donna!" The man ran to his car, got in it and sped away. My mother had run down the stairs to find out what I was screaming about.

Mom said that by the time she got to us, the man was too far away to see who it was or the see the license plate. As my mother related this story to me the month before she died, I had what I thought were flashes of memory.

Over the years, she told me many stories of my childhood that had the same effect on me. I have quite an imagination so, maybe they are memories or, maybe I just made pictures in my head to fit the stories she told me.

Psalm 127:4-5
4: *As arrows are in the hand of a mighty man; so are children of the youth.*
5: *Happy is the man that hath his quiver full of them: they shall not be ashamed, but they shall speak with the enemies in the gate.*

My mother may not have been happy with the three husbands she chose but, she was happy with her children. Not all the time but, she loved, cared for, provided for, enjoyed spending time with and was proud of what we eventually did with our lives. I say eventually because two of us had some pretty rough teen years.

She also loved her seven grand-children, looked forward to being with them and, secretly provided for them. Countless times, as I spoke with people in our mother's life that were not really in ours, they would let me know how much our mother bragged about us and our children.

2
DON'T EAT THOSE
JUNE OF 1965

My mother's second husband's mother decided that we did not love her any more so, she moved to Puerto Rico. I was a month shy of my fifth birthday and do not remember if my mother told me why we were going to visit Grandma Grace.

I remember so many things about that tropical island that I loved. I went outside to climb a palm tree and discovered jumping frogs and lizards which distracted me from my original purpose of getting a coconut.

I remember walking through the airport on our arrival and seeing a bag of marbles which, when I asked, my mother purchased them for me. I had them for many years afterward, until I discovered Hotwheels.

I remember watching Batman in Spanish and thinking it was the strangest and funniest thing I had ever tried to wrap my head around. I will also never forget the warm water and beautiful beaches.

One thing that was not so good but that I will never forget is waking up on the floor in pain. I began to cry because, I not only was hurting but I could not seem to stop shaking. My mother came into the room, sat on the floor and pulled me into her lap.

I thought that I woke her up with my crying so I began to say over and over that I was sorry. She asked why I was apologizing. When I said, "Because I woke you up", she said that I did not wake her up, the earthquake did.

I asked her what an earthquake was. After telling me, she further explained that I was on the floor because it shook me out of the top bunk I was sleeping in. She also made me understand that I was hurting because I fell on the floor.

But, the thing I remember most about that trip was saving the life of my two-year-old cousin. One afternoon, she spiked a fever. My aunt took her to the doctor and he simply recommended Bayer Chewable Baby Aspirin.

Just before two o'clock in the morning, I was awakened by a sound that came from the bathroom. I looked over to see my cousin coming out of the water closet after turning out the light. Since my brain could not understand what would make that sound, I went into the rest room to figure it out.

I do not know how much plastic was in use at that time but, the bottle of aspirin was made of glass. The sound I heard was the noise the bottle made when she dropped it in the metal trash can.

I have been accused of having more than my share of intelligence and, in 1972, my IQ was registered at 162. Seven years earlier, I must have made a little more than the average five-year-old because I did not think eating an entire bottle of medication was good.

I woke up my mother who woke up Grandma who woke up my aunt and we all rushed to the hospital. After they pumped out her stomach, the doctor came over to me, placed his hand on my shoulder and said, "Young man, you just saved your cousin's life."

Until I discovered sex, that was the most wonderful feeling I had ever experienced.

Psalm 107: 8 Oh that men would praise the LORD for his goodness, and for his wonderful works to the children of men!

Over the years I have said many times, "Luke was a physician 2,000 years ago and, if doctors are still practicing medicine, you should not allow them to practice on you." There are times though, that physicians can and do have their place. I thank God that this was one of those times.

3
WHERE DID IT GO?
STARTED JULY OF 1971

When I was eleven years old, I was rescued from a bad situation by my mother. I had been living with my father and his second wife. When I returned to live with my mom and sisters Donna and Lisa, Donna thought it was her job to take care of me.

One of the ways she accomplished that was to clean my room for me. I know that most parents have a problem with their children's rooms. My mother did for a while too but, after realizing by way of explanation and demonstration that my room only looked like a mess, she relented.

I was allowed to keep my room any way I wanted as long as the door was kept closed. It may have looked like a hand grenade went off in my room but, I knew where everything was at any given moment. That is, until Donna got to it. I guess because my sisters had to share a room, they developed the habit of being neat.

Once in a while Donna would see my room and decide that she needed to help her poor slob of a brother. I would be gone and she would clean my room, putting everything in what she thought was its place. After each white tornado blasted through my room, it would take days, weeks and even months for me to find things.

It was not so bad if she was around because I would just ask where she put it. It did get very frustrating though when she was not available. Then I got married. At this time, I was also losing enough sight to make things difficult.

Since I did most of the cooking I knew where things were in the kitchen. Then Trish, my first wife, would decide to cook. I was never able to understand how she could take an herb or spice from its place, use it, and then put it somewhere else.

Man was it frustrating to be in the kitchen after her. Then there were the many times I would put something in the fridge to eat later or to take for my lunch the next day. Trish would eat it and I thought I was going crazy. I would take everything out of the fridge looking for it.

Granted, we were poor so there was not an abundance of food in the fridge but, it was still frustrating. Then I would tell her what I was putting in the fridge, that I did not want her to touch it and that I intended to have it later. When later came, at least ninety percent of the time, it would be gone.

Our marriage was not good after the first year and a half. After begging her for a few years to leave, she did. Now I was so happy because I lived alone and there was no one to move anything from where I placed it. That lasted for two years.

For the past fourteen years I have had to learn to be patient with those who have little idea of the difficulty in trying to find something that someone has moved from where you last knew it to be. At one point, as my wife Jovanna and I were renting rooms in our home, we had a man live with us who did not and would not understand this.

He had used the bathroom and had left the door half open. I had told him many times before to not do that. As I went into the bathroom, I hit my head on the corner of the door and cut my forehead.

When I went to him and showed him the result of his carelessness, his response was unbelievable. He asked me, "Why don't you walk around the house with your hands in front of you?"

When I asked him which was more reasonable, his opening or closing the door all the way or my having to walk around my own house with my hands in front of my face, he responded that it should be my job, not his. Needless to say, more problems arose after that and, I asked him to move out.

Though I still get frustrated at times, I have learned a little more patience and have even discovered the humor in some of the situations. For instance, sometimes at a restaurant my wife will take my plate to cut up my food. In making the area more accessible she will move things around like my water glass.

I have often been seen moving my hand up and down around the area where my cup had been. I love to hear the puzzlement in the voices of people who have asked me, "Ummmm, what are you doing?" With one of my friends, Guido, it has become a game.

He will sit near enough me at the table to move things on me. The first time he did it he asked, "Ray, what the heck are you doing?" He had me going for a while but, now that I know, the first time I cannot find what I am looking for I just say "Guido!" and he and others will laugh as he replaces the item.

I find it amusing when I am waving my hand around looking for something and a person comes up to me with the question, "What are you doing?", You can tell by the way they ask that the real question being held back in their mind is, 'What is your problem?'

All of this reminds me of my parent's dogs Cookie and Ronzoni and their first snow fall. I went to let the dogs out of the basement to the back yard. They were always so excited to get out that they ran up the five steps as I opened the door.

When they got to the threshold, they stopped so fast, I would swear you could hear the screech of breaks. There were about four inches of snow on the ground and they stood there looking at it as if to ask, 'Where did my back yard go?"

I could not get them to go outside unless I went first. They were so tentative initially that it was comical. Once they realized that it was okay, they started running around in their new playground. I made a snowball, got their attention, tossed it to them and almost fell down laughing when they killed it with their teeth and ran around looking for it.

I did it again and again with each of them and, every time they were just as puzzled as to where the ball that was in their teeth had gone. Now I understand much better how they felt.

Luke 15: 9 And when she hath found it, she calleth her friends and her neighbors together, saying, Rejoice with me; for I have found the piece which I had lost.

Unless you are blind, you cannot understand the frustration of misplacing or dropping something and having to spend a ridiculous amount of time trying to find it. So I can understand that woman's joy in finding, what was then, a month's income.

4
THE DIAGNOSIS
JUNE OF 1972

I had been living with my father and his wife for two years when my mother came to fetch me. I spent the next year visiting the doctor to get my Asthma under control. I visited the dentist to get 13 of my 25 cavities filled. I visited the Ophthalmologist to get fitted with glasses. I joined the Boy Scouts and joined a gymnastic organization.

I begin my story this way for two reasons. The first is to let you know that my body was under a lot of stress for those two years and that with good care I was able to go from a fifty-nine pound eleven-year-old sick weakling to a much healthier and very coordinated twelve-year-old in one year. I firmly believe that the stress I was under exacerbated my eye condition. I believe that if my body had not undergone such stress, my eye disease would either have taken many more years to show or maybe not even shown up at all.

The second reason is related to the first in that it is a warning, caution or advice to anyone who has a family history or marked propensity for sickness or disease. God has given our bodies a remarkable ability to heal themselves if given the proper tools. Those tools are plenty of clean water and lots of fresh, ripe, raw fruits and vegetables. This is especially important for children because their bodies are still growing. If we do not provide our children with the proper building blocks and good exercise habits, their bodies will suffer and sickness and disease will be their legacy.

My mother had seen me play football and had been to some of my gymnastic exhibitions so she was well aware of my physical abilities. The fact that I was beginning to excel in sports made what is in the next paragraph very puzzling to her.

The fact that my sisters liked changing the furniture in the living room every month made it very painful for me. They are two and four years younger than I and had no idea that there was a problem. They just liked seeing things from a different perspective each month.

Many times I would come running into the apartment and bang my shins into the coffee table or chair and then proceed to fall over them as if I was auditioning for the opening scene of the Dick VanDyke show. My mother would admonish me time and time again that I needed to be more careful.

We had no idea that anything serious was wrong. We were in the eye doctor's office and my mother was telling him about my habit of falling over the furniture. He put me back in the chair and got so close in examining my eyes I thought he was going to kiss me. Hasn't anyone ever told eye doctors that they ought to suck on breath mints all day so their patients will not pass out because of their breakfast or lunch. Anyway, after a few minutes he said, "I think I know what the problem is but, I want him to see a retinal specialist." So we went.

After a battery of tests and questions we went to his office to talk. If you have seen the movie "Mask" with Cher, what follows will seem vaguely familiar to you. The doctor asked my mother if I could please wait in the hall so he could talk to her about my eyes. Her response was, "They're his eyes, tell him." The doctor proceeded to tell me that I had retinitis pigmentosa and that I would probably go blind by the time I reached eighteen.

I know now where the strength came from that made me take the news so well and to do what I did when I got home but it would be six years before I would be introduced to Him. We went home and I put on a blindfold, a bandanna really. I wanted to know if I would be able to cook, shower, clean and do everything else I needed to do in order to live. After three days I had decided that I could live just fine without seeing. I then made up my mind that I was going to try as much as I could before losing my sight completely so that in later years, I would not sit around moaning that I did not get to do certain things.

I will not regale you with the details but I will say that I had mild aspirations of being the next Evel Knievel. The doctor was close in his diagnosis. By the time I was eighteen years old I had lost most of the vision in my left eye. Even before that I had dropped out of high school because I was no longer able to see the blackboard and reading my books was extremely difficult. One of the most disappointing times in my life was not being able to graduate with my friends and knowing I would never be able to attend a high school reunion.

Most people back then and many today, over thirty years later, do not understand that there is a lot between great vision and total blindness. My teachers were not equipped to help someone in my position. I thought I hated learning but have come to realize that I love learning, I just hate the obstacles to that knowledge.

Being told I would go blind was not disturbing to me for many reasons. One, at the age of twelve, I could not fathom the whole meaning. Two, at that age, you do not really believe anything is going to happen to you that you cannot recover from. Three, in reality, going blind is not that tragic, at least not in the big picture.

When I was 18, I received a spiritual diagnosis that was worse than being told you will go blind and much worse than anything I could possibly have imagined. I was told I was going to die a second time. I was made to understand that, if I did not change my ways, I would spend time in a place called Hell, which was worse than being blind because it was palpable darkness and that I would be separated from God. I was further informed that, after that time of solitude, I would spend the rest of eternity in a lake of fire with no hope of getting out.

I was grateful to the doctor who caused me to pay attention to the light I had left. I was much more grateful to the person who let me know that, not only could I escape the darkness and torture to come but that I could instead have a personal relationship with the Creator of everything. Till that point I had no relationship with any of my three fathers and ached for what was being presented to me.

I have been in love with the LORD since August 8, 1991 and know that, though I might be blind for 60 years or more in this life, I will have all of eternity to behold His glory and that which He has prepared for me. So, I encourage you to hold fast to Him, use that which He has given you, good and "bad" to point others to Him and, urge you to meditate on the following verses:

Lamentations 3:21-27
21 This I recall to my mind; therefore have I hope.
22 It is of the LORD's mercies that we are not consumed, because his compassions fail not.

23 They are new every morning: great is thy faithfulness.

24 The LORD is my portion, saith my soul; therefore will I hope in him.

25 The LORD is good unto them that wait for him, to the soul that seeketh him.

26 It is good that a man should both hope and quietly wait for the salvation of the LORD.

27 It is good for a man that he bare the yoke in his youth.

5
TIC, TOC, CRASH, BANG, BOOM!
October of 1972

There is a Bible verse that goes, "Pride goeth before destruction, and an haughty spirit before a fall." This is true in more ways than one. I was so concerned about what people would think and say about a boy who could function perfectly well in the day time but would walk around in the dark with a cane so, I chose to not use one.

I was already suffering at the tongues and hands of most of the neighborhood children because I was so skinny that if I turned sideways and stuck out my tongue, I looked like a zipper. In addition, being so blond that my hair was almost platinum and having the last name of Whitehead did not help matters. I decided that I did not need any more help in order to be tormented by the other children so, when I was offered a cane, I reluctantly took it. Thanks to that cane I never tripped over anything or got lost in my closet.

One of my two best friends lived about one block away. If you made a right out of my apartment, went to the corner, crossed the street, made a right and went half way down the block, you would be at his apartment. I decided to go to his place. When I stepped out the door, it was so dark that I could not see anything but, since I knew the way to his place so well, I decided to go anyway.

I was only a few steps from the corner when I felt a stinging in my shins and started falling forward. I put my hands out to brace myself for contact with the pavement but, there was empty space where the cement should have been. Then I hit something very bumpy and began sliding down it to the right. When I tried to get up to discover what had broken my fall, I found out that it was a keg of beer.

There was a bar at the corner called the "TIC TOC." They were unloading a truck and the metal doors to the cellar were open. My shins had hit that and, I had fallen on a set of metal rollers they used to send the beverages down the stairs. I do not know if I had screamed as I fell but, as I attempted to rise, one of the workers was by my side helping me up. They must have been very concerned because one of them helped me home.

My mother cleaned up all the blood and put so many bandages on me that I felt like an Egyptian mummy. Though I deserved one, I do not remember getting a lecture on the proper times to use my cane. You would think that I might have learned a lesson from this experience, well, I did. I learned to walk slower and listen better but I did not yet learn humility or how life and injury saving a cane could be. I also learned that gravity sucks.

You might be tempted to cut that twelve-year-old some slack, my current self would as well. However, more than that type of grace being given to me, I wish I had learned my lesson.

Over and over again as the years passed by, I found myself falling because of my pride. Sometimes literally but more often, metaphorically. Because I chose to care more about what those around me thought than what my LORD thought.

Proverb 16:18 Pride goeth before destruction, and an haughty spirit before a fall.

Thankfully, these hard lessons are fewer and farther between. I look forward to the day when, not only will my Savior remove every tear but, He will also remove the possibility for me to sin. I do not know how our relationships will work in Heaven but, I do know that I will finally care more about His opinion than any other.

6
SALT AND PEPPER PLEASE
March of 1973

This story has nothing to do with my lack of vision at all but, since it is related to another story and since it is so funny, I thought you would enjoy it.

In another story, I have related that my math teacher had exempted me from the work paper rule. Well, she was out sick one day and we had a substitute teacher named Mrs. Star. It was obvious that she did not know or was not interested in teaching from her looks, attitude and posture. Also she did not even open her book or tell us to take out our books.

Instead, she just put a six-foot-long algebra problem on the board and told us that we had all period to solve it. After handing out yellow paper to each row, she said that there would be no talking in the class and then she stood at what I recognized to be, ATTENTION, at the front of the class.

I did not take a sheet of paper but passed them on down the line. I got to work on my problem and had solved it about ten minutes later. I raised my hand and after being called on, told the sub that I was finished. She said that it was not possible that I had finished and after assuring her that I had, she asked to see my work.

When I told her that I did not have any work because I did it in my head and that my teacher said that I could, she made a face that would have been the perfect picture for Webster's Dictionary next to the word, "doubt." I did not think her look could sour any more than it had until I told her the answer that I came up with. Now her picture would have fit next to the word, "satisfaction."

After trying for a minute to convince her that I could not be mistaken I suggested that she allow me to prove it at the board. She said, "If you are correct, I'll eat my hat." I turned to my best friend Ronald and said, "Ronald, go to the teacher's lounge and get some salt and pepper." My classmates thought that was funny but she did not and told my friend to sit back down.

I approached the board and began to solve the problem. After a few minutes I stood back and had the same answer that I had come up with before. She was not happy but could not deny that I had the correct answer after examining my work. Once she conceded that I was correct I asked her if she would like her hat now. She was not amused.

When my teacher came back to school, I told her what had happened thinking that she would be proud of me. She rebuked me instead. I learned at least two valuable lessons from her that day. The first was that, even if your elders are wrong, they still deserve our respect. The second was, it is much more meaningful when someone that cares about you and that you love and respect, rebukes you.

Proverb 27:6 Faithful are the wounds of a friend; but the kisses of an enemy are deceitful.

Misses Laborski was a much older lady and my math teacher but, she was definitely my friend. She not only taught me much about math, she taught me that no matter how smart you are, you were not born with that knowledge. Everyone had to learn everything they know which makes us all even.

7
BEEP, BEEP, FIVE DEGREES LEFT
JULY OF 1973

One of the hardest things to get the fully sighted to understand was, and still is to a large degree, the fact that there is a lot between 20/20 and blind. When I first started to lose my sight, it was so gradual that I was not aware that I was losing anything. I thought that everyone saw the same way I did. Even after I had completely lost the ability to see at night, my brain did not comprehend that there was now a great difference between me and my friends.

Like most children, I did not want to be different. My mother worked from five in the evening until two or later in the morning so, I was frequently out on the streets very late. At first, whenever we, that is, Ronald and I, wanted to go somewhere, I would either stand on the axle of his back wheel or sit on the handle bars and he would pedal us there. This is good training if you want to develop strong legs or a hard butt however, Ronald came up with a better idea.

Since he and I were both expert riders, he decided that I should be able to take care of my own transportation with a little bit of bat sense. He would ride in front of me and beep every second so I could stay on track. If there needed to be an adjustment of more than two degrees, he would say 3 degrees left or right. If we needed to make a hard turn, like 90 degrees right, he would say right turn and, on the word "Now" I would execute the turn and he would go back to beeping.

Even as I am writing this it amazes me that I did not have one accident during the many years we used that system. I was however hit by many cars as a pedestrian and while on my bike when Ronald was not around. God obviously had other plans for me because, though a few of the accidents were serious, I lived to tell about it.

Psalm 91:11 For he shall give his angels charge over thee, to keep thee in all thy ways. 12 They shall bear thee up in their hands, lest thou dash thy foot against a stone.

This is a Messianic Psalm and too many Christians use it personally. Though God allows us to dash our feet against stones occasionally, we have no idea how much He has saved us from in order to give us enough time to choose His Son Jesus.

8
WE ARE GOING TO DIE
JULY OF 1973

My mother was a single mom for many years. Though we were poor, we, the children, did not know it. Sadly, one of the things that is missing in our society is discipline. When I say discipline, I do not mean just the negative aspects. I mean the demonstrating, teaching, leading, guiding along with the physical chastisement that comes out of loving and wanting the best for your children.

Though my mother did not have the benefit of God's word, she did wonderfully well at raising her children with what she did have. She taught and guided so well that we were actually shocked to see the behavior of other children. There were many times that my siblings and I would remark that there was no way we could ever get away with that, referring to a disobedient child.

That was enough to amaze me. It did not stop there though. It is amazing how much smarter my mother became as I grew older. Now, as I look back, I am in awe at what my mother accomplished with so few resources available to her. I now know that she made great sacrifices in order to provide her children with opportunities.

One of the things she provided for us was the chance to go up in a small airplane and fly over parts of New Jersey and New York. We did not know until we got there what was going to take place. My two sisters and I were very excited to find out that we were going to go up in a plane.

We climbed up into the plane. Donna was sitting in back of the pilot and Lisa was sitting in back of me. I got in the front passenger seat and went to close the door. The pilot told me to leave it open a crack. My sister Lisa immediately turned green. The pilot noticed and assured her that everything was perfectly fine.

Just in case she did not believe him, he told her where she could find a barf bag in the pockets on the back of my seat. After doing his check list, we took off. After flying for a while, Lisa seemed to recover. Then it happened. The pilot asked me if I would like to fly the plane. When I said yes, my sister utilized the bag she had found. Donna however, was jealous, she wanted to fly the plane.

I flew over the Hudson River and over New York for a bit and then the pilot said it was time to go back. He instructed me in the technique of banking the plain for a return to the airport. My sister began to panic and asked in a frighten voice, "Are you going to let him land the plane, he can't see that well?"

The pilot assured her that I would shortly be relinquishing the controls so that he could land the aircraft. I am surprise that my sister will even get on a plane anymore, but she does. The next year we were treated to a helicopter ride but the pilot would not let me touch anything much less fly the bird.

There are many amazing things in our lives and flying is one of the many I have had. I believe that one of the reasons the LORD allows us to have these experiences is to prepare us for what is ahead if we surrender ourselves to Him. It gives us a better understanding of the following verse.

Isaiah 40:31 But they that wait upon the LORD shall renew their strength; they shall mount up with wings as eagles; they shall run, and not be weary; and they shall walk, and not faint.

9
WHAT ACTING CAREER?
SEPTEMBER OF 1973

In the grammar school I attended in Guttenberg, New Jersey, you did not start moving around from class to class until you got to the seventh grade. So, when I finally reached that magical grade, it was a little difficult to get use to all the extra teachers and all the moving around. I do not remember how to spell her name so I will just refer to her as Mrs. B. Mrs. B was our music teacher.

I learned two things quickly about myself while in her class. The first is that I cannot sing. She would have each child approach the piano and then she would play some scales. She would ask you to follow her by singing the scales. At the time I had no idea what scales were and did not know enough about music to keep myself from being embarrassed.

When it was my turn, I sang with the music she was playing, or at least I thought so. She informed me that I was going the wrong way. Since I was just standing there, I could not understand what she meant by, "Going the wrong way." When I just kept on singing, she said, "You need to go higher." Again, I had no idea what she meant.

She decided that I probably could not go higher so she began playing the music in a lower key. After a moment she was going lower than I was and told me to go lower. Still not comprehending her meaning I stopped singing. She stopped playing and asked me what had happened. When I told her that I had no idea what she wanted me to do, she decided that perhaps I should act rather than sing.

After working the rest of the children through the same process, she came over to work with those she had chosen for the play. She started with giving us directions as to our positions. After we were all where we were supposed to be she began giving us lines.

My wife and I homeschool our two children. Naturally we are interested in the best way to teach them. Within the past few years, we have learned that there are four major learning types. My son is a kinetic learner. He learns best when his body is in motion. At first, I thought that he could not possibly be listening to me while playing with something in his hands or while bouncing off the walls.

I decided to test him. I would be teaching him something and when he was the most physically active, I would ask him what I had just said. I was shocked to learn that he was able to repeat what I had just said, word for word. I further soon realized that if I wanted him to explain something, he had to be in motion. I would try to have him sit by me and explain it but, it did not work. As I reflect back, I realize that I too was a kinetic learner.

Now I know why what happened, happened. As my teacher gave me the lines she wanted me to say I began to move around a little while trying to memorize them. When I thought I had them down, I looked down to find the spot where I was supposed to be standing. As I moved over to it, I fell off the stage. Because I had taken some martial arts classes I knew how to fall and I quickly jumped up without a scratch.

Though I was not harmed physically, my mind never recovered from that trauma. I immediately quit the play and never tried out for another one again.

Years later I saw Ronny Milsap on stage. He had pre-arranged with his crew to play a little joke on the crowd. He pretended that he did not know where on the stage he was. He then walked to the edge of the stage. He told the audience that his crew was telling him that he should keep walking. The crowd began to shout for him to stop.

I remember thinking that I would be petrified to be up there without a cane having to rely on the shouts of strangers for direction. Though there is no stage, I do drama for the children in my church and now wish my teacher had made me stick with it back then.

Who knows, maybe Bruce Willis and I would be friends now since we had lived in the same city for a while back in the eighties.

Romans 11:29 For the gifts and calling of God are without repentance.

10
ALL YOU CAN EAT
February of 1974

When I was eleven years old, because of my poor health and other reasons, I was only 59 pounds. I had no strength, energy or coordination. I spent the next year trying to fix those deficits and was successful. I ended up with such great hand-eye coordination that, when I joined a little league baseball team, I was the pitcher. When I played football, I was usually the quarterback.

The only drawback to my improvement was hunger. Second servings was a given and a third plate full of food was not unusual for me. I have no idea how my single mother managed to feed six people every day when there were only four of us in the house. I joined a bowling league and had an average of 146 which was not bad for a 13-year-old. My mother, her boyfriend and my sister Donna also were on teams at Castle Lanes on Kennedy Boulevard in, I believe, Jersey City New Jersey.

Across the highway and about a block down was a Chinese restaurant called, Mai Kai. After my mother's evening league was done, she took us to that restaurant because they were having an all-you-can-eat special. I took advantage like you would not believe. to keep me from looking like a pig, my mother made me limit my plate to 5 ribs at a time.

When I was digging into my thirty-third rib, the owner/manager came over to me and actually asked me if I could stop eating. When I reminded him that the sign said "all-you-can-eat" for one low price. He said, "I know, but if everyone ate like you, I would lose money." I do not think that he was serious because, my family laughed and he smiled as he walked away. I think he just wanted to see how this skinny boy could pack away so much.

In July of 1976, my mother, her new husband, my two sisters, myself and three of my step-siblings took a car trip to Disney World. On the way, we stopped at a restaurant we had recently seen a TV commercial for. That restaurant was Pizza Hut and, you guessed it, they had an all you can eat sign in the window. For $2.99 per person, the eight of us dined well.

My step-brother Billy and I went up at least six times. I stuck with pizza, spaghetti and lasagna. Billy went for things like muscles, shrimp and clams. He is the only person that was able to keep up with the volume I could put away.

Because my sight was getting worse, I was not able to see details like facial expressions from more than three feet away. I am pretty sure that seeing the frowns on the worker's faces would not have affected my appetite anyway. I believe that because, when I sat down with my fourth plate of food, my mother said, "You should see the managers faces.", and I just kept eating.

As customers left the restaurant, at least one manager would be standing at the door handing out balloons and lollipops. When we were finally ready to leave, Lynn, Lisa, Toni and Donna each received their parting gifts. Billy and I just received stern looks.

Neither my step-brother nor I cared about balloons or candy. Balloons would have looked stupid to us at our ages and lollipops were much less interesting to us than all that good Italian food we had just consumed. I say, "good", only because it would be several more years before I discovered real Italian food and fell in love.

The last of dozens of stories about this little piggy happened in the summer of 1977. My friend Kevin and I decided to go to, what was then, Hudson County Park, to play football. We had four other friends with us and, since I cannot remember all their names, I will not mention any of the rest of them so as to not hurt any feelings. Kevin gets mentioned by name because he and Ronald were my two best friends.

Anyway, after playing football for about ninety minutes, we decided to take a break and have lunch. The restaurant, White Castle, was across the street from the ninetieth street park entrance which was close to where we were playing. After ordering and getting our food, we sat together and, everyone commented on my two bags of food. I had gotten 20 cheeseburgers with mustard and ketchup, a large soda and some fries.

My friends had gotten four, five or six burgers each. Naturally, they all started teasing me. Then, someone brought up the movie, Cool Hand Luke. In that movie, Paul Newman eats fifty hard boiled eggs to win a wager. I ended up betting my friends $200 that I could eat fifty White Castles in an hour. They took the bet at forty dollars apiece to my two hundred and we set the bet for two weeks from that day.

The following week, we were playing football again and had lunch at White Castle again. Like a fool, I ordered twenty burgers again. That was not the foolish part. What was unwise was my eating them as fast as I could and, in fifteen minutes, I had eaten all of them plus my fries and soda. They canceled the bet.

Philippians 4:5 Let your moderation be known unto all men. The Lord is at hand.

I know that these stories seem like the opposite of what the verse above is stating. That may be true but, I did not know the LORD yet. Once He found me, I did start learning how to be a little more reserved in my eating habits. However, I sometimes still find it hard to back away from the table when the food is especially good. That is why, when I am able, I focus on the last five words of the verse. When I pay attention to the fact that He is always near, it is easier to abstain.

11
THAT WAS DISGUSTING
April of 1974

When you attended first through sixth grade at Anna L Klein grammar school, hearing the name Misses Espizito made you shake. She was the history and geography teacher for seventh and eighth grades and, though you had no choice but to take her class, you did not want her for homeroom.

Guess whom I got for homeroom both years. We were all petrified until you got to know her. That took a few weeks. I was always the class clown but, had to figure out more subtle ways of being funny because, at first, she did not seem to have a sense of humor. It turned out that we were wrong.

She did have a funny bone but, learning and decorum were more important to her. I found out years later that, Misses E was the most visited teacher by her former students. I went back to see her and a few others twice.

On this particular day, Misses E had to go to the teacher's lounge for something. We were about eight minutes from the end of class. She told us that, when the first bell sounds, we were to put everything away and line up outside the classroom. We had to line up in size order with the girls on one side of the hall and the boys on the other side.

We were also instructed to keep quiet. Well, most of them were quiet. I say them because I was not a quiet one. I began swallowing air so I could burp the alphabet. The second bell, which indicated that we were to move to our next class, was about two minutes after the first.

When I thought I had swallowed enough air to burp the entire alphabet, I began. I got to the letter "T" when I heard the door behind me close. I turned to find Misses E staring at me with a frown on her face. After a moment of that look, she said, "Mister Whitehead, come over here."

I walked over to her with a smirk on my face because I knew what was coming. The reason she had gotten such a fierce reputation was because of her discipline methods. If you were a girl, she would ask you to put your hand out palm up and she would strike it with a thick wooden ruler which always left a red mark. Too bad our teachers are not allowed to do that anymore.

For the boys, she would pull your sideburn as she lectured you. Did I forget to mention that she was short in stature? Maybe I should say that she was really short. She had blocks of wood attached to her brake pedal and accelerator and she sat on a couple of phone books.

She was so vertically challenged that she could not reach my sideburn without having me bend down. So, when she commanded me to bend down, I refused. She instructed me again to bend down and, when I refused again, she kicked me in the shin. What do you do when kicked in the shin? You lift your leg while reaching for the damaged area as you bend down.

As I bent, she grabbed my side burn. I immediately forgot about my shin as she twisted and yanked my sideburn as she told me, "That was the most disgusting thing she had ever heard." Of course, most of my fellow students were amused, which I guess was the effect I was going for in the first place.

Job 36:9, 10
9 Then he sheweth them their work, and their transgressions that they have exceeded.
10 He openeth also their ear to discipline, and commandeth that they return from iniquity.

I will not say that I never again transgressed her rules, however, I never forgot the lesson. I fell in love with her at that moment because she did not put up with any student's nonsense. I did not learn much history or geography from her because I hated those subjects but, I did learn things from her that were much more important.

I remained class clown in grammar school, in high school and in college. to this day I still love to make people laugh. My wife told me a few years ago that, one of the reasons she fell in love with me was because of my humor. We laugh together every day.

12
UP IN SMOKE
MAY OF 1974

I started at the age of eleven delivering papers for the Jersey Journal. I really liked the job because I not only made good money, I met several people that became friends. There was George the barber on 68th street just off Bergenline Avenue.

Mrs. Lipps who had two daughters that were so beautiful that I wished they were not married. There was the owner of Dick's Florist, I bet you cannot guess his name. There was the most famous person I ever had on my route, Larry Csonka, who moved into the penthouse of the Galaxy Towers and, when he shook my hand, I thought I would lose it.

Then there was the old Polish couple. They did not take a paper but, I saw and waved to them six days a week. They sat on their covered porch every day as I went by and waved to me. One day, I decided to stop and talk with them for a few minutes.

My sister Lisa's grandmother Grace was from Poland so, I was familiar with the accent and enjoyed talking with them. After seeing them every day for two and a half years, one day, they were not there. I was concerned so, I got off my bike, went up on the porch and knocked on the door.

They did not answer and, since there was no door bell, I tried the window. Still no response. Then I realized that I could smell natural gas. I tried the door and windows but, they were all locked. As I was banging on the window, a neighbor across the street was leaving their home.

I yelled to them, asking them to call the Police about a gas leak. They did and, a few minutes later, the Police showed up. Two minutes after that, the fire Department arrived. As the fire department was preparing to break into the dwelling, my friends turned the corner.

Did I forget to mention that they were chain smokers? Well, they had just finished lunch around the corner and were each smoking a freshly lit cigarette. I ran up to them informing them of the trouble and asking them to put out their smokes.

They unlocked the doors and allowed the Firemen to open all their windows after turning off the stove. It turned out that she had a ten-gallon pot on the stove atop two of the burners and, when it boiled over, it put out the flames but, the gas continued unabated and filled the house.

When the excitement was all over, the Fire Chief approached me asking if I was the one that reported the gas leak. When I answered in the affirmative, he said that, "Not only did you save their lives but, you kept the surrounding five buildings from being blown up as well. Who knows how many lives you saved today?"

From the next day on, every time I stopped by, the lady offered me some form of dessert.

Numbers 16: 35 And there came out a fire from the LORD, and consumed the two hundred and fifty men that offered incense.

What these men were doing was wrong which is why God fried them. Sometimes what happens to us is because of our sin, sometimes because the enemy hates us and, occasionally because of mistakes. This was simply because she put too much water in the pot. I am glad that they were not devoured by what could have been a conflagration.

13
CLIFF HANGER
JUNE OF 1974

Ronald became one of my three best friends during my teen years. He became a friend when he came to my rescue as another boy from my school was kicking me into the sewer on the corner by our grammar school. William had stolen my lunch in class and when I loudly complained about it, he got in trouble. He promised to get me back which is what he was doing when Ronald came along.

Ronald grabbed him by the shirt and pinned him to the brick wall of the school. He told him that if he ever bothered me again, he would be sorry. William never did bother me again but there were a few times when you could almost hear the wheels in his head spinning, trying to figure out a way. A few years later, as one of my sisters began developing into a beautiful young lady, William actually made a few attempts to become my friend.

After Ronald saved my life, he came over, picked me up out of the gutter and introduced himself. You see, I was the new boy and did not know anyone yet. Ronald and I became fast friends, initially because he saved me but, more because he and I had a lot of the same interests. One of those interests was bicycles.

We loved to ride them, fix them, take them apart to see how they worked and to try to make them better. We used to ride around the surrounding towns and, whenever we saw a bike or part of a bike being thrown out, we would take it home. We would take it apart and keep the good parts. This was good training for my later becoming a bicycle Mechanic. There was one point where I had twelve ten speed bikes.

Since I did not care what they looked like, they were mostly ugly. I would have one colored fork, a different colored body, two or three different colored brake and shift cables and different style and color brake pads. I learned the hard way that if the bike looked great, it was a target for theft. If it looked horrible, no one wanted it.

Once we had maxed out on bikes, we shifted to motor bikes. The first one was acquired by Ronald; it was a Honda 70. After fixing it up we took it to the tracks. Down along the Hudson River there were Railroad tracks and piers. People would fish and crab off those piers. The first time we took it down I found a set of railroad car wheels. to use an expression, "They weighed a ton", in reality, they weighed over seventy pounds.

Ronald guided the bike while I rolled the wheels. We decided to roll the wheels off one of the piers to see what would happen. Not much, they just shot into the water like a bullet. We decided that when we built our two-man submarine, we would try to find those wheels again.

We then took the bike to a wooded section of the tracks and started riding. Ronald would go first and blaze the trail. He would then come back and tell me where to go. My eyes were having more trouble now and going in and out of shade was becoming difficult. You could not call it bravery, I now think it was stupidity but then, I thought it was trust, maybe it was. I would listen to his directions and then follow them without question.

On this particular trip, he came back excited because he had discovered a long trail. The object was to stay out of sight so that the Police would not come and hassle us for riding around the tracks. I again listened to his directions and followed them. I took off alongside the tracks and into the woods. As I came up to the rise I was supposed to turn right. In that area the trees were a little thinner so the sun was shining in spots.

My eyes were hit by the sunshine and then they would take too long to adjust to the shade again. Well, I missed the turn off because I had just been hit by the shine. I was going about twenty-five to thirty miles an hour and the bike was going up a hill. Now Ronald did not tell me why you had to turn and I just thought it was because there was a better trail. Boy was I wrong.

As I reached the top of the hill, I realized that there was nothing but horizon before me. Then I looked down. It was too late. The bike and I were flying through the air. Below me was a drop of about forty or fifty feet into a crater. Within the crater were three huge piles. One of stone, one of sand and one of dirt.

I fell twenty feet or more before landing in the pile of dirt. The bike stalled and I sat there not injured but stunned. After a few minutes I turned around to see from whence I had come. As I looked down, I saw the rest of the drop. I realized that if I had been going ten miles an hour slower, I would have probably fallen the whole way to my death.

What next? How in the world will I get the bike back up there? As I sat, contemplating my options, I didn't really see any, I heard a voice from on high. No, it wasn't the LORD Jesus Christ speaking to me as He spoke with Saul on the road to Damascus. It was Ronald, standing at the launch site.

Once he heard the motor cut off and not come back on again, he began the search. He followed the trail I was supposed to take but did not find me. He backtracked and went up the hill, and there I was.

I have always been fond of long Victorian or Elizabethan names so I always called my friend Ronald. Even when I found out that Ronald was his middle name. Since that is how he introduced himself, that is what I figured he wanted to be called. Over the years I have always introduced myself as Raymond. Unfortunately, many people decide, without permission, to shorten your name. That, I do not like. Others however decide to give you a nickname. That is what Ronald did.

That voice from above asked, hey R.W., what the hell are you doing down there?" He was not really wanting an answer. I knew this for two reasons. One, I knew my friend and his tone assured me that he was just giving me the needle. Two, because he immediately started climbing down to come help me.

Landing in the stones would have hurt. Landing in the sand would have been worse for the bike and my eyes. Landing in the soft dirt was the safest but also the most difficult to dig out of. After much trouble we managed to get down off the pile. After a little driving around, Ronald found a way back up.

I think that the experience of flying off the cliff on a mini bike gave me an understanding of why Evel Knievel kept going. Did it make me more cautious? I think so but, you would need a Micrometer to measure just how much more careful I became.

Ronald will always be my first best friend. My wife is now my best friend. However, as with Moses, the LORD Jesus Christ is my very best friend.

Ronald saved me, befriended me, looked out for me, taught me things, including how to defend myself and, since I had a lousy example as a father, was the closest picture of the LORD I ever saw until 20 years after we became friends.

Exodus 33:11 And the LORD spake unto Moses face to face, as a man speaketh unto his friend.

Ronald and I spent many years speaking face-to-face. And, though I have heard the LORD's voice twice and experienced His working in my life many times, I cannot wait to meet Him face-to-face.

14
SIX WHEELED BIKE
June of 1974

We had a bulk trash night once a month on a Thursday. That meant that everyone put their items out on Wednesday evening. Since my mother worked from six in the evening until two in the morning, I was free to roam the streets.

My mother did not know that I was out until two in the morning each month picking through other's trash to find my treasures. I once found a Sony stereo that was worth over six hundred dollars at the time. Mostly what I was looking for were bike parts.

There was a time when I was sixteen that I had twelve ten speed bikes. I was giving them away because I had no more room. I also had parts for smaller bikes as my sisters and a few of my shorter friends had twenty-inch bikes. It was not until a few years later that I actually earned money for fixing bicycles.

One of my grammar school classmates was Eileen Moony. She had a younger sister named Jeanie who was about three years younger. One day, Jeanie saw my sister Lisa riding her bike with a friend named Mimi. I noticed that Jeanie looked very sad. I went up to her and asked her what was wrong.

I was surprised when she told me that she wanted to ride a bicycle but her mother would not let her. When I asked her why, she said that her mom was afraid that she would get hurt. You see, Jeanie had cerebral palsy and because of that, she had poor balance. Also, with her hands and feet twisted inward, it would have been hard for her to pedal and steer.

I know I should have asked but, at the tender age of fourteen, I already had an attitude against people restricting what those of us with disabilities could do. So, I went to the basement and created a special bicycle for Jeanie. The handle bars were twisted in a way that fit her hands better than your standard bars.

I made the breaks hyper sensitive so she would not have to squeeze too hard to stop and placed them on the rear tire only so she would not accidentally flip the bike. I placed leather straps from a pair of roller skates on the pedals so her feet would not tend to slip off.

The most important modification I made was to put reinforced brackets on the training wheels that I placed on both wheels. That way, she could learn a lot more than normal and still not fall over. Once it was done, two days later, I waited to see her come out of her house.

When she did, I asked her to come to my apartment because I had something for her. She followed me and, when I presented her with the bike, she was speechless with surprise. I showed her the modifications, helped her on it for the first time, showed her how strong it was, that she could trust her weight to it and let her go.

She was having so much fun riding up and down the sidewalk with the other children that I think I was happier than she. That is until her mother saw her and made a beeline for her. When I saw what was going to happen, I intercepted Mrs. Mooney. She started freaking out on me and I asked her to shut up and look at her daughter.

She was so shocked that someone the age of her middle daughter would speak to her that way that, she actually stopped talking. I asked her to please look at her daughter's face to see her huge smile.

I explained how I created the bicycle especially for Jeanie and that it was strong enough to hold her weight, even around the corners. She was still not happy but, acquiesced. Her parting shot to me was, "Okay, she can have the bike. But if she gets hurt, I will hold you responsible."

Proverb 24: 23 These things also belong to the wise. It is not good to have respect of persons in judgment.

Okay. I could make myself sound really wise here. However, I was only fourteen and already reeling from the prejudices of others regarding my vision loss. So, truthfully, I just wanted her to shut up and see how happy and normal her daughter felt.

15
COMMON SENSE
April of 1975

I have had the following experience so much that I have trained myself to not look when people call from across the room or across the street or even honk their car horn.

On this one particular day I was walking down the block about one hundred feet from my mother's house when I heard a car horn. As a reflex I turned my head in the direction. When I realized that I could not see who was in the car, I turned back to the path I was on.

A few days later I was in school talking with a classmate. Rather, I was talking and he was not listening with an attitude. When I realized that he was irritated, I asked him what was bothering him. He shot back with, "Nothing, what's your problem?" After going forth and back for a while it finally came out that he was the one in the car that had honked at me.

Because I did not smile or wave at him, he thought that I was upset at him so, rather than ask what the problem was, he just gave me the cold shoulder. It took a few minutes to explain that I could not see him and that turning toward the honked horn was just a reflex. Believe it or not, the same person got mad at me for the very same thing a few months later.

After having this happen to me a few times, I decided that it would be easier to train myself to ignore car horns and shouts from a distance rather than try to explain over and over again why I did not wave to them. Before adopting this drastic measure however, I did try one other thing. I waved to anyone that could possibly be attempting to get my attention. That backfired in three ways.

One, some people would see me later and remind me of the incident of which I had no recollection. Two, others would actually say that they thought I could not see well enough to recognize them so, "How come you could see me the other day?' Third, As I thought someone was trying to get my attention, I waved to him. He then asked me, "What the f___ Is your problem?" It turns out that he was trying to get the attention of someone else.

Now that I ignore possible petitions for my attention, people are starting to think that I am deaf as well as blind. You just can't win.

to paraphrase a song by Ricky Nelson, you can't please everyone so you just have to please the LORD.

Romans 8:8 So then they that are in the flesh cannot please God.

Though I do not wish to hurt others, I have finally learned that you please the LORD first, others second and let the chips fall where they may.

16
SCIENCE PROJECT
MAY OF 1975

I went to a grammar school named Anna L. Klein in Guttenberg, New Jersey. The town consisted of forty-five blocks and had forty-seven bars in it. The school had kindergarten through the eighth grade. For Kindergarten through sixth grade, you stayed in the same room with one teacher. For seventh and eighth grades, you went from class to class. This was to help you get used to what high school was going to be like.

I do not remember if it was just the last two grades or if every grade had to do a science project each year. Memory fails me so I do not know what my seventh-grade project was. However, very few people can forget what my eighth-grade project was. By the time the eighth-grade science project came around, I had begun drinking, smoking and using Mary Jane.

One of the things my buddies and I discovered about pot was, if you smoked it green, you would get a headache. For my project, I decided to grow a control group, one dosed with Anacin and the third was laced with aspirin. I thought that, if the pain reliever was already in the marijuana plant, it might prevent the headache from coming on.

I will never know if it would have worked because, during the science fair, my principal approached me saying, "Raymond, you do know that I cannot let you have those plants back, right?" I just smiled as I replied, "I was not sure anyone knew what they were." He then informed me that he would have to let my mother know. I did not realize that he meant immediately.

When I arrived home, the eight feet tall pot plant in my room was gone. When I asked my mom what had happened, she told me that Mister

Farenza had called her with the good news. I passed the science project with an A but, he could not give back the plants as they were contraband. When my mother asked him for an explanation, he described the plants. When he did, the light bulb went on.

She went to my room, cut down the plant and threw it in the garbage. Since it was ripe for harvest anyway, after she went to work that night, I retrieved it, took it to my friend's house and we cooked it. We got a lot of seeds from that plant and became creative in finding locations to plant them.

Proverb 3:9 Honour the LORD with thy substance, and with the first fruits of all thine increase:

It is certain that I was not honoring the LORD as I did not know HIM yet, I was breaking the law and, I was abusing my body. It is funny how time changes some things. It is no longer a crime to smoke or have a certain amount on your person. Also, over the years it has been found to treat some conditions including pain and depression.

I do use it occasionally for the pain caused by the Traumatic Brain Injury I received in January of 2011. I also need it to fall asleep once in a while and can only use edibles because I have severe asthma so, cannot smoke. Being completely blind, the alure of getting stoned is no longer attractive to me.

17
WHAT CAN YOU SEE?
JUNE OF 1975

My mother has always been a very observant person and has taught her children to be the same way. We were driving home and had stopped at a light. While waiting for the light to turn green, my mother began to look around. It was late at night and the headlights were on.

Someone rode up on a bicycle across the street to our right and made a right turn onto the road straight ahead of us. As they began to ride away, the reflectors on the pedals were the only thing you could see bobbing up and down.

At that moment my mother's brain began to process all the things I had told her over the years about my vision or, lack thereof. The light turned green and she began to drive again. I became a little concerned because it seemed that she was paying more attention to the world around her and less to her driving. Just to let you know, we arrived home safely.

She would see something and try to point it out to me. She would use the directions, up, down, right left, and, sometimes she would grab my arm and point it directly at the object when I was not able to find it otherwise.

Once I located the object, if I could at all, she would have me describe exactly what I saw. Then she would tell me what it was. Suddenly she said, "Look over there" and pointed my arm toward the right. She was pointing to a black gentleman who was wearing dark clothing and white sneakers. He was running across our path.

Needless to say, the only thing I saw were the sneakers running down the road by themselves. When I described that to my mother, she burst out laughing because she was beginning to realize what things must look like for me.

It has been difficult over the years to describe to people my visual condition. First, because it changed from day to day, second, because it depended heavily upon the light source. Also, since my field of vision was greatly diminished, there would be times when my eyes would land in just the right spot while most of the time it took a great deal of effort and adjustment to lock on to something if I could at all.

I am grateful that, though most of the rest of the world could not or would not understand, I could always count on my mother to try to put herself in my place and then, after having both points of view, try her best to help me overcome an obstacle or accomplish a task. Thanks mom!

Mark 8:22 And he cometh to Bethsaida; and they bring a blind man unto him, and besought him to touch him. 23 And he took the blind man by the hand, and led him out of the town; and when he had spit on his eyes, and put his hands upon him, he asked him if he saw ought. 24 And he looked up, and said, I see men as trees, walking.

I saw, for years, the way the man above saw for moments. Fortunately, Jesus did not leave him that way.

Mark 8:25 After that he put his hands again upon his eyes, and made him look up: and he was restored, and saw every man clearly.

He will not leave me blind either. Whether here or in Heaven, someday the LORD will give me perfect vision as well, and you too if you but ask Him.

18
THE MAYFAIR
JUNE OF 1975

It has been so long since it happened that I do not remember the name of the girl but, she and I were going to the Mayfair to see a movie. The theater was about 7 blocks from my home. We were walking there and had gotten to within one and a half blocks of it when we began to argue about something. She was so mad that she stomped away saying that she was going to go home.

It was already getting dark and I considered going home but decided that since the theater was much closer than home, I would go see the movie by myself. Since I had been there many times before, I knew the setup and figured I could pull it off on my own.

I walked up to where you purchased the tickets and gave them my money. They handed me the ticket and I went through the door between the velvet covered cattle directors. I could sense that there were people in front of me so I moved up slowly and managed to get to the ticket collector without incident. As I approached the ticket collector, I held my ticket out a little and pretended to be looking through the doors. I figured that he would see that I was not paying attention to him and that he would grab my ticket, tear it in half and place the stub in my hand, and he did.

I walked through the doors very slowly and a little to my left where I knew the wall behind the first row should be. I then followed it until it ended. I made a left and began walking down the aisle, angling toward the right so I would find the middle row. When I found it, I continued walking down the aisle looking at the screen to judge the best place to sit. When I found it, I began side stepping into the row.

Every time I have been to the theater and walked into a row with people seated there, I could feel their knees against the backs of my legs." I figured that if I walked slow enough and paid close attention, I would be able to find an empty seat. There it was, about seven seats in, a seat with no knees in the back of my legs.

I sat down only to jump back up again immediately. Just as my but touched what should have been the seat cushion, I felt a skinny pair of legs. I was attempting to apologize but the owner of those legs was obviously not able to hear me above her screams for help. She was still hitting me with her purse when the usher with his flash light on came down to ascertain the trouble.

The man lived up to his title because he grabbed my arm and ushered me out of the theater. He was making grunts and other noises of disbelief as I tried to explain that I was blind and did not know the lady was seated there.

At that moment my x-date came in to the theater and saw that I was in trouble. She asked the usher what the problem was and when he explained what had just occurred, she explained to the gentleman what I had been trying to tell him for the last few minutes.

I guess the shock of that experience was greater than I had realized at the time because I cannot remember what the movie was or if we even saw it or were asked to leave.

I know that most of you probably expect me to put the verse, "Hell hath no fury like a woman scorned." However, that is not from the bible. The following is, though.

Proverbs 21:19 It is better to dwell in the wilderness, than with a contentious and an angry woman.

That may have described my date that evening, but the following describes my wife since April 25, 1992.

Proverbs 31:10 Who can find a virtuous woman? for her price is far above rubies.

19
FEEL THIS
AUGUST OF 1975

My friend Ronald and I were invited to a party in Secaucus, New Jersey. When we got there, a bunch of teens were gathered by a chain link fence that was eight feet tall and had barbed wire at the top. We walked over, introduced ourselves and asked what was going on.

They told us that they had been playing frisbee and it had gone over the fence. When I asked why no one climbed over to get it, they told me that it was the guard dog that had discouraged them. I could see the frisbee about fifteen feet from the fence and started to climb.

They all started to yell for me to stop but, since I had little fear of dogs, I continued. As I climbed, the dog remained out of sight. As I got safely over the barbed wire, I jumped to the ground, ran to the frisbee, started running back to the fence, threw the disc to the crowd waiting to see if I would be eaten by the guard dog, and, jumped as high on the fence as possible.

The dog had lunged for me as I could tell from the reaction of the onlookers and from the fence below me shaking from its impact. By the time angry dog tried for me again, I had one leg over the wire and the other one was too high to reach.

We spent the next couple of hours enjoying the party, drinking and playing frisbee. When it started to get dusk, I had to bow out of the game because I could not see well enough to continue playing. The group became quiet and, a few minutes later, they all came over to where I was standing.

They all began to inquire about my vision deficit and, when they were satisfied that, in the dark and with no flashlight, they could move on with their evil plan. One of the boys went behind me and said, "We want you to feel something."

Now, there was a girl there that I was attracted to and, when I asked what they wanted me to feel, he mentioned her name. By this time, it had grown so dark that I could not see anything in front of me. So, when they lifted my hands as if to place them on her breasts, I pulled back.

It was not because I did not want to have that pleasure, it was because I did not want an audience. Though I struggled, I failed. There was one person holding my left and, one on my right and, at least one person pushing me from behind.

When my hands finally made contact with someone's chest, it was one of the guys. I was so relieved because, I was afraid that the girl was also being forced. We all had a great laugh and, I ended up dating the girl for a few weeks.

Proverbs 5:19 Let her be as the loving hind and pleasant roe; let her breasts satisfy thee at all times; and be thou ravished always with her love.

Here we are again, talking about my two favorite subjects. At the time of this story, I did not know the LORD. Now that I do, I am even more glad that I was reluctant to grab that girl and happier that it turned out to be a joke.

I know that my next thought is not popular but, until you are married, and I do not mean the ceremony, you should refrain from touching that intimately. Humans have very little self control. The evidences of that are sexually transmitted diseases, unwanted pregnancies, divorce and broken families.

20
GYMNASTICS BY STROBE LIGHT
SEPTEMBER OF 1975

My mother was a single parent doing a great job of raising her three children while not letting us know that we were poor. She worked, struggled, saved and cut corners in order to provide us with opportunities.

One of the greatest opportunities she gave me was gymnastic lessons. I fell in love with gymnastics quickly and to this day I cannot listen to a routine without crying. Our gym had a few adult instructors and, once we reached a certain level of proficiency and the age of 14, we became instructors.

We were in New Jersey and would occasionally travel to other states for competition. We would also hold many exhibitions. Most of the exhibitions were for the younger children but, once in a while we would have an exhibition for the older gymnasts.

By this time, I had lost all night vision. The exhibition the adult instructors wanted us to do was around the music by the rock group "Queen." They had selected the pieces "We will rock you" and "We are the Champions." They had also decided that we would do it with black lights.

It is possible that my memory has failed me but, I do not remember practicing the routine in the dark with the strobe lights, the way we did it before our audience afterward. We had set up the mats in an x in the middle of the floor. We had a mini tramp at the end of one arm of the x and a horse at the end of the arm next to it.

We had two lines at the other two ends of the cross. to the beat of the music we were supposed to cris cross each other while doing cart wheels, flips, twists and vaults. Though form was always uppermost in the minds of our teachers, on this occasion, with the strobe lights flashing and all of us wearing black clothing with reflective patches, timing was the most important item on the agenda.

I am so glad that we practiced that routine so much because, once they turned out the lights, I could not see a thing. I know that it is mostly due to the grace of God that I did not get hurt nor did I hurt anyone else. Thinking back, if we had practiced it in the dark, I think I would have bowed out because of the fear of injury. As it is, I am thankful that the LORD allowed me the chance, the fun, the thrill and the wonderful memory.

I am not ashamed to tell you that as I wrote the last paragraph there were tears in my eyes. If you are reading this and have a degenerative eye condition, I encourage you to get out there and do what you can now so that you will not regret later that you did not try.

My mother had encouraged me to get into gymnastics because she felt it would put some meat on my bones and help my asthma. She was correct about both. I did not know at the time the sacrifices she had to make in order to pay for my classes. I think however, that she felt compensated in full when she breathlessly and half in shock, watched her blind son fly through the air with the others that day.

Isaiah 9:2 The people that walked in darkness have seen a great light: they that dwell in the land of the shadow of death, upon them hath the light shined.

The people sitting and watching that night would have said that the lights they saw jumping, twisting and flipping in that darkness were great, especially my mother. However, The Greatest light is Jesus and, if you follow Him, you will have greatness for eternity.

21
CAN I GET A LIFT?
NOVEMBER OF 1975

Unless there was a lot of snow on the roads, I rode my bicycle to school every day. After my tires were flat while chained to the bike rack in front for the second time, I got permission to chain it around back in the teacher's lot. My math teacher had obtained the pass for me when I told him what had been happening.

Now, at the end of the school day, I could walk through the weight room to the back and get my bike. I had been doing this for a few weeks and, every day I was taunted by the wrestlers and football jocks. I ignored them until this day.

I had not joined either team because I did not like their superior attitude nor the way they tortured those beneath them. I was so tired of listening to their taunts that I stopped and asked, "Which one of you can bench the most?" I told the guy that responded to place the weight on the bar and move away.

I laid on the bench and two of them came near the bar to spot so I told them that I did not want a spot. I picked up the weight, slowly brought it to my chest, lifted it back up slowly and racked it. I then got up and told them that, "Pound for pound, gymnasts are the strongest people in the world."

I then went to my bicycle, went to the newspaper office, delivered my papers and went home. From the next day on, not only did they stop taunting me but, they greeted me and offered to lift with me. I had to decline because of my paper rout but no longer ignored them.

Some of them even greeted me in the halls. That caused some of my friends to question my loyalties until I explained what had happened.

Judges 16:2 And it was told the Gazites, saying, Samson is come hither. And they compassed him in, and laid wait for him all night in the gate of the city, and were quiet all the night, saying, In the morning, when it is day, we shall kill him. 3 And Samson lay till midnight, and arose at midnight, and took the doors of the gate of the city, and the two posts, and went away with them, bar and all, and put them upon his shoulders, and carried them up to the top of an hill that is before Hebron.

Okay, the jocks did not want to kill me and I did not carry away doors that weighed hundreds of pounds each. But, the Gazites had no idea how strong Samson was until he proved it to them and, they never bothered him again once he did.

22
TWILIGHT ZONE
April of 1976

In our lunch room, we played several table games once we were done eating. I know, by now you are thinking, 'Were you ever done eating?' Yes, because next to food, which for me was fuel, I loved sports. We played hockey with three coins or football with a standard sheet of paper folded into a triangle.

We will start with football which, other than girls, was my greatest love. Take a piece of paper, fold it in half the long way, then fold it in fourths by putting the edges inside the already folded area. Now you have a sheet that is two and an eighth inches by eleven.

Now take the paper and fold the bottom right corner up and to the left so you end up with a triangle. Now fold the right end toward the left at the vertical edge of that triangle. Keep folding the paper toward the left making triangles until you do not have enough to make another fold.

Tuck that last piece into the fold and voila, you have a football suitable for a high school cafeteria. Now to play. Place the long end of the triangle at the edge of your side of the table and flick it toward the other side.

The "goal" is to get part of the football to hang over the edge of the opponent's side in four flicks if the table is four feet wide, three if it is three feet wide. Let us stick with a four feet table as that is what we had. If you get it to hang in three flicks, you get six points.

If not, you can try for a field goal. The field goal and extra point are the same process. The opponent holds his hands up like he is going to frame a camera shot with one thumb overlapping the other. You place the tip of the football on the table, balance it by holding the other tip with the pad of your index finger and flick it through the uprights with your other index finger.

Now for hocky

Hold three coins in the palm of your hand and drop them onto the table. Flick one coin through the other two and repeat the process until you are ready to shoot for a goal. The opponent holds his index and pinky on the table with the ring and middle fingers bent down and against the table's edge.

The fingers forming the goal must be parallel or wider. At any time, including just after the drop, you can shoot for the goal. If you hit the knuckles of the ring or middle finger, Score! If not, it is the other person's tern. It does not matter how many times you zig zag the coins.

Sometimes my friends would get fancy and even shoot them backward a few times to let me know how good they were. For some reason, a contest started in our school to stick pennies into the drop ceiling tiles. I have no idea how much money ended up in the tiles of our school but, I envied the janitor who got to spend the entire summer pulling out the coins.

When we were done playing hockey one day, my friend Kevin and I decided to see who could get a penny to stick first. He won.

Segue to a Twilight Zone episode:

A man was standing next to a pile of newspapers with a box for coins on a table. People would take a paper while walking by and throw the price of that paper into the box. A man walks by, grabs a paper, throws a quarter into the box and, it stands on edge.

For the rest of the day, the quarter chucker can read minds. He forgets to take the paper home with him after work so stops for another at the same stand. As he throws a coin into the box, he knocks down his quarter from earlier and his ability to penetrate the craniums of others ceases.

Back to the story:

Kevin's penny stuck on the first shot. Mine did not so, I tried again. It did not stick on the second try either but, after bouncing on the table two or three times, it stood on edge. I was hoping I would be able to read minds but, after marveling for a moment, Kevin knocked my penny down.

I got just as frustrated with him as the paper seller did with his customer. No, I was not able to read minds unless you count the fact that I knew Kevin would not let my coin stand for long.

Hebrews 10: 16 This is the covenant that I will make with them after those days, saith the Lord, I will put my laws into their hearts, and in their minds will I write them.

Knowing what is sometimes in my mind, I am glad that I was not granted the ability to read other's thoughts. As that episode of the TZ showed, knowing other's thoughts can be very damaging. I am much better off having God place his laws on my mind, though I sometimes try to erase what He places there.

23
LOOK WHAT I CAUGHT
MAY OF 1976

I had been rescued by my mother from two years of torture just after my eleventh birthday. I was completely blind in my left eye, legally blind in my right, had twenty-five cavities, was doubled over with debilitating asthma and weighed only fifty-nine pounds.

If it had not been for one of the three most wonderful women I have ever known, Mom-Mom Margarete, I would have died. When she realized what was being done to me, she arranged for me to spend a lot of time at her home. She fed me and gave me some of her asthma medicine.

As my mother took me to the eye doctor, dentist and asthma doctors in order to try to get me healthy, she also tried to help me gain weight. No matter how much I ate, I could not seem to put on pounds. That is when she had me drink Carnation Instant Breakfast drinks with my food.

In addition, she encouraged me to join the Boy Scouts, try out for sports and join a gymnastic organization called Sokol Hall. Those three activities, more than anything else, helped me regain my health. I played baseball and a lot of basketball but, fell in love with football.

Gymnastics not only helped me gain muscle mass that I sorely needed, it taught me leadership skills. At the ripe-old-age of fourteen, I became a gymnastic instructor. I and a few friends started teaching the five to twelve-year-old boys.

We were coming up on an exhibition for the younger children so, we were training them hard. The younger student's show for their parents was very different than the demonstrations put on by those of us that were thirteen and older. There were three spots that people could watch the youngsters from.

I and my best friend Kevin were spotting and directing the young men on the side horse vault. I was standing slightly forward of the horse to keep the boys from hurting themselves while Kevin directed them back around the apparatus so traffic would flow smoothly.

If you had been one of the parents, you might have thought that I was not paying enough attention because my friend and I were carrying on a conversation. You would have been mistaken though. I was paying such close attention that, those watching could not believe what they saw.

If you are not familiar with the side horse vault, it goes as follows. You run toward the horse. Through hundreds of practice runs, you figure out where your launch spot is. When you hit that spot, you jump and land on the white line that gives you the maximum spring.

Then, you fly toward the horse with your hands out like Superman. You place your palms on the horse, stiffen your arms, straighten your torso up, bend your knees, have your feet land on the horse and stand up with your arms spread up and out in victory.

After a pause of two or three seconds, you jump down and allow the other instructor to guide you back in line to do it again. This time however, as an eight-year-old boy hit the spring board, he flew too high. As he was about to land head first on the oak panel floor, you could hear the intake of breath of several mothers.

As he flew by me, I reached out and grabbed his ankle, held him in midair, placed my other hand on his stomach, folded him in half and placed him on his feet. As they realized that the child was not going to smash his head on the floor, the sound of relief from those paying attention was almost surreal.

Proverbs 4:20 My son, attend to my words; incline thine ear unto my sayings.

I know that my instructors were not my parents. But, Judy, John and the others were parental figures. We listened to the instructions they gave us which were designed to help us become better athletes. We also listened to the directions they gave regarding our responsibilities for those we were training.

Within two years of this incident, I had to retire as a gymnast and as a trainer as I had lost too much vision to continue safely.

24
YOU'RE WHERE?
MAY OF 1976

Across from my friend Kevin's house and to the right was our gymnastic organization. to the right was a parking lot for something I cannot remember. Across the street from that lot was a set of garages. This made for a wonderful place to play games.

We played stick ball, wiffle ball, frisbee, hocky, running the bases and, a lot of football. For hockey, we used a crushed soda can so, if one of us got too exuberant, little or no damage would be done to cars, walls or other property.

Running the bases was easy since we were all great at catching the ball. One person would stand on a man-hole-cover, another would stand on the next cover and, everyone else had to try to get to one of the covers while the ball was in play.

It amazes me that, as fast as we threw the ball to each other and, with as many as five of us in the middle, no one ever got hit in the head. The other games are self-explanatory so we will move on to the game we played the most, FOOTBALL, YOU BET!

Six of us were playing football this day and, as good as we were at most of the aspects of the game, we all sucked at kicking. It is surprising that, as many times as we hit cars, windshields, houses and windows, we did not cause any damage.

James lived on the other side of the street from Kevin and, on fourth down, he decided to kick the ball rather than throw it. It ended up on his roof which was two stories high. We were all bummed because we did not have another football available at that time.

I loved climbing things and, with James' grudging permission, I placed my butt and hands against his father's home and my feet on the house next door. I walked up between the two buildings until I reached the top.

Because I had studied Kung Fu as well as gymnastics, I was able to push off with my feet, do a back roll with a twist, land on the roof and roll, all without getting hurt but, not without noise. Moments later, Mister M came out the front door yelling, "What the hell was that?"

When James told him that I had climbed onto the roof to retrieve our football, he yelled for me to come down. I refused because he was so mad and I did not want to be physically chastised upon my descent. When I told him that I would come down if he went inside, he refused.

I threw the ball down to Kevin and proceeded to hop from building to building until I got to the home just before the projects. Then there was a problem. The project fence was about ten feet tall but, the building I was on was more like sixteen feet tall. So, I hung off the edge, pushed off, did a half twist in the air and grabbed the chain links toward the top.

I then climbed over the fence, walked through the projects, got to my home, took a shower because I was filthy and called Kevin. Mrs. S was preparing dinner when she answered my call. She was surprised that it was me on the phone and asked where I was.

When I told her, she yelled for Kevin. When he got on the phone, he was a little freaked because there were three police cars and two fire engines out front looking for me. They had searched all the buildings, alleys and back yards but could not find me.

Because they thought I must be hiding somewhere, they continued to search until Kevin went out front to let the police know that I was home. When he got back to the porch, where all the guys were waiting for them to find my body, he told them that I was on the phone.

It warmed my heart to hear them bust up with so much laughter and so many comments. When Kevin got back to the phone, I told him that I would return once I had something to eat because the officials should be gone by the time I arrived.

Jeremiah 23:24 Can any hide himself in secret places that I shall not see him? saith the LORD. Do not I fill heaven and earth? saith the LORD.

I may have been able to hide from the police and from the fire department but, though I tried for many years, I was not able to hide from God. He found me in 1978 and I tried to continue to live for myself for the next thirteen years. Finally, I came out of hiding and have been serving Him since August of 1991.

I had looked forward to the day that I would have served the LORD longer than I had lived for the devil. That moment came on September 12, 2022 at 3:48am. That is, assuming that I gave my life to Jesus at 3:48pm on August 8, 1991.

I am sure of the date and, it was after 3:30 that afternoon so, I just decided to claim that time. I know that it is silly but, I love numbers and could not help myself but to figure it out.

25
SAFE!
JUNE OF 1976

My mother and step-father wanted some time alone so, I was asked to take my sisters and step-brother on an outing that Ronald and I had planned. We were going to ride our bikes along the March of Dimes twenty-five-mile trail that we had walked over a year ago.

We would start at Hudson County Park, which has since been renamed to, "James J. Braddock Park." We would then travel along Kennedy Boulevard to Washington Park in Jersey City. Once there, we planned on having lunch and resting for a while before heading back.

Until the age of nine, we lived on Poplar Street in JC and, since we were approaching it, I turned my head to yell at the gang behind me that we were approaching that street. I had been riding my bike with no hands because I had a drink in my left hand and a sandwich in my right.

Just as I turned my head around, a semi-truck was emerging from the street I was about to cross. I heard my sisters scream as the truck driver hit his breaks and scared me into action. I shoved the last of my sandwich into my mouth, grabbed the handle bar, hit the brakes and slid sideways under the truck.

We were now completely blocking traffic in one direction of Kennedy Boulevard as well as the side street he had come from. He jumped out of his rig, ran over to me and, when he realized that I was unharmed, he threw me a fifty, ran back to his cab and took off.

I guess he did not want to hang around for a police report to be created. After brushing myself off, we went down the street to see our old apartment and our favorite neighbors, the Zambeckies. The rest of the trip was without incident and, I do not believe anyone ever told my mother. This might have been the first time I recognized that my peripheral vision was diminishing.

Proverbs 4:1 Hear, ye children, the instruction of a father, and attend to know understanding.

Change the word father to mother and, you will realize that I was not obeying the principle of this verse. Parents are always telling their children to be careful and, after a while, as they say, "It goes in one ear and out the other." I do not know who "they" are but, they are right. As someone else has said, "The older I get, the smarter my parents were."

I suppose that I paid more attention from that point on, at least until the next day.

26
TACKLED BY A BEE
JUNE OF 1976

My step-father Tony, was a Pop Warner football coach. When he entered our lives, I was fifteen. I loved playing and watching football so went to many of the games he coached. I even ended up helping him as some sort of assistant.

The team he coached was from Weehawken, New Jersey so, every Saturday that they had a game there, I would ride my bike to the field. I had been studying carpentry in school and took the opportunity to use my new knowledge a few times.

Once, the screws that held the strike plate for the supply room came loose and, none of the men could figure out how to fix it. There were quite a few smokers in the crowd so I went around until I found someone with a book of matches, they would let me have.

I love how people used to look out for each other back then. Before handing them to me, he warned me about the dangers of smoking. I took three of the matches out of the book, ripped the heads off of them, placed them one hundred and twenty degrees from each other and put the screw back in.

Not only did it hold securely so you could once again lock the door but, the men all proclaimed me to be a genius. I rarely went to any away games because I preferred to be playing football with my friends and teams from the surrounding towns than spending hours in the car.

There was one away game that I went to in Saddlebrook, New Jersey. My mother wanted us to all go as a family, so I agreed. It turns out to have been a good decision for one of our cheer-leaders. It turns out that she was allergic to bees and got stung during warm-up.

The best hot dogs in the world are by the Sabrett company. They also have the best mustard, sour kraut and onions in red sauce. After arriving, I went right for the concession stand to see if they had my kind of hot dogs. I was just about to place an order for three hot dogs with mustard and sour kraut, French fries and a large root beer when I was paged over the stadium speakers.

A side note about me and hot dogs. Once, when on my way to work at Davis Toys, I decided to walk. I was in the mood for hot dogs and, since the walk was only two miles, I figured I could get a few on the way. I started at seventy fifth street but did not find a vender until sixtieth.

At the first stand, I got a Dirty Water Dog with mustard and sour kraut. As I walked to the next stand, I ravenously devoured the first one. At the second stop, my choice was mustard and red onions. As I have traveled around the country, I have found that, unless you are from New York or New Jersey, everyone thinks that red onions are diced red onions.

If you are from New York or New Jersey, you know that red onions are onions simmered to death in a red sauce. My third stop yielded a dog with mustard and chili and my fourth gave me one with mustard, sour kraut, onions and chili.

You might find this hard to believe unless you knew me before I hit thirty-five but, I repeated that pattern twice more. That is correct, I had a total of twelve hot dogs in twelve city blocks.

Many of the children in my neighborhood knew how much I could eat and would walk up to me and knock on one of my legs. Why you ask? Because some little person once heard my mother utter, "He has a hollow leg." It morphed into my having a wooden leg and the youngsters wanted to find out which one of my legs had been a tree once.

Back to the real story.

I heard my name, emergency and return to your team. Though the teams were on the field practicing, I ran straight across, treating the word emergency seriously. When I arrived, I was brought to the girl that had been stung. The bee's stinger was still in her inner thigh so I took over.

She was dizzy, faint and, the area around the stinger was darker than the rest of her skin. I asked one of the men nearby to help me carry her to a shady spot behind the bleachers. I had someone run for some water and someone else run for something to cover her with and to use as a pillow.

I also had someone run to call for an ambulance. Once we got her in position and made her comfortable, I removed the stinger, gave her some water to drink, used some of the water to make a mud poultice and applied it to the injury.

This was before it was common to have EMS at sporting competitions. A few minutes after applying the mud to her leg, we heard the ambulance approaching. It was so weird to see a vehicle drive across the football field, straight for us.

After giving her a shot of adrenaline, they placed her on a stretcher. They tried to roll it to the van but, there were too many rocks. They lowered the gurney down again and carried her to the ambulance.

Once they secured her in, one of the EMS workers came over to me and asked, "Good job, where did you train?" When I said, "The Boy Scouts.", he told me to think about becoming an Emergency Medical Service Teck.

I continued to study medicine and first aid but, I never did try to become an EMS worker. At last count though, I have saved the lives of thirteen people and led nine people to give their lives to Jesus Christ, a more important way of saving lives.

1 Corinthians 15:55 O death, where is thy sting? O grave, where is thy victory?

Of course, this verse is talking about accepting God's gift and avoiding the Lake of Fire. If I had heard this verse just after saving the cheer leader, I would have shouted, "Ha!"

27
YOU EAT TOO MUCH
JUNE OF 1976

This story has more to do with ignorance, mental blindness, than it does with physical blindness. It has been said that many times when we often claim to have forgotten something, not heard something or not seen something it is out of convenience rather than true impairment. By this time my left eye had developed a cataract and my vision was starting to be affected more than just at night.

I had a paper route for the last four years and had made a lot of money but, I wanted to make even more money and to be able to make it more quickly. After looking in the paper and considering many items, I decided to go to Carvel and apply. I was accepted and began working the following week.

Since I was familiar with the items, having eaten most of them, it did not take long to master making them. Most of what people wanted was custom stuff anyway. The one thing that I did not master was giving the customer the least amount of ice cream on their cone while still being able to dip it in the chocolate or sprinkles without losing the ice cream in the process. You were supposed to put a little in the base of the cone and press the ice cream in circles on the rim so that it compressed enough to not fall off.

I suppose if I had practiced more, I would have gotten the hang of it but instead, I smashed the base of the cone full of ice cream to anchor it. Though the boss said that I was doing a good job, he took me off the line and had me start making the ice creams.

You would make sure there was enough mixture in the machine, usually the vanilla machine. Then you would get a five-gallon container and layer the bottom with strips of ice cream you cut off with a knife and laid side by side. The trick was to put down each layer so that it looked tight but had plenty of air. Then you would put in a layer of fudge, fruit, mint or chips, depending on what flavor you were making.

I had a lot of fun making the different flavors because until this time, I had not considered how in the world they were made. When I was hired, I was told by the boss that as long as you were working you were allowed to eat whatever you wanted except the cakes. I took him up on the offer.

While I was working front for the first two days it was hard to eat because you were constantly waiting on customers so you had to put your snack down. This caused most of the workers to default to shakes or malted. The instant he put me on making the stuff, I discovered how to work with one hand while eating with the other.

The boss was present most of the time. He would walk around giving directions as to what needed to be restocked or cleaned or how someone could do something more efficiently. The first day he gave me a lot of directions on the best ways to make the different flavors but, by the second day of making them, my third day at work, the only directions he gave me were what flavors to make.

The end of the week came and the boss called me aside. I had no idea what he was going to say but I certainly did not expect to get paid yet because I was told when I was hired that I would not get paid until the second week. I was surprised when he placed a check in my hand and even more surprised, shocked even, when he said, "I am sorry but I am going to have to let you go."

When I asked him why he said that I ate too much. I repeated his instructions that we were allowed to eat as much as we wanted as long as we were working. He then said, "That is true but, usually the workers get sick of the stuff after two or three days and stop eating, you just kept on going." I was too stunned to think of an objection so I just pouted and left. As I stopped to get a hotdog with mustard and sour kraut from a street vender I thought of the question I should have asked. I considered turning around and asking it but figured it would do no good so I just walked home eating my hot dog.

Though I lost a job I liked doing it was a good experience because it put me on the road to being able to respond quickly and intelligently.

I decided that I was never again going to be fired without exhausting all the angles or without a fight.

Proverbs 23:21 For the drunkard and the glutton shall come to poverty: and drowsiness shall clothe a man with rags.

Obviously, because I was a glutton, I lost my job and, temporarily was poor. However, I learned my lesson and never took advantage of fringe benefits again.

28
FOREST FIRE
JULY OF 1976

I was now a Junior Assistant Scout Master in charge of thirty-three children from twelve to seventeen-years-old. We were camping at Nobebosco camp which we found out upon arrival, was not exclusively a Boy Scout Camp. We had a wonderful Friday but, when I woke up the next morning, I smelled smoke.

I know, we were camping so, smelling smoke should not have caused alarm bells to go off in my head. Even when you bank a fire before going to bed, you do not smell its smoke in the morning. What I was smelling was thick and smelled like more than just fire wood. I got two of the older boys up and asked them to help me locate the source.

Though I could smell the problem, I could not see well enough to locate the smoke and trace it back to its location. What we found was the next camp sight, about two acres away, blazing. The campers had built their fire too close to the cabin they were staying in. During the night, it caught fire and, rather than getting help, they took off.

By the time we discovered the conflagration, at least a half-acre was involved and spreading quickly. I had my two friends wake up the entire camp, had them send two boys to the ranger station to call the fire department and got to work. I had the older boys get axes, hatchets and saws while sending the younger boys for the Indian pumps and buckets.

If you do not know, Indian pumps are five-gallon containers you wear on your back, have an opening at the top and a hose with a pump at the end. I know it sounds like foolish pride but, when the Scout Master arrived with our two assistants, because I was already leading the effort, he let me take charge. I had the three men begin clearing brush, digging ditches and chopping trees that were on fire into the main blaze.

I had the bigger boys use the pumps to wet the brush, ground and trees that had not yet caught since they could see the direction of the sparks. The younger boys were running between the water source and the pumps to keep them filled, allowing the pumpers to work non-stop. Some of the smaller guys had to carry an empty bucket so they could turn it upside down and stand on it to reach the top of the containers.

I had my back to the fire so I could chop enough of the tree so it could be pushed into the fire. By the time the fire truck arrived, it had been over two hours of hard work. Whenever I hear the phrase, "Go jump in the lake", it reminds me of that fire because, that is just what we all did once the Firemen took over. Except for what happened next, it was actually a wonderful experience.

Once we were done washing up and had started on our delayed breakfast, the Ranger came over to speak with our Scout Masters. He accused us of having started the fire. The Scout Master had the Forest Ranger speak with me and to ask questions and gather evidence. It was hard for me to keep my temper as I had first, second and a few third degree burns from helping to put out what others foolishly started.

However, after going over the smoldering mess, pointing out what was left behind by the other campers and having him go through the records to find out who had rented the cabin, we were cleared. A few months later, our troop got an apology letter and a citation for preventing a greater disaster. I, Howard and Phil Junior were named in the document.

Philippians 2:14 Do all things without murmurings and disputings: 15 That ye may be blameless and harmless, the sons of God, without rebuke, in the midst of a crooked and perverse nation, among whom ye shine as lights in the world.

In the Boy Scouts, we have very specific rules for building, retaining, banking and putting out fires. We knew that we were innocent and it wrangled us to be accused. As verse fourteen suggests, we did the work of containing the fire, not only without murmuring, we did it with excitement and joy. We may not, as verse fifteen suggest, seemed blameless in the Ranger's eyes. However, as Shakespeare said, "The truth will out!" It may have taken three months for the truth to come out, but it did.

29
TAKE HER OFF MY HANDS PLEASE
JULY OF 1976

My mother had a dear friend that she discovered at APA Trucking Company. For about fifty years, my mother worked for two trucking companies. The first one I just mentioned and she worked there about fourteen years. The second one was New Penn where she worked for thirty-five years.

Her friend, Anne Guill, was known to us as Aunt Anne. She lived in Ringwood, New Jersey and drove one hour to and one hour from work each day. One day, my mother told us that we were going to visit Aunt Anne and that we should take our bathing suits. I thought that meant that she had a swimming pool.

Instead, she took us to a place called, "Shepheard's Lake." It is a spring fed lake of about seventy-four acres. It has a sand beach, woods surrounding the lake and a large picnic area. Once we discovered it, we returned many times each year.

In the span of a week or two, our parents each rescued a puppy from their jobs. Since my step-father Tony was one hundred percent Italian, he named his dog, Ronzoni. Since the puppy she rescued loved cookies, my mother named her Cookie.

I do not remember why but, we took the dogs to the lake. Except for the liquid in their bowls, they had never seen water. As we got close to the water, we let the dogs go. Still being puppies, they had boundless energy and ran full tilt at the lake.

They must have thought that it was a great wide-open place to run because, that is what they tried to do. After taking a few steps into the water, they both turned around, ran out of the lake, turned back around to face the lake and began to growl and bark.

I have often wondered what it would be like if animals had a balloon over their heads like in comic strips. I imagine that Cookie's barks were saying, 'I don't like being tricked like that! I thought you were ground that I could run on!" I figured that Ronzoni's growls were saying, "I hate being this wet and want to know why you did this to me?"

Months later, when the lake was open for business, I and my best friend Ronald went up there for the day. While I was swimming beyond the float ropes, I heard the life guard whistles. Since I had been a life guard in the Boy Scouts, those sounds kicked me into action.

I immediately looked toward the stand to see in what direction they were running. When I noticed that their direction would have taken them about fifteen feet to my right, I sunk under the water and looked in that direction. I saw a little girl, about eight-years-old, sinking toward the bottom.

I swam over to her, grabbed her under the arms, lifted her above the water and swam toward her rescuers. I lifted the float rope and handed her off to the young men when they arrived. I was surprised when they started chastising me for what I had done. When I told them that I was a life guard, they calmed down a bit but still looked unhappy.

I was more surprised when later, as I passed the stand, I asked how the girl was and was given the terse reply, "She's fine but you should not have tried to save her." I replied, "I should have just let her drown?" When he said, "We would have gotten her.", I just walked away shaking my head.

Song Of Solomon 8:7 Many waters cannot quench love, neither can the floods drown it: if a man would give all the substance of his house for love, it would utterly be contemned.

I rescued the little girl because I love little people and wanted to help. The attitude of the guards made me feel like their only impetus was that they were getting paid to do a job. I could be wrong but, I believe that if I had been in their situation, I would have been grateful for the assist.

30
HONKEYS
JULY OF 1977

Until July of 1977, we lived at 211 69th Street in Guttenberg, New Jersey. My mother and Tony got married in February the previous year and began looking for a house because the apartment we were living in was too small for the five of us plus occasionally having one, two or three of Tony's children living with us.

As noted in the story, 'Tic Toc Crash Bang Boom', I had lost my ability to see at night by the age of twelve. We lived in such a small town that it was not hard for me to get everywhere I wanted to go without seeing much more than the street light, traffic lights and the head and tail lights of the cars around me.

My two best friends lived just one and two blocks away from me. Ronald was half a block down the street, make a right, go another half block and cross the two-lane street. He lived between sixty eighth and sixty ninth streets. Kevin lived in the other direction on Seventieth Street.

to get to his house I had to cross two streets that were one lane and one street that was two lanes though it was only two blocks away. Ronald and I listened to music, smoked legal and illegal substances, talked about girls, drank a lot of beer and rode our bikes until we purchased a 1964 and a half classic Mustang together.

It was in bad shape which is why it cost us only one hundred and seventy-five dollars. After doing all the work on it ourselves and using it for two years, we sold it for four thousand dollars and bought a Gremlin.

Kevin and I were gymnasts together, played a lot of football, pool and poker with some of our other friends. Once we moved to 219 75th Street in North Bergen, New Jersey, it became more difficult for me to get to their places in the dark. On this particular evening, I was walking to Kevin's house to play pool and poker.

Because I did not want to run into the crazies in front of the pizza place after closing, I crossed the street and turned right. When I got to 73rd Street, there was a truck waiting at the corner to cross. I waited for them to pass but, when I heard the driver yell out his window that I should go, I began to walk across the street.

When I was in front of his truck, he blasted his horn which almost gave me a heart attack. I continued to walk to the other curb while cursing them as they laughed loudly. For a long time, I had many evil thoughts against those boys. However, once I gave my life to Jesus, I began to pray for them instead.

I know that I have done some things to people over the years that I would love to go back and apologize for. So, my prayers for them were that they would remember what they did, be truly sorry for what they did and, come to know the LORD and His forgiveness.

Matthew 6:15 But if ye forgive not men their trespasses, neither will your Father forgive your trespasses.

This is a very hard one for me because, it is my opinion that forgiveness cannot be given unless it is asked for. No one gets into Heaven unless they repent to Jesus so, since He is my example in everything, I do not forgive until I am asked. That does not mean that I continue to stew over those that have wronged me. Instead, I give them over to the LORD to deal with.

As has happened many times, they eventually come to me asking for forgiveness and, without hesitation, I give it. I love how God has restored many relationships this way over the years.

31
OVER THE TOP
JULY OF 1976

I, two sisters, two step-sisters, one step-brother, my new step-father and my mother packed into a station wagon and headed for Florida. We were on our way to Walt Disney World. On the way we stopped and spent a day at Water World, at least that is what I think it was called. In my opinion, we should have just spent the whole vacation there.

Once we had gotten to Disney World, we discovered that the greater part of the time was spent standing in line, waiting and getting sunburned. Yes, some of it was fun but, if it takes more than ten minutes to get on a ride, that is too long.

I do not remember many of the rides at Water World even though we did go on many of them. There are two that stick out in my mind very well. The first was a slide that you lay down on belly first. You slide ten to fifteen feet and end up diving into the water. I suppose I could blame what happened on many things but, I will just admit to having had a "Blond Moment."

I was facing the water even though I could not see it or more precisely, because I could not see it. I have been around water enough to know that you tuck your head in when you dive. As my face connected with the water, I thought that my eyeballs had popped out. It was so painful that I was not able to open my eyes for a while. That was a mistake that I have not repeated to this day.

Since my sister Donna was right behind me, I yelled to her. My sister however, despite my warning, ended up doing the same thing. Perhaps she did not hear me.

The second ride was a body flume. You had to walk up quite a few sets of stairs to get to the launch point. Once there you had two options. You could take the six-hundred-foot slide or the six-hundred-and-sixty-foot slide. Naturally the line was longer for the longer slide but, since we all wanted to go on the longer one, we decided to wait.

Once my eyes began to be affected during the day, they became highly sensitive to sun light. Until glasses that could filter out the ultra-violet light became available, I had to ware darker and darker sun glasses each year. By this time, I was having trouble seeing some things because of the glare and I missed something very important at the beginning of this ride.

I found out after the ride that there was a sign that said you could only go down face up and feet first. Not knowing this, as soon as they gave me the go ahead, I dove into the body flume. I immediately herd people yelling at me but, I was having too much fun to try to figure out what they were saying.

I was picking up a great deal of speed and was enjoying the ride immensely. I came to a serious turn. I began to ride up the wall and at one point was so high that I could see the structure holding the flume together. I could also see down to the bottom, which seemed to be about three hundred feet straight down.

I thought my life would be over in seconds. I managed to spread my legs enough to cause sufficient friction to keep me from going over the edge. It was then that I began trying to hear what the people screaming at me were saying, "Turn around!" So I did. It took a lot of effort to get the job done while speeding down the tube and being thrown up against the left wall and then the right.

When I had finally gotten my feet forward, I lay back and enjoyed the rest of the ride. Upon splashing into the water below I was informed that I would not be allowed to ride that flume again because I broke the rule. I did not think they would be able to pick me out of such a huge crowd if I waited a while and then went up again.

After swimming around for a while I again went up the stairs. I figured that if they did pick me out, I would simply tell them the truth. I had plenty of people with me who could back me up. As it turned out, I reached the top and no one recognized me so, I rode down the flume many more times that day. Of course, I went down feet first.

Job 36:11 If they obey and serve him, they shall spend their days in prosperity, and their years in pleasures.

It was so much more fun going down the flume without the fear of dying and to not be confronted by the workers at the end of the ride.

32
I CANNOT BEAR THIS
JULY OF 1976

I had just been promoted to Junior Assistant Scout Master of Troop 379 in Palisades, New Jersey. I had, just the month before this honor, been voted into the Order of The Arrow. These honors are still two of the proudest moments in my life though they happened forty-eight years ago.

Our troop was going on a two-week camping trip to Floodwood, New York and, because of my recent promotion, I was given much more responsibility over the 33 boys that were attending. One of those responsibilities was the charge of a 11-year-old hyperactive boy named Gary.

His mother agreed to my terms so I took charge of the money she gave him and made her take the 5 pounds of candy that was in his duffel back home with her. It took him three days to come down from the constant sugar high he had been on for the few months I knew him.

We arrived at our camp site, chose our tents and tent mates, unpacked, placed all of our supplies in a locker six feet off the ground under a tarp and had dinner. After the meal, we cleaned up and sat around the camp fire swapping stories. Then we went to bed anticipating the five-mile hike we had planned for tomorrow.

When we arrived back to camp after the hike, we discovered that a bear had destroyed it. He or she had broken into the storage cabinet, eaten most of a loaf of bread, opened a jar of peanut butter, broken a plastic jar of jelly and left behind a thank you.

Most of the boys were freaked out but, when the Ranger came into our camp, gave us some tips, talked with the younger boys and assured all of us that the bear was not dangerous, we cleaned up and had dinner. After some more stories around the camp fire, we were dismissed to bed.

Because I was the senior most Scout in our Troop, I had a tent to myself. As I was preparing for bed, and had stripped down to my Fruit-of-the-Loom's, I heard a crashing noise in the woods behind my tent. I then heard a growl that sounded like a bear.

Rather than wait for him or her to come into my tent to say hello, I ran out the front of my tent. Not more than two steps from the front of my tent, the entire troop had gathered there and was laughing. It turned out that the Scout Master and the two Assistant Scout Masters had arranged an initiation for me.

There was no bear, just the older boys in back of my tent making noise and the younger Scouts slapping the sides of my tent. It was a good prank and, helped me to sleep well that night because all of the adrenaline in my glands had been dumped into my system in less than thirty seconds.

What happened to Gary. Well, because he was not allowed any treats that were heavy with sugar, he became a docile, obedient and helpful young man. When we arrived home, his mother did not even recognize him at first. When I explained what happened, his mother assured me that she would keep sugar away from him. She kept her word, for three months that is.

1 Samuel 17:34 And David said unto Saul, Thy servant kept his father's sheep, and there came a lion, and a bear, and took a lamb out of the flock: 35 And I went out after him, and smote him, and delivered it out of his mouth: and when he arose against me, I caught him by his beard, and smote him, and slew him.

I have always considered myself to be brave. However, I was not brave enough to wait for the bear to enter my tent so I could grab it by the beard and smite it like David did.

33
WHERE ARE MY PANTS?
July of 1976

This story took place the day after the story "I Cannot Bear This." I and another member of our troop, Henry, had gone down to the lake to complete part of our survival training. This part required us to enter the water in our clothing and go out to the part that would be over our heads.

We were supposed to take off our sneakers, tie the laces together and hang them over our heads. Then we had to take off our pants, good thing there were no girls around. Next, tie the ends of each pant leg, whisk them over our heads to fill the legs with air, place one leg on either side of our heads while scrunching the waist together to keep the air in.

This only worked for a few minutes at a time. The purpose was to help keep you afloat to prevent exhaustion if you were trying to traverse a large body of water. Well, the sneaker part went well for both of us. Unfortunately, Henry decided to drop his pants and they sank twelve feet to the bottom of the part of the lake we were in.

He had more pants back at his tent but was mortified at the prospect of walking back to the camp site in his undies. He had a little more ballast than was good for a twelve-foot dive and, no matter how hard he tried, he could not make it.

He begged me to try. I did not think I could possibly find them as my night vision was almost non-existent at this point. But, because I never like to hear a friend whimper, I tried it. He spotted them and helped me to migrate over them.

He must have had glow-in-the-dark pants because, once I got about eight feet down, I saw something at the bottom that was much lighter than the mud. I swam toward the object and, when I put my hand on it, I realized that it was his pants. He was almost hysterical with relief when I came up with them.

Time for a rant:

Why is it a pair of pants? Does that mean that each leg is a pant? If that is true, what do you call the hip and waist area? Why is it not a pair of shirt? If you have two pears, why is it still only a pair? It is no wonder so many people have trouble with the English language!

Back to the story:

Henry untied the legs of his pants and put them on. Putting on wet pants while swimming is not as easy as it might seem. Once he had them on, he quit. I tried to convince him to keep going but, he had enough and went back to the camp for a snack.
I completed the program which included some swimming under ice that winter among other things I am glad I survived but would never want to do again.

Proverbs 18:24 A man that hath friends must shew himself friendly: and there is a friend that sticketh closer than a brother.

I do not know if he had any brothers but, if he did, they could not have been any closer than we were that day. I do not think he could have been more grateful to a brother as, a sibling would probably have used it against him in the future.

34
DUELING BLIND MEN
AUGUST OF 1976

I guess the reason this story got as far as it did is because the few bad things that had happened to me by this time because of my blindness. My bad experiences had tainted me and caused me to pay less attention than I otherwise would have. I know that I have become more of a detective because of this incident.

I was at the corner of the block where my mother's house was. Having just left there. I had made a right hand turn and walked only a few feet when my cane struck something. It was still light enough out that, if I had tried to, I could have probably seen what was going on.

In addition to my previously stated attitude, I had developed a habit that I was not really aware of. In fact, it was not until decades later that, through reading a book by someone who had improved her eye condition through exercise, that I realized what I had been doing.

For me, sunshine became more and more painful to be out in and would give me headaches. Some inside lighting could do the same thing so, I developed a habit of not trying to see. For years, if the subject would hold still long enough and I would concentrate, I could eventually see what I was trying to look at. Since staring at people made most of them uncomfortable, I paid less and less attention to what was around me because it was easier to have someone else explain the necessaries and to do without the rest.

Well, back to what I struck. I figured that someone was playing a game with me and I was not in the mood to play. I said excuse me and tried to go around the person to the right. As I did, they moved to their left and we again were in each other's way. I then said, "Excuse me but

I am blind and I am trying to get by." The other man responded with, "Very funny, can I get by now?"

I then went to my left thinking that the person may have had enough fun by now and would let me pass. You guessed it, he moved to his right and we again were in each other's way. Just as he started to tell me that he was blind and that I was not being very nice, someone came running across the street to us.

She instructed me to stay right where I was and she went to the other man and helped him to get around me. She then said that the path was clear and I could go. As I started walking away, I could hear his cane tapping on the ground. It turned out that we were both blind and both were thinking that the other person was trying to play a joke on us.

I wanted to turn around and find out who he was and to apologize for the way I acted. I have often wondered how our encounter has affected him, I know it changed me.

Luke 6:39 And he spake a parable unto them, Can the blind lead the blind? shall they not both fall into the ditch?

I suppose that we would have eventually figured it out. However, I am glad that we had a sighted person to help us around each other's "short-sightedness."

35
HAVE A NICE TRIP
AUGUST OF 1977

We moved six blocks away and went from Guttenberg to North Bergen, New Jersey. Now instead of having at least one bar on every block, we had at least one pizza place on every block.

By now I had started to wise up and use my cane. If I had used a little more wisdom I would have crossed the street to get where I was going. It was dark and I was going to a friend's house to shoot pool. Though I could not see a thing at night, my day vision had not yet become effected.

I had become a good player. I would walk into a bar and not be able to see a thing because it was so dark. I would walk over to the pool table, that I could see because it always had a bright light over it, and place my money on the table. I would then stand back and wait for fifteen minutes or more for my eyes to adjust enough so I could see an empty seat at the bar.

Most of the time I would get the table and keep it for the rest of the night. It would start out with the looser paying for the game and progress to the looser also buying the drinks and finally, the looser would walk away with less cash in his pocket.

But I digress. Back to the reason I should have crossed the street. Of all the pizza places I had to pass by on my way to play pool at my friend's house, there was one that was always rowdy. I cannot remember the name of it but, they would oftentimes have dough fights outside because they would be closing soon and would just throw the dough away anyway.

Some of the participants were indifferent to me but others did not like me for some reason that I never found out. As I was approaching the doorway to the pizza place, I heard a few boys talking in a low voice. I did not hear what they were saying but got the feeling that it was about me and that it was not good.

The next thing I knew I had become subject to gravity. I put my hands out to protect my face from the sidewalk because my cane went flying when they tripped me. Amidst their laughter, I was able to get up, find my cane and continue my journey.

You may ask why I would put this story in when it is the opposite of funny. The answer is not, (Because they thought it was funny). I guess the reason is that, we have all done things to others that we thought were funny at the time but later came to regret. We will all have opportunity in the future to do or say more of those things.

Though I did not get hurt physically and did recover emotionally, I believe that those boys have carried around a scar because they have never been able to apologize for their misdeed. I am sure that there are a few people out there that are rotten and nasty without any encouragement. I do believe though, that most of the time we give into pressure to do or say something hurtful to others that we would have not even thought of had we been by ourselves.

I believe that we often do, and especially say things under the guise of humor that hurt others. I hope this little story will encourage you to express yourself in a loving way, even and especially when there is peer pressure trying to get you to do what you know is wrong.

to come up with a verse for this story, I searched the Bible for the word forgive and came up with 112 entries. Most of them had to do with the LORD forgiving us. However, there were quite a few that had to do with us forgiving others.

Luke 3:3 Take heed to yourselves: If thy brother trespass against thee, rebuke him; and if he repent, forgive him.

However, in this case, the people that sinned against me are long gone and I have had no opportunity to challenge them. Since I have had no chance to accept their apology, I have chosen to let it go since holding on to anger does no good and I am sure that there are people out there that wish I would have asked for their forgiveness.

36
QUEER CUE
SEPTEMBER OF 1976

As I have already mentioned, I liked to play pool and had become pretty good at it. The main reason I did so well was because of a friend whose father purchased a regulation table and placed it in their finished basement. At first the father was reluctant to allow his son's friends to play on it unless he was there but, after a while and once he realized we would be careful with it, he relented.

Well, on this particular night I had arrived at my friend's house and they were already playing. I pulled out my four-piece cue and put it together. I do not remember what happened, but somehow my cue got damaged. As a joke I unscrewed the tip from my cue, did the same to my walking cane and screwed the cue tip onto my cane.

I played for a while but soon realized that the cane was not true so I undid the process. I put my cue into its case and placed my cane in the corner. I then got a cue from the wall and played for a few hours before going home.

The following Monday I got on the bus to go somewhere and as I sat down, I began to fold up my cane. I noticed that the joints were unusually hard to loosen. One of them was so stuck that I did not think it would ever come loose. Later however, I was able to get it apart with the aid of two pair of pliers.

As I sat there on the bus with my partially folded cane, it dawned on me why my cane was so stuck. The impact of playing pool with it a few days earlier had caused the trouble. Though I have joked about it ever since, I never again used my cane as a pool cue.

1 Corinthians 14:40 Let all things be done decently and in order.

37
CATCH HER
NOVEMBER OF 1976

I attended North Bergen High School until the middle of my junior year. Because I was unable to see the blackboard anymore and reading books was literally a headache, I quit. On January 21, 1977, I walked into the disciplinarian's office and handed the following note to him.

"Dear Mister D, I quit, signed, me," and walked out of the school.

Unfortunately, there were very few things that captured my attention during those two-and-a-half-years. I can only think of four things worth remembering. The first was lifting more weight in the bench press than the football and wrestling jocks to get them off my back.

The second was having a beautiful girl named Mercedes ask me out during a bomb scare. The third was the wood working class I took in my freshman year; the two classes I took during my sophomore year and the three wood working classes I had during my junior year.

The fourth thing happened only two months before I left high school for the last time. I was on the landing between the second and third floors on my way up. You were always supposed to keep the railing on your right side. As I was walking up the last flight, I noticed a girl wander to the wrong side of the stairs.

As I was about to say something, I noticed that she looked dazed. I thought that she was stoned. As she drifted back to the correct side, she started to fall. I moved to her side and caught her. I lowered her to the landing and was shocked at how little attention was being paid to this girl.

She was shaking so violently that I realized she was having an epileptic seizure. This was confirmed moments later when a friend of hers came down the stairs to help me. I had nothing to put between her teeth to keep her from biting her tongue so I placed my fingers in her mouth.

Fortunately for me, she did not bite. I found out later that you should never place your fingers in the mouth of someone having a seizure. I turned her head to the side to prevent the blockage of her airway and waited for the shaking to stop.

When it finally ceased, it seemed long though it was only about ninety seconds, her friend took her to the nurse's station. I suppose that the dozens of students that passed us by could have figured that we had things under control. However, they just seemed callus to me.

Luke 10:31 And by chance there came down a certain priest that way: and when he saw him, he passed by on the other side. 32 And likewise a Levite, when he was at the place, came and looked on him, and passed by on the other side.

I know that none of the teens passing us were Priests or Levites, but is sure felt like no one cared and everyone wanted to get away as quickly as possible.

38
WATCH OUT FOR THE PITCH
MARCH OF 1977

I lived in Baltimore, Maryland from February through July of 1977. When spring came around, my father decided to coach little league baseball and he wanted me to help him as his assistant. Though my eyesight was getting steadily worse, I could still see well enough to help.

At the risk of sounding like a male chauvinist pig, I had no idea that girls were now playing little league baseball. If a woman can actually do the same thing a man can do, she should be paid the same or get the same benefits and perks.

Since this book is not meant to be an equal rights treatise, I will not go any further on this topic. Suffice it to say that it took a little adjustment on my part to get used to a female pitcher. After watching her for a while, the phrase, 'You throw like a girl', went out the window.

After trying all the youngsters at each position, Raymond SR. wanted a confab between home plate and third base. I thought we were done so I turned to the girl and asked her to throw the ball to me. I was going to test the throwing and catching ability of each player.

Since she did not respond to me directly and my father wanted to tell me something else, I turned my face toward him. I guess my sight was not as good as I thought because, she threw the ball to me and I missed it. That is to say, I did not catch it but, it did not miss me.

When the ball hit me in a place that changes the pitch of a man's voice, I hit the ground. I was squirming on the ground and trying to keep my hands away from my crotch when the coach said, "Get up, you're making the girl feel bad."

I wanted to hit him in the nuts with a baseball and note his reaction. Instead, I got up, tried to breathe and, spent a week walking it off. Okay, maybe it was more like ten minutes.

Galatians 4:12 Brethren, I beseech you, be as I am; for I am as ye are: ye have not injured me at all.

I certainly wanted my father to be as I was after his insensitive comment. And, truthfully, though I was in pain for a while, she did not injure me.

39
STICKY SITUATION
JUNE OF 1977

If you have never played chicken, I will tell you how it goes. I am not talking about two cars racing for a head-on collision to see which one turns away first.

My best friend Ronald and I used to play two games in the woods. One was chicken which I will explain second. But first, stretch. You have a knife and are standing with your feet together, face to face, with your feet 1 foot away from your opponent's.

You take the knife and throw it into the ground to the side of the other person's foot. If it sticks, they must stretch their foot to the knife, remove it from the ground and take their turn. Whomever cannot stretch to the knife or falls down in their attempt loses.

We were both very good at the game but he was better than I. We had gone into the woods with our girlfriends, food, drink and something to smoke. to impress the girls, we started playing the game. Ronald beat me a few times and I was a little frustrated.

I was about to lose another game when I spotted a large tree about ten feet away. I figured that everyone would laugh when my knife bounced off the tree and I lost. So, I threw the knife with no fear of losing it in the woods as I had great aim. to my amazement, it stuck in the tree.

I turned to my friend and said, stretch! The girls broke out in laughter, almost falling off the log they were sitting on. Ronald just said, "You win R W." He got my knife out of the tree and graciously handed it to me.

Now for chicken. It is the opposite of stretch and much more dangerous. You stand facing each other with your legs stretched as far apart as possible. Being a gymnast, I could stretch much wider than Ronald. to make it more interesting, and, if you are brave enough or stupid enough, you play in bare feet.

At this time, I was visiting my brother and sisters in Baltimore MD. Danny heard the stories about the two games and decided that he would challenge me to a game of chicken. He did want us to keep our sneakers on though.

We each had sheath knives but, neither of us wanted to damage them in the rocky dirt of our father's back yard. We decided to use darts instead. to make a little more interesting since we were keeping our footwear on, I climbed the hill which was 8 feet higher and about 8 feet away.

We faced off, stretched and I threw my dart between his feet. After moving the closer foot to the dart, Danny picked it up and threw it. It landed in my right shin. I looked down in surprise, reached down to pluck it out, watched a drop of blood trickle down my shin and looked up.

I was not upset because that is part of the game. If you get stuck, you have only yourself to blame. I was prepared to take my turn but, he was not there. As I looked toward the side yard, I noticed him running down the block. I yelled for him to come back because I was not upset.

I suppose you can understand his reluctance since this was the first time playing the game. I had not explained that one of the rules in the game is, 'no retaliation.

Psalm 38:5 My wounds stink and are corrupt because of my foolishness.

No, my wound did not stink or become infected though the game was foolish. Thank God for His common grace toward children and fools.

40
I DON'T WANT TO GET A SHOT
JUNE OF 1977

My brother Dan's best friend lived just a half block away. I was in the back yard when I heard Danny yelling my name as he ran from Carl's house to ours. He sounded so frantic that I ran down the side yard to meet him.

When he told me that Buckle, his friend's nickname, had slashed his wrist, I jumped on my bike and got to him as fast as possible. It was hard to believe that someone so small had so much blood in him. It was all over the front door, porch, stairs and sidewalk.

He was running around like a head with its chicken cut off. I grabbed him, made him sit down, told his sister to call the police, call their parents and get me a kitchen towel., It turned out that Carl and his sister were having an argument.

As she went to shut the door in his face, he reached out and his hand went through one of the twelve panels of glass that made up the door. A piece of glass slit his wrist completely across on the inside. I removed the glass that was still in the wound, lifted his arm up and applied pressure to the artery.

The blood flow stopped a few minutes before we heard the ambulance coming. Unfortunately, we heard the siren going down the wrong street. I asked his older sister to hold his arm up so I could get back on my bike and point the emergency driver in the correct direction.

Once they were headed to the right house, they went so fast, it took me thirty seconds to get back there. After lying to the paramedic that I was his guardian, they started working on Carl. I almost fell down laughing when I heard what he was saying.

This little boy with his wrist slit open so you could see tendons and muscle was having a fit because he did not want to go to the hospital and get a shot. The emergency workers refused to take him to the emergency room until I assured them that his parents would meet them there.

Exodus 20:16 Thou shalt not bear false witness against thy neighbour.

I have heard thousands of times that you should not lie. Though I believe that is a good guideline, it is not from the Bible. The Bible tells us to not bear false witness, which is a lie. However, it says, "against thy neighbor."

So, though you should keep from lying whenever possible, sometimes a lie can actually be a blessing and is not breaking the ninth commandment. Only when a lie of commission or omission is designed to harm or best someone is it not acceptable.

41
VOLLEYBALL OR BASKETBALL?
JULY OF 1977

I was such a good volleyball player in my grammar school that our gym teacher, Mr. Pisante, said that I was the best player he had ever taught.

I, my two sisters Donna and Lisa and a few of my good friends were in a gymnastic organization in Guttenberg, New Jersey called Sokol Hall. We were offered the opportunity to go to Chicago for an international gymnastic meet. The trip would take a full day there and a full day back on a bus.

We would be in Chicago for five days competing and one day on a football field executing a routine we had been working on for six months. I was told by someone that over forty-two thousand youngsters were on that field. It was a beautiful thing to see on film later.

Try to imagine all those gymnasts executing a five-minute routine that included flips, twists, hand springs, cartwheels and dance moves and having it look like we had all been practicing together for months. In reality, there were hundreds of organizations from across the USA, South America and Canada that got together one day to accomplish this feat.

My favorite piece of equipment was the still rings followed by the parallel bars and then the horizontal bar. We, the boys, had to compete on those three as well as pommel horse, vaulting and floor exercise as individuals and as a team.

In addition, there was an indoor volleyball competition that our team had qualified for. When we did have some free time, I liked going to the pool to enjoy the view of dozens of females that were in great shape and looked fabulous in their bathing suits. When I was not at the pool, I could be found at the pizza place playing pinball.

I had gotten so good at pinball that I almost missed our first volleyball game. I had racked up so many free games and could not find any more challengers. This turned out to be the second time I would have to leave a machine with over ten free games on it. The first time had been in South Carolina the previous year.

After four days of gymnastic competition were complete, we started the volleyball tournament. Because I had been so good at serving aces, I was selected to serve first. We were hoping that, after an ace or two, the other team would lose their confidence.

I had not only never practiced on that court, I had not even touched a ball yet to test its bounce.

Because I was slowly losing my vision and had just run into a building that was much dimmer than the bright sunshine outside, I was having trouble seeing everything and everyone. I got into position, was handed the ball, served it and scored two points.

How can you score two points on a serve you might ask. I will tell you, I hit the ball too hard and it went into the basketball net. So those points did not count in our game. I did get a lot of boos and teasing from my teammates as well as cheers and laughter from everyone else.

Once I settled down and my eyes adjusted, I did much better. When the serve came back around to me, I was able to nail a couple of those aces after all.

Proverb 21:5 The thoughts of the diligent tend only to plenteousness; but of every one that is hasty only to want.

42
MANHOLE COVER
JULY OF 1977

This story is not as funny as it is amazing, in fact, it is a miracle. I am not proud of what I was doing when this incident occurred but, I wish to be accurate so I include the detail of our illicit activity.

Though our school had a police officer come in once to tell us about all the bad things that can happen to you if you take drugs and though we did have one class on one day in science that showed us more of the evils of addiction, I began smoking pot. I remember listening to the officer and teacher and being firmly convinced that I would never do those things.

Two of my friends and I were walking under a set of buildings that were under construction. I was walking in the middle and we were passing a joint back and forth. I believe that if we had not been stoned, one of them would have seen the danger.

The buildings were Called the Galaxy towers and were being constructed on the Palisade Cliffs in Guttenberg, New Jersey. My friends and I used to hang out a lot on those cliffs before they started construction so, we figured that, until the buildings were finished, they were still our cliffs.

Just as I handed the joint to one of my friends I felt a pain in both of my arm pits at the same time. I stood there for a minute, at least I thought I was standing, trying to figure out why both of my pits were hurting. Then I noticed that my friends were still walking and I called to them.

They turned around and looked but did not see me at first. When I noticed that they were having trouble locating me I realized that they were much taller than I was. I then said, "I'm down here guys." They both looked down and were astonished to find me hanging by my arms in a man hole. I still had no idea what had happened as they approached me.

They each reached down, grabbed an arm and lifted me up. Once I was on solid ground and had rubbed my arms for a minute, I looked down to find a two-hundred-foot drop straight down. It turns out that someone had removed the cover and had not replaced it.

Since I was not a Christian at the time I could only be amazed at my good luck. I now know that, though Satan was trying to destroy me, God had other plans and, though I did not know Him yet, He knew me and had a purpose for me that had not yet been fulfilled.

Ephesians 5:18 And be not drunk with wine, wherein is excess; but be filled with the Spirit.

I know this is not exactly the same. However, whereas my body and mind used to be filled with alcohol and drugs, it is now filled with God's Holy Spirit. I have had more fun, joy, thrills and excitement since August 8, 1991, the day I got saved, than the previous 31 years ever held for me.

43
PAIN IN THE NECK
AUGUST OF 1977

It might seem that retiring from gymnastic competition at twenty-four is young. Giving up competition at seventeen is really young. Unfortunately, I had no choice. I was trying to do a move on the still rings where I would let go of the rings, twist one hundred and eighty degrees and grab the rings again.

I was too stupid to realize that my diminishing vision would be a problem. Several times I was able to grab one of the rings but, not both yet. When doing moves like this, rather than the one-inch-thick mat, we would place a four-inch mat under ourselves. It was a good thing I did or I probably would not be writing this book.

The last time I tried my new move; I missed one ring completely and only got my fingers on the other one enough to cause a problem. I could not hold on and that caused me to flip upside down. I landed on my head and sprained every muscle, ligament and tendon in my neck.

It took six months to recover and, by that time, I had lost my left eye to a botched surgery. Without the depth perception that two eyes give you, I could no longer safely do gymnastics. It was hard to give up. When my wife and I purchased our first home, she bought a fifteen feet round trampoline for my birthday.

It took me three months to land a perfect front summy. I, my children, other relatives and many neighbors enjoyed that bounce toy until my insurance company refused to cover our home unless we got rid of it.

Genesis 45:14 And he fell upon his brother Benjamin's neck, and wept; and Benjamin wept upon his neck.

I have made reference more than once that I love humor. The following verse is one of those examples. I was teaching Sunday School with five, six and seven-year-olds when reading this passage. When it mentioned that Joseph fell upon his brother Benjamin's neck, I stopped reading and yelled, "Ouch!"

Most of the children laughed and, over the years I have even gotten an adult to chuckle. Now back to something less funny.

1 Samuel 4:18 And it came to pass, when he made mention of the ark of God, that he fell from off the seat backward by the side of the gate, and his neck brake, and he died: for he was an old man, and heavy. And he had judged Israel forty years.

I was young unlike Samuel and thin, about one hundred and thirty-five pounds. The Bible does not try to be politically correct; however, it accidentally is in this verse. What it really means is very fat. So, when he leaned over too far, fell backwards, hit his head on the wall, he broke his neck and died.

I thank God that, though I fell from over six feet in the air and landed directly on my head, I did not die and, it did not break. Too often, as my wife Jovanna keeps pointing out to me, when something bad happens, we have to remember that, "It could have been worse."

44
WHOOPS, I DID NOT MEAN TO GRAB THAT
September of 1977

It was late at night and I was headed for my mother's house. I was using my cane but, as I turned the corner to head up the third of a block to her place, I folded my cane. I knew every crack in the sidewalk, every tree, pole and I would know exactly when I came to her home.

One of the things I developed as my sight deteriorated was the ability to listen. Now some people seem to think that if you lose one of your senses, the others get better. That is not true. What really happens is you rely on them more. For instance, if I am walking through a neighborhood and there is any noise, a car, air conditioner, music or electrical wire buzz, the sound changes as objects get between you and the noise.

There is an apartment building on the corner which has an alley way between it and the next building which is a warehouse. The apartment building is set back further from the street then the warehouse so, I can tell by the change in sound when I am even with the alley and that lets me know to listen for the warehouse or I will smash my nose on it.

I know that I am in front of my next-door neighbor's house because it is set back a little from the warehouse and the texture of the sidewalk has changed. I am now walking on their driveway and only a few feet from my mother's gate. There is the change from blacktop to cement which lets me know that I need to take three more steps, make a left and put out my right hand for the gate latch.

My hand landed on something that was not supposed to be there. It was the left breast of a woman who is now yelling at me. As I realize what has just happened, I raise my cane and told the woman that I was blind and did not know she was there. After a few minutes of answering her questions like, "Why weren't you using your cane if you are blind?", she finally gave up and accepted my apology. As a parting remark I said, "Besides, I did not expect anyone to be standing in front of my mother's house."

In the emotion of the moment, I forgot to ask who she was and I did not recognize her voice so, I have no idea of her identity. I often wonder if she lived in the area and if she kept her eye on me after that.

2 Chronicles 16:9 For the eyes of the LORD run to and fro throughout the whole earth, to shew himself strong in the behalf of them whose heart is perfect toward him.

Whether she kept her eye on me or not is not important, what is though, is that the LORD has.

45
FOLLOW ME
NOVEMBER OF 1976

My mother had a friend we called Smokey. I remember three things about him. He smoked eight packs of cigarettes a day which is how he got the nickname. My mother and one of my sisters went to clean his house once and they said that the dust on top of everything was so thick that when you tried to wipe it away you ended up making mud. Lastly, he helped me get a job with the state through a program called Ceda. I have no idea what it stood for.

I do not remember what my official title was but I called myself an Assistant Forest Ranger. I took that title because that is what I did most of the time. I rode around with a Forest Ranger helping him carry out his duties. Sometimes we counted dead deer, sometimes we supervised the prison workers as they chopped and loaded firewood and sometimes we emptied trash cans. There were many other things we did as well and I really enjoyed it.

Those of us that worked there, High Point State Park, lived in a few cabins near the highest point in New Jersey. After work most of us would meet in the social hall which had a bumper pool table and a music room. I soon became the master of the table and could win more than half of the games in one turn.

There were many times I could win the game in five shots. This did not go over well with the rest of the players for two reasons. First, they did not like losing their money. Second, they did not believe that I had a problem seeing because I was such a shark at the table.

After seeing me fall off things, run into things and hit my head on things, most of them began to believe that I was either sight impaired or just plain stupid. One day the crew decided to play a game of volley ball.

Though I had been great at the sport, my sight outdoors had worsened to the point that I could not play the sport any more. Another bone of contention for those who had lost to me at the table.

A little side story:

There was one guy named George. He was very tall, very skinny and a vegetarian. As they were playing the game, George and a girl on his team went up for the ball at the same time and George ended up on top of the girl on the ground. I yelled out, "Hey George, I thought you were a vegetarian." That got a lot of laughs from everyone and somehow eased the tension between me and them.

A few weeks later one of the leaders drove up to the social hall. Later, one of the other leaders drove up there too. The second person had someone meeting them there and asked the first leader if he would drive his car back to his cabin for him. Well, it was Friday and the guy wanted to relax so he decided that he would take care of it later.

Later became so late that everyone but he and I were gone. It had snowed a few inches while we were inside and he was not looking forward to having to drive his friend's car to his cabin, walk all the way back up the hill to the hall and then drive his car to his cabin. I half-jokingly offered to drive his car back for him.

He responded with, "I thought you were blind." Because of his response, or mor accurately his tone, I decided to see how far I could push this. After suggesting that he put his flashers on and drive in front of me slowly, he agreed. I could not see a thing other than his flashers the whole way back to the cabins and, except for one moment when I thought I was going to drive off the edge of a cliff, there were no mishaps.

Once we arrived at his cabin safely, he was very grateful and greatly relieved. Fortunately for me he did not tell anyone of our little convoy and neither did I, until now.

1 Corinthians 4:15 For though ye have ten thousand instructors in Christ, yet have ye not many fathers: for in Christ Jesus I have begotten you through the gospel. 16 Wherefore I beseech you, be ye followers of me.

Following that car in the dark was fun, however, following Jesus through this life has been much more rewarding.

46
CAN YOU DIG IT?
JANUARY 11, 1978

By the age of 12, I started having trouble adjusting from light to dark. Within two years, it would take minutes rather than seconds for my eyes to get used to the dimmer circumstance. Also, by the time I was 14, I had no night vision left.

In order to get to my Scout meetings or my gymnastic club in the dark, though I did not realize it, I started using echo location. I could still see the lights and used them as a general guide. I thought that I was feeling the obstacles in my way when I was really hearing the changes in the surrounding sounds as I came upon a trash can or other object in my path.

When there was new snow, the problem was just as profound as it was in the dark. On January10, it started snowing in the evening. By the morning, there was over three feet of snow everywhere and 4 feet drifts in places. My mother and step-father Tony both worked from six pm until two or three in the morning.

When I got up on the morning of the 12th, Tony asked me to dig his car out. Though the streets had been plowed, it was still so bright from all the snow-covered cars and sidewalks, that it hurt my eyes. Even so, I made it to the place where Tony said his car was.

Because I was squinting to keep from getting a headache, I did not realize that the car was parked over the crosswalk lines. I began to remove the snow from the car and throw most of it on the next vehicle. After about an hour of work, I realized that it was not my step-father's car. I had to go slowly to keep from scratching the paint and to keep from cracking the glass.

I was so upset that someone had parked illegally that, as I began to uncover the correct vehicle, I threw the snow onto the offending car. I did this with abandon and delight for a while but, slowed down as I grew tired. When I returned home, I regaled everyone with the tale. Tony began to berate me for not paying attention. He still did not believe that I was going blind.

Isaiah 42: 18 Hear, ye deaf; and look, ye blind, that ye may see.

The context of the above verse is salvation. However, the word look also means pay attention and the word see also means perceive. If I had paid a little more attention coupled with the perception that my stepfather would have told me if he had been parked illegally, I might have avoided the trouble. As "they" say, 'live and learn'.

47
WRONG ACCENT
MARCH 10, 1978

My mother and I had been going to see an eye surgeon in Jersey City for a while and this was our last visit before the surgery. We had arrived early so we could eat at our favorite Chinese restaurant across the street from the medical center.

She tried something different each time we went. I loved their pork fried rice. She was reading the menu aloud and, smart ass that I have always been, decided to repeat what she said in my Chinese accent.

We were having so much fun that, when the waiter arrived, I forgot to go back to my regular voice and ordered my dish in, what was probably a very bad accent to him. After my mother ordered her items, he left. She said, "You should have seen the look on his face."

Then, in a very serious face and voice she said, "You know that he is going to spit in your food." Then we both busted out laughing. Her comment was so funny to me because, she could see the expression on his face, while I could not. My food tasted the same as it always had so, I do not think he utilized sputum to increase the moisture content of my dish.

Another time that using accents got me in trouble was on my sister Donna's twenty fifth birthday. I was walking around the streets of New York when I remembered that it was her day to celebrate. I called her from a pay phone but, her answering machine came on and, I left the following message.

"Donna, I wanted to wish you a wonderful day but, since you are not there, I am going to give your phone number to a bunch of people on the street and ask them to call you." I hung up and called back five more times using the following accents, Chinese, French, Indian, British and Spanish.

A few days later, she called me outraged that I would give her number to strangers. When I explained that I had made all those calls, she did not believe me until I repeated the message I had left in my Chinese voice.

Proverb 24:28 Be not a witness against thy neighbor without cause; and deceive not with thy lips.

Unfortunately, I did deceive my sister with my lips. Until writing this, I had not thought of her distress over the next two days as she expected strangers to show up at her apartment unannounced.

48
NO TIME FOR SWIMMING
MARCH OF 1978

There is a park in New Jersey called James J. Braddock. It starts at Seventy Ninth street and goes to Ninetieth and begins at Boulevard East and goes to Bergenline Avenue. It is one hundred and sixty-seven acres, contains a lake that has a walking path a mile around with an island in the middle that Canadian geese live on.

It has baseball diamonds, football fields, tennis courts and a playground with a wading pool in it. At the entrance of seventy ninth street, there are two roads separated by a strip of grass which has a mulberry tree growing on it. My sister Donna and I used to fight the aunts for the berries.

We would climb up so high you could not see us and we would eat berries until we were full. The first time we did this; our mother was upset at the stains on our clothing. We did try to keep from messing up our clothing from that point on but, were not successful

On this particular day, I entered the park at the ninetieth street entrance from Bergenline avenue. I went in there because I had just finished off twenty White Castle cheeseburgers and the restaurant was just across the street from that entrance.

I rode my bike two miles through the park to get to the playground. It was closed after Labor Day but, if the weather was still good, there would be an ice cream truck parked there. I loved to get three Toasted Almond bars. I would be able to break the almonds off in large chunks from the first bar.

By the time I was done with the first one, the second would have warmed up enough to pull the almonds off in larger sheets. Then, the third one would have softened enough for me to enjoy the almonds and ice cream together.

Much to my chagrin, the truck was not in front of the closed gates. As I was looking around, I noticed that there was a car near the pool and that there were several children near it. I lifted my bike over the fence, climbed over it and rode my bicycle over to the car.

As I got closer, I realized that it was my friend, Chester the cop. As I pulled up, I asked him what was going on. He told me that a girl had fallen into the pool and he was waiting for an ambulance. As I looked down into the pool, I noticed that she was tangled in her bike in a pile of leaves.

When I asked my friend why he was not helping, he said, "Her parents could sue me if I touched her." The pool was three feet at the deep end which is where she had fallen. I jumped down, checked her pulse, made sure she had feeling in her feet and then disentangled her from the bicycle.

I stopped the bleeding from her neck with a little pressure, asked three of her friends for their jackets, placed one under her head and covered her with the other to keep her as warm and comfortable as possible. After figuring which of her friends had parents that knew the girl's family well enough to have their phone numbers, I sent them off to make phone calls.

I asked Chester how long before the ambulance would arrive, he said, "Another forty-five minutes." He said that they made the request forty-five minutes ago. When I asked why it was taking so long considering that Palisades hospital was only a few miles away, he told me that there was a strike.

I sat next to the girl making sure that she could still feel her feet and hands and made her talk to keep her awake. She was so annoyed with me but, you are not supposed to let someone with a concussion fall asleep so, I continued to bother her until the ambulance arrived.

When it did, there was only one young man. He seemed a little dazed so, I suggested that we place the girl on a back board, put her in a body bag and strap her to the stretcher. He allowed me to help with all the afore mentioned steps, closed the door and rode away.

As we were gingerly placing the girl in the bag, her friends came back and told us that the parents would be waiting at the hospital. I called the medical center a few hours later and was told that since I was not a relative, they could not tell me anything.

It did not matter to the woman I spoke with that I was the one that saved her life. A day or two later, my mother showed me the article in the newspaper describing me. Either they forgot my name or I forgot to give it to them. About three weeks later I was approached by one of the girl's friends.

I was walking up seventy fifth street and passing the grammar school when I heard a young man shouting, "Hey mister, hey mister." I was not yet eighteen so did not consider myself a mister yet. He not only continued shouting but, he was getting closer to me.

As I turned around, I realized that he was one of the girl's friends. He told me that her parents had been trying to find me. I gave him one of my business cards, asked how she was doing and said goodbye. I thought I would hear from her parents in a day or two. I never did.

Psalm 30:10 Hear, O LORD, and have mercy upon me: LORD, be thou my helper.

Though I did not know Him yet, He knew me. I started studying medicine at the age of fourteen, I had gotten merit badges in life saving, emergency preparedness, first aid and had studied chiropractics and massage for two years.

All these things gave me the skills that caused me to save more than thirteen lives and to help many other people in bad situations over the years. He has definitely been my helper because, though I have been in many life-threatening situations, I have never felt panic.

49
SCARED STRAIGHT
JUNE OF 1978

I was working for a company in Secaucus New Jersey which was only a few blocks from where my Step-Father was working. He worked a little later than I did so I would walk over to his job and wait for a ride home. While hanging around one day I asked him if I could drive his car around the trucking yard.

He gave me the keys and I drove around for a while. After a few days of this, I decided to become a little more adventurous and drive on the road in front of the trucking company. There was very little traffic on that road so, day by day I gained more confidence and went further.

Though I did not turn onto the main road, I did drive up and down the whole length of the access road. I had just turned around at the far end of the road and was headed back to the trucking yard when I heard a siren. Knowing that you are supposed to get out of the way of those types of vehicles, I pulled to the side of the road. Actually, I pulled into the ditch on the side of the road.

I was afraid that the siren was a cop wanting to pull me over. Fortunately, he whizzed by me and after my heart returned to a somewhat normal beat, I tried to pull out of the ditch and back on to the road. I was leaning so far to the right I thought that we would have to call a tow truck and that I would be in for it. Thankfully, the car eased out of the ditch and back on to the road without a scraping sound.

There was no damage to the car and I slowly drove to the docks. After parking the car I went in, found my Step-Father, handed him the keys and never asked for them again. One and a half decades later, in general conversation, he remarked about my driving his car outside the trucking yard. I did not know that he knew and we both had a good laugh when I told him of the Police car that scared me into not driving his car any more.

Hebrews 13:17 Obey them that have the rule over you, and submit yourselves: for they watch for your souls, as they that must give account, that they may do it with joy, and not with grief: for that is unprofitable for you.

It would have been unprofitable for me to have been pulled over by an officer of the law. He would have found out that I had no license and would probably assumed that the car was stolen. It is unfortunate that we often have to have a scare before we will obey the rules.

50
LEARNING THE HARD WAY
JULY OF 1978

Soon after giving up on driving, I got a part time job with the company, ATSL Trucking, where my Step-Father worked. I probably would have asked for the keys again if I had not started working with him because I would have gotten bored waiting for him to be done for the day.

Because of the peculiarity of my eye condition, it was hard for some people to understand that I was limited in what I could see and in what light I could see it. My step-Father was one of these people. In the beginning, he refused to believe that I had any problem at all. He thought I was making it up and using it to my benefit.

No matter how many times and how many ways my mother and I would try to explain, he just would not believe that I had a visual problem. After all, how could someone drive a car up and down the road if they had eye trouble. I found this mind set to be more prevalent than I would have imagined. Even today, more than a quarter of a century later, I run into, sometimes literally, people that just cannot fathom a person who can see in some settings but not in others.

After working for eight hours at a clothing warehouse, Ormond, making boxes and packing them for one of their 83 stores across the country I would go to work for four hours unloading and loading trucks where my Step-Father worked.

Most of the time I would take items off one truck and load them in the warehouse against the wall in one of fifteen piles for the fifteen trucks that had to be loaded later. When I arrived at work this day, I was given a carpet truck to unload.

Because carpet was so large and bulky, and because carpet would go on the bottom anyway, instead of making piles, I took the carpet directly to the truck it was to be loaded on. The truck I was unloading was in the first bay and the other fifteen had empty trucks.

I began to unload and, when I came to a carpet that had to be taken to truck fifteen, all the way at the other end, I decided to see if I could locate any more pieces for that truck. I was able to find two more and loaded them on a dolly. It was dark in the dock because all the bays were filled and the light, incandescent bulbs, did not really help me.

I was able to identify each truck because there was a sliver of light coming through each bay so I could count the trucks and keep everything in order. I was walking toward the last truck with my load of three rolls of carpet. As I got to the dock I began to turn in toward the trailer. Some of the trucks were lower and some were higher than the dock, this one was lower.

Some of the drivers were great at docking and others were lousy, this one was lousy. He had parked far enough from the dock that you had to be careful not to fall to the ground between the dock and the trailer. Well, before I knew it, I was tripping over a dolly that someone had left in front of the trailer. I smacked both shins on the dolly, fell forward and over it, rolled toward the truck and fell down between the trailer and dock. I was able to hold on to the trailer with my right arm and the dock with my left so that I did not fall to the ground but I was still pretty cut, scraped and bruised.

Sometimes to this day, when a sighted person remarks to me that they cannot understand how I do the things I do without seeing, I tell them that I can see but am just faking it for the attention.

My Step-Father had been watching me walk across the dock wondering how I could claim to be blind when I could move so well around the docks when he saw the accident. After icing my shins and bandaging my other cuts he remarked that there must be something to my claim because no one would have been so stupid as to do that on purpose just to make others think that he had trouble seeing.

I agree. Though I like money as much as the next person, I do not think that I would have repeated that trick for a million dollars. There have been many people over the years that have seen me trip over things or walk into things which began them rethinking their view of my viewers. The things you have to do to get some people to believe.

I was going to use the Scripture, "There are none so blind as those who will not see." However, that is not a verse from the Bible and after going through every line with the word blind in it, I could not find anything even close. So, what I decided to use is this verse:

Deuteronomy 27: 18 Cursed be he that maketh the blind to wander out of the way. And all the people shall say, Amen.

At the moment I read this passage, I decided to pray for everyone that has ever mistreated me because of my blindness, that they might be saved, rather than cursing them.

51
BANK ROBBER?
AUGUST OF 1978

My friend Paul Rovetto, some other friends and I were playing football in front of our houses. Now, please do not get bored because this story has a similar beginning as, "YOU'RE WHERE" Believe me, it does get more exciting. The part that is the same is that boys will be boys.

Paul's team decided to punt the football on fourth down rather than throw it. These friends were just as bad as my other friends when it came to kicking a ball accurately and, it landed on the roof of a bank. The bank was two stories while the building next to it was over thirty feet tall.

I decided to do my climbing trick here as well. See, I told you it was similar. Now for the differences. There was a treasure trove of stuff on the bank's roof. I threw down frisbees, wiffil balls, tennis balls, pinky balls, flying rings and our football down to my friends.

Some of that stuff had been up there for years and some of my friends recognized a few of the items with glee. As I threw our ball to Paul, a police car drove up. One of the officers got out of the car and asked me what I was doing up there. I thought it was obvious as I threw the football but, I decided to explain anyway.

When I was done, the officer asked me to come down. I said that I would once they were gone. The second cop chimed in with, "That's not gonna happen." I then suggested that they get in their car and back it up half a block. They refused so, I held my arms akimbo, moved my hip out a little and put an attitude of incredulity on my face and waited.

They finally agreed when they realized that it would be a hassle to get a ladder here. They got in their car and backed up a little. I waved them back more and, reluctantly, they obeyed. As I started down, I kept my eyes on them. When I was about halfway down, they started pulling forward.

So, I climbed back atop the bank, resumed my previous stance and waited for them to back up again. When they did, I began shimmying down, making a point of staring at them. When my butt was about seven feet off the ground, I dropped, ran around the corner and hid.

I am sure that, if they had chosen to, they could have gotten my address from one of my friends but, as soon as I hit the ground, they all scattered. They probably had not paid attention to the direction of any of them since they thought they could catch me.

They probably also figured that, since there was no attempted break in, they could just write it off.

> Proverb 29: 2 *When the righteous are in authority, the people rejoice: but when the wicked beareth rule, the people mourn.*

I believe that these police officers were righteous because, once they knew that no law had been broken, and that they had fixed the problem, they moved on. There are many people that abuse their authority, Senators, Congressmen, Judges, police officers and bosses. They will get theirs someday. I am glad that I did not get mine that day.

52
BUMPER POOL CHAMPION
December 12, 1978

By the time June of 1978 rolled around, I had held over seven jobs. The only reason for losing most of these was because they would hire people to work for 29 days and fire them before they were eligible to get into the union.

My mother had a friend who got me a job with the state in a place called High Point State Park. This was part of a state funded program named CEDA. They helped young people get jobs, most of which no one else wanted but that needed to be done.

My title was "Assistant Forest Ranger." Though I did help the Forest Ranger in our area at times, the job was much more dynamic. When I helped him, it was to inspect state owned buildings, count dead deer hunters shot but did not track; and to empty 55-gallon trash cans.

Other than that, we did plumbing, carpentry, masonry and electrical work on 100-year-old buildings, we picked up trash from the property of those same buildings, from roads and picnic areas and we trimmed trees and bushes.

Because I had finer carpentry skills, I made wooden signs for those areas. And, I just remembered that in the foundation of a building in Port Jervis, there is a penny and my initials in a foundation that I poured.

When not working, we played basketball, volleyball, and bumper pool. Of course, some of us smoked pot and drank beer in the woods. One Saturday, four of us went to the woods to party. Three of us brought Coors in cans. One guy brought bottles but forgot to bring an opener.

I grabbed a bottle to show him how to open it between two rocks when he tried to get his cap off more forcefully. The neck of the bottle broke and, though all three of us yelled for him to not drink from that bottle, he did anyway. We rushed him to the hospital but, since it took over an hour to get to the car and another to get to the medical center, he did not make it.

I started dating a girl who worked in the kitchen named Sandy Brown. Can you guess what color her hair was? I had become the pool champion of Port Jervis and, until Sandy, that is where I could always be found after work.

This day, we were on a date so others were running the table. When we got back, she wanted to get something to eat so I went to the table. I placed my dollar bill on the table behind three others and waited for my turn.

I had become so good at the game that I could win in five shots 90 percent of the time. Since the winner got to keep the loser's bill, I could have quit the job and made a better living at the game. That is, except for the fact that if you were not working in the program, you could not stay there.

The second-best player hated my guts because, once I had mastered the game, he could never beat me. He tried many times each night and became cash-strapped because of it. While Sandy was eating, I was sitting on the radiator waiting my turn.

He came over and offered me a toke on his joint which I accepted. I did not know that it was an attempt to compromise my game. It turned out that the pot was laced with pcp. A few minutes later, I felt myself floating while hearing a very loud base drum beat.

What had happened was, I fell from my perch, hit the ground and started banging my head on the ground. I came back to reality with Sandy holding my head in her lap and trying to bring me back from the trip. When I finally became lucent again, I went looking for the culprit who had vanished. He stayed out of my way for the rest of my time in the program.

Ephesians 5: 18 And be not drunk with wine, wherein is excess; but be filled with the Spirit.

Since the only drug of that day was alcohol, that is what is mentioned in the verse above. However, the principle is the same. Once I gave my life to Jesus, I knew that I had to put aside the desire to lose myself to beer, wine, whiskey, pot or any other substance that would overrule good judgement.

As Mattie said to Rooster Cogburn in the movie, "True Grit," when he offered her a drink, "I will not put a thief in my mouth to steal my brain.."

53
CATCH THIS
SUMMER OF 1979

My ninth job, not counting tutoring and odd jobs, was with a company named Excello Maritime, which supplied neighborhood stores and pharmacies with everything from tooth brushes to watches. My main job was to unload the truck at the docking area. We only had one bay which had a conveyer belt to its left.

Most of the time you would take a fork lift into the truck and offload the skids full of products. Then they would be driven to their storage area. The conveyer belt to the left of the dock went for about twenty-five feet. Then it met with a belt that went up to the next level which was the equivalent of the third floor.

If the items needed to be stored on the next level, the skid would be parked at the bottom of the conveyer belt going up. Then someone, usually me, would be at the bottom unloading the skit and putting the items on the belt. Someone at the top would take them off.

The loading of the delivery trucks would be done at a different spot in the warehouse. There was a set of doors where the delivery truck could drive into the warehouse. Then the person in charge of order fulfillment would bring all the items to be delivered that day to the truck area. Then three of the workers would load the truck.

On this particular day one of the guys did not show up for work. I was asked to help load the truck. One person would be on the floor throwing the boxes up to the person on the truck. He would then slide them in back of him where the next person would stack them in order of what store they had to go to.

Being young men and full of energy, the guys liked to play practical jokes on each other. Because I could not see well, I ended up being the butt of a disproportionate number of jokes. I decided that I would bide my time and get them back somehow.

It seemed that no one liked the job of throwing the boxes up onto the truck because it was the most tiring. Guess which job I got. Well, I have always liked jobs that were more physical so I jumped right in. I decided to play a joke on the catcher. I took a box that was small but heavy and threw it up to the catcher, making it look like it did not weigh much.

When he went to catch it, thinking it was lighter than it was, it shocked him and pulled him down and smashed his fingers. It did not hurt him because he was wearing gloves and he thought it was very clever. A few minutes later I came upon a larger box that did not weigh much so, I threw it to him making it look heavy. In bracing himself for the weight, he ended up losing his balance and throwing it over his head.

After getting up off his but, he decided that it would be a great game. Although I did get him once in a while after that, none were as good as the first two. Everyone else adopted the game and it made the work go faster and more enjoyable. No, we did not damage any of the product though some of the boxes were a little crumpled.

Proverbs 26:18 As a mad man who casteth firebrands, arrows, and death, 19 So is the man that deceiveth his neighbour, and saith, Am not I in sport?

The reference above refers to deceiving your neighbor. Most people think that means you should not lie. Though lying is usually not a good idea, this verse is about trying to profit from fooling your neighbor. The heart of this verse is the attempt to deceive for gain. Since all had fun, no one profited above anyone else. Besides, the Bible tells us hundreds of times to be joyful.

I used to work with a girl who loved to tell you something she thought you did not want to hear and follow each statement with, "Just kidding." This was an attempt to get in a dig without suffering the consequence of retaliation.

54
WHAT A VIEW
SEPTEMBER 17, 1979

Have you ever been parasailing? I have and it was an amazing experience. At first, the people running the ride did not want to allow me to go up in their rig. They thought that because my sight was limited, I might be a liability. Once my mother and I explained things to them, they reluctantly let me go up.

They were very detailed in their instructions and, I went up without a hitch. I was told later that I was four hundred feet over the water. By this time, only my right eye was functional. That might explain in part why the ocean floor seemed only twenty feet under the surface.

When taking off, I only had to walk two steps forward, when the rope that was attached to me and the boat five hundred feet in front of me, began to pull. Then I was in the air. I saw what I thought was a shark on our side of the reef and, it was.

When I got back down and told the men in charge of the ride what I thought I saw, they informed me that it was a nurse shark. They said that nurse sharks rarely attack humans. I later found out that they only bit people that are aggressive toward them.

Once my twenty minutes were up, I felt myself descending toward the floating launch pad. I landed on the boards with no problem as if I had just jumped off a four-inch curb into the street. When I asked how deep the water was here, I was told that it was over four hundred feet.

Distance is almost impossible to judge when you have only one working eye. It is even harder when the usable eye is 20/400. Basically, that means, what someone with 20/20 vision can see clearly at twenty feet, needs to be twenty times that size for someone with 20/400 vision to see clearly.

Funny enough, the man who went on the ride after I did, missed his landing and ended up in the water. Fortunately for him, he did not get hurt, only very wet. When the boat driver realized that the man was sinking in the water, he sped up which pulled the man back up out of the ocean. They went around again and, the second landing try was successful.

Mark 8:24 And he looked up, and said, I see men as trees, walking. 25 After that he put his hands again upon his eyes, and made him look up: and he was restored, and saw every man clearly.

I know what it is like to see blurry trees moving around. It is wonderful to know that, someday, Jesus is going to heal my eyes perfectly as He did for this man.

In the story, "What can you see?" I used verse twenty-four. As anyone that knows me can tell you, I hate repetition. So, why am I using it again? Because his seeing men as trees was not the end of the story. His being healed completely is.

It is wonderful to know that, if you surrender your life to the LORD Jesus Christ, you will get a body that will have no defects, will not feel pain, will not suffer hunger and will never be subject to sorrow.

55
HOW MANY TIMES
DO I HAVE TO SAVE YOU?
September 19, 1979

My mother, my sister Donna, my sister Lisa and I were in the Bahamas for a week. After spending the day traveling, the girls were tired but I was not willing to go to sleep yet. So, I went down to the hotel bar to get an idea of the night life.

As I was sitting there with a drink and looking around at all the pretty girls, one of them parked at the bar near me. I could not believe what I found out during the normal opening questions. It turned out that the attractive young lady was a cousin vacationing from Alaska.

We talked until the bar closed. She was staying in a different hotel and was going home the next day. We said goodbye and I went to my room to finally go to sleep. The next day, my sisters and I rented motor bikes and toured the islands that were attached by bridges.

We were returning from one of our excursions and rounded the corner only to find that we were once again on the wrong side of the road. As we were repositioning our bikes to get over to the correct lane, our headlights moved over a wall. It was about twenty feet long and thirty inches high.

It was covered with shiny black stones that looked polished smooth and bright from our lights. We brought our cycles closer, put them on their kick stands and walked toward the wall. As I reached my hand out to touch one of the stones, they parted.

My sisters screamed and ran back to their mopeds and I backed away slowly to see what would happen. The Water bugs reformed and the wall was once again completely covered. That was a weird but fascinating experience I am glad I had but would not want to repeat.

I do not understand their fear of bugs as we all played with ants, water bugs and spiders when we were little.

The next day our mother arranged for us to take a boat ride to a private island. While on the flat bottomed, see-through boat, the captain passed around a jug of wine. Most of us had a sip or two but two girls named Pam and Pam decided to imbibe quite a bit more than the rest of us.

When we arrived at the side of the island, the captain instructed us on how to get off the boat and where and how to climb up the little cliff to the isolated island. I have always tried to be a gentleman so, I helped Pam and her friend off the boat.

There was a coral filled ledge to step onto before turning to climb up the twelve feet of cliff. Of course, I was polite in allowing the girls to go ahead of me. It did not hurt that I enjoyed the view. It was a good thing that I was carefully watching Pam climb up the cliff.

When she was about seven feet up, she slipped. I have always had quick reflexes and took a step backward to be in a better position to catch her. According to our tour guide, Captain Morgan, If I had not caught her, she would have been cut to ribbons by the coral.

I did not doubt that she would have bled to death because, when I caught her, a piece of that coral cut through my flip-flop and punctured my big toe. She promised to make it up to me, but I think the alcohol prevented her from remembering that promise.

I really enjoyed that island because it was the kind that gave women the option, to wear or not to wear. After a few hours, we got back in the boat, passed around another jug and sang songs on our way back to our pier. Yes, the Bobbsey-Twins rehydrated themselves again.

I again offered them a hand off the boat and, since they were the last two, I was walking behind them toward the parking lot. As the Pam who fell into my arms stepped off the curb, a taxi came screaming around the corner. Since her observational skills were challenged, she did not notice.

I ran and tackled her to keep her from being flattened by the vehicle. Because I was a gymnast and a football player, I was able to twist on the way down so she would land on me and not the hard ground. Unfortunately, as the car passed us, it hit and sprained my ankle.

You guessed it, she promised to make it up to me. The next day, she invited me to her hotel to go swimming. After a few minutes in the water together, she took off. When I found her a little later, she was sipping something at the floating bar.

I did not, and still do not have a problem with alcohol. In fact, God tells us to celebrate his goodness with wine and strong drink. However, there is a difference between loosening up and functioning below par. Once I realized that getting drunk was all she was interested in, I left.

Deuteronomy 14: 26 And thou shalt bestow that money for whatsoever thy soul lusteth after, for oxen, or for sheep, or for wine, or for strong drink, or for whatsoever thy soul desireth: and thou shalt eat there before the LORD thy God, and thou shalt rejoice, thou, and thine household,

Unfortunately, many religions have taken Scriptures out of context and made absolute rules around them like this verse:

Leviticus 10:9 Do not drink wine nor strong drink, thou, nor thy sons with thee...

They forget to finish the verse and place it in its context.

...when ye go into the tabernacle of the congregation, lest ye die: it shall be a statute for ever throughout your generations.

This is not for everyone nor is it all the time. Otherwise, why would Jesus have created eighty gallons of the best wine this side of Heaven?

John 2:7-11

7 Jesus saith unto them, Fill the waterpots with water. And they filled them up to the brim.

8 And he saith unto them, Draw out now, and bear unto the governor of the feast. And they bare it.

9 When the ruler of the feast had tasted the water that was made wine, and knew not whence it was: (but the servants which drew the water knew;) the governor of the feast called the bridegroom,

10 And saith unto him, every man at the beginning doth set forth good wine; and when men have well drunk, then that which is worse: but thou hast kept the good wine until now.

11 This beginning of miracles did Jesus in Cana of Galilee, and manifested forth his glory; and his disciples believed on him.

56
ANIMALS COMMUNICATE
February of 1980

My mother began rescuing animals when we were living in an apartment in Guttenberg, New Jersey. It began when my sisters and I were playing in the backyard. There was an alley between the house we lived in and the VFW next door.

It was barely wide enough to squeeze through sideways if you were small. We heard a noise in there and, upon investigating, one of my sisters saw a white rabbit trying to hide from us. We were able to scare it out of the alley and into our mother's arms.

I wanted to be more creative but, mom went and named the rabbit, Bunny Bunny. We rescued two more rabbits, Honey Bunny and Red, before figuring out that each rescue took place soon after Easter. People would purchase a bunny for their child as an Easter present and, when they got tired of it, they would leave it outside to fend for itself.

This infuriated our mother and, without success, she tried to find the "criminals." This became hard on me because I was allergic to the rabbits and ended up taking twenty-two pills a day to keep from spending my life in the emergency room.

The only animals we had until our first rescue were fish and, I was not allergic to them. Well, mom finally got a house of her own and began the animal rescue in earnest. At one time, just before leaving home for good, she had forty-nine cats, seven dogs, one dove, two guinea pigs and two parakeets.

One of those cats was an orange tabby called Preston. My stepfather was now part of the rescue mission. He worked at a trucking company called Preston so, when he rescued his first cat, that is what he named him.

My room was off limits to everyone. It had weather stripping around the entire door frame to keep out as much animal dander as possible. At times, many of the cats tried to get into my room as I unlocked it and went in. At first, several cats would gather around my feet, waiting for the door to open.

However, as I always gently pushed them away from the door, they got the hint and stopped trying. That is, all except Preston. He tried getting in from the left, from the right, charging in at the last moment from across the room and jumping off the kitchen counter as the door opened.

That last one worked and I had to toss him back into the kitchen. Well, I got home from work one day and, before opening my door, I looked around for Preston but, he was nowhere in sight. That is, until he slapped me on the head from atop the refrigerator.

By this time, my vision had narrowed to the point of looking through a McDonald's straw. That is why I missed him. He had jumped on the counter to the left of the fridge, climbed on top of the covered fish tank on that counter, climbed onto the back of the fridge, pushed all the cereal boxes forward and sat there waiting for me to return.

If I could have seen the thought bubble over his head, this is what it would have read, "I am going to get in there someday." He did not use words but, he communicated perfectly. I was so impressed with his hard work that I wanted to allow him in my room for a few minutes but, that would not have been good for my lungs.

I know that animals will be in Heaven but, I do not know if our pets/friends will be there. I have no proof of this but, I believe they will. I am so looking forward to asking Preston why he tried so hard to get into my living space.

Genesis 3:1 Now the serpent was more subtle than any beast of the field which the LORD God had made. And he said unto the woman, Yea, hath God said, Ye shall not eat of every tree of the garden? 2 And the woman said unto the serpent, we may eat of the fruit of the trees of the garden:

Numbers 22:28 And the LORD opened the mouth of the ass, and she said unto Balaam, what have I done unto thee, that thou hast smitten me these three times? 29 And Balaam said unto the ass, because thou hast mocked me: I would there were a sword in mine hand, for now would I kill thee.

Yes, I believe that we will be able to talk with animals as the four verses above show us. Since Heaven will be perfect, why would we not be able to communicate with our furry friends? Whatever God did twice, He can do again.

57
PROFESSOR WHITEHEAD
MARCH OF 1980

I will tell you in the story "Watch Out, Coming Through" that I became a math teacher. Well, here is the rest of the story. After teaching in that program for a while, I was invited to an awards presentation at the college. I did not want to go but my colleagues were urging me to attend, so I went.

Much to my surprise I was called up and given an award and the title of Professor Whitehead. From that day on for many years, even when I was not teaching, people called me Professor. I have to admit that I liked it.

Once the presentations were over, we started down the stairs. I had started dating someone who was with me at the presentation and she was guiding me. As we got to the bottom of the stairs she said, "One more step." I put my foot forward and down as if to go down one more step and, the people closest to us heard the snap.

It hurt and swelled but I did not think it was that serious. However, when I went to the doctor the next day, the x-ray showed that I had broken my ankle. I have to admit that I do not like to listen to doctors because they are still practicing medicine and I want to wait until they are done practicing and have it right before I am willing to let them work on me extensively.

I also have a high tolerance to pain so, when the doctor recommended crutches and rest, I did not listen to his directions for long. Once the swelling went down, I went back to work. I will probably be able to forecast the weather through my ankle when I get older but, so far, I have no problems with it.

I have been walked into things by many people. Most of the time it involves the face or the chin. Once in a while I encounter what I like to refer to as, "Voice Changers." Objects that hit a male in just the right spot to cause doubt to form in his mind as to whether he will ever be a father.

Though running into things is painful, there is perhaps something worse. It is the opposite of what caused my ankle to break. When you are walking up the stairs and you think there is one more step up and there is not. I cannot describe the feeling of coming down hard with your foot, expecting it to connect with the ground at any nano-second only to pass that point and have to put the brakes on.

Your whole body is poised to begin an upward motion and is leaning forward and then, you have to try to stop. Your entire body jerks as if you just received two hundred and thirty volts in your rear and your heart is pretending to be a herd of wild horses on the run.

If you are sighted and ever help a blind person up or down the stairs, please make sure you tell them the correct number of stairs. A broken ankle sure was a lousy way to end an otherwise great day.

Isaiah 58:11 And the LORD shall guide thee continually, and satisfy thy soul in drought, and make fat thy bones: and thou shalt be like a watered garden, and like a spring of water, whose waters fail not.

The word "fat" in the verse above means strong and healthy. Once I lost too much sight to do the sports I loved, cycling, football, basketball and frisbee, I started lifting weights to keep healthy.

Because I have chosen to honor the LORD above anyone or anything else, He has caused me to be spiritually and physically strong as the verse suggests.

58
WATCH OUT, COMING THROUGH
JUNE OF 1980

I lived with my father and his second wife from my ninth birthday until my eleventh birthday. My step-mothers parents became my grandparents and I called them mom-mom and pop-pop. That is the way grandparents are generally referred to in Baltimore, Maryland.

My school was about the same distance from my father's house as it was from my grandparent's home, though in the opposite direction. I would often go to mom-mom's house after school to help clean the dog droppings, mow the lawn, rake the yard or shovel the snow. After doing those things there was not much else to do but watch TV.

I did not like watching TV that much so I went around their home trying to find other things to do. I discovered a typewriter and fell in love. I would sit there for hours typing things. Soon I gave up on the letters and concentrated on the numbers. I discovered patterns within the numbers and became fascinated with math.

A few years later, when I was in the sixth grade, I had a math teacher who recognized my skill and she drew it out of me. She also gave me a lot of leeway and responsibility. We were supposed to write all of our work down on yellow sheets of paper in order to show how we came to our conclusions.

Once I was able to demonstrate to her that I did all the work in my head, that using the paper would be a waste of resources and would slow me down, she excused me from having to do so.

She was such a good teacher because she would pay attention to each student and figure out how they learned best and teach them that way. Many times, she set the class to task and put me in charge while she helped those few students that were struggling with the latest concept.

Sometimes she would even let me teach the class. She even took to recommending me as a tutor to the parents of students that were having a tough time keeping up.

While waiting to take my test for my GED, (in the story, "I see, you hear"), I began to help other students. I could hear some of their frustrations and since I was ready to take my test the first day, I began helping them. As I said in the other story, they did not like me helping at first but, after a while they relented.

After watching me for a while, they offered me a teaching position. I eventually got an honorary degree from the college for my work with the students. I taught two classes a day which were one and a half hours each. The students ran the gamut from recent dropouts trying to get back into school or into a vocation to the disabled trying to prepare for college. They ranged in age from sixteen to sixty-eight.

One of the students was a woman in her sixties bound to a wheelchair. I had just finished my second class and was about to leave when I heard this woman talking with someone about an appointment she needed to keep. She was trying to get someone to help her to the building just a block away. I excused myself to her for having overheard the conversation and asked if I could be of assistance.

She was not certain at first, but after assuring her that with her directions and my muscles we could get the job done, she agreed. We headed out the door and made a left-hand turn. Perhaps because I was so concerned for her safety, I noticed more people on the sidewalk than ever before, even though there were probably the same number of people. It became a challenge for her to give me directions because she was so fascinated with the reactions of the people around us when they realized that a blind man was pushing her wheelchair.

After a while she began to laugh and try to explain to me the looks on people's faces. We made it to the corner, across the street and found the building she needed to go into. We got inside, found the elevator and got in. We got off on the floor she needed and found the room where her appointment was and, after making sure she would have a way back, I took my leave.

She later told me that was the most fun she had in quite a while and wouldn't mind doing it again. That was not a true case of the blind leading the blind, but it was close enough.

Isaiah 35:5 Then the eyes of the blind shall be opened, and the ears of the deaf shall be unstopped.

Those of us with infirmities, and that is most of us, have the hope of being perfect in mind and body when the LORD returns for us. That should make the eighty or so years we have to live with our problems, more bearable.

59
I SEE, YOU HEAR
AUGUST OF 1980

I had to drop out of high school in my junior year because back in 1977, in my High School at least, they could not figure out how to help me. I was unable to read the board or my books and was beginning to fail some classes. At that time, you only had to be sixteen to sign yourself out of school. Since I was seventeen, I wrote the following note, "This note is to inform you that Raymond J. Whitehead Jr. will no longer be attending school. I signed it, "Me."

I had a newspaper route at the time but was now looking for ways to earn more money. Over the next few years, I had more than ten jobs. Some of them lasted thirty days because they did not want you to get into the union so, they let you go the day before you would qualify. Some of them let me go once they discovered my vision problem which was still only prevalent in dark and dimly lit places.

It seemed as if I was not going to be able to get a good job unless I went back and got my GED and then perhaps went back to school for a degree. I ended up in a program called Newstart. This was a state funded program affiliated with the local college. Once in the program I discovered how easy it was going to be to pass the test for my GED.

Even though I felt that I could pass the test right away, they made me stay in the program for the full six weeks before allowing me to take the test.

During that time, I started helping other students who were struggling. At first the teachers would tell me to get back to my desk but, after a while they allowed me to help. Later they even offered me a teaching position. I had often taught in my grammar school's math class and tutored other students in math for pay at the ripe old age of twelve.

While I was waiting to get my GED, I met Juanita. She was a deaf student at the program. We were about the same age and we started hanging out together. I wouldn't really call it dating because I was not interested in dating anyone that most of the people I knew, knew.

We were going to see a movie together, something with Bruce Lee in it. We were quite early so we decided to go to the pizza place nearby. While waiting for our pizza we decided to play the pinball machine that was between the counter and the door. We developed a plan. Since she could not hear, I would squeeze her arm, poke her in the side or shake her shoulder whenever there was a sound. Since I could not see, she would tell me when to flick the paddle.

It was strange not being able to see the game since at one time I had been so good at pinball. I almost missed a gymnastics competition that I had gone all the way from New Jersey to Chicago, Illinois for. I had piled up so many free games that I hated to just let them go. At another time, in Florida at a sandwich shop, I had piled up so many games that my two sisters, my step brother, and my two step sisters played the game until the owner closed the store. There were still twenty-six games left on the machine which the owner refused to pay me for.

Juanita and I made a good team but you should have seen the looks and heard the comments we got. We were having so much fun with the pinball machine that our pizza got cold and we ended up being late for the movie. So late that we decided to go back and play pinball some more instead.

Exodus 4:11 And the LORD said unto him, who hath made man's mouth? or who maketh the dumb, or deaf, or the seeing, or the blind? have not I the LORD?

Since the LORD'S original creation was perfect, there would have been no one blind, deaf or with any other disability. However, since we fell, many people have had to suffer the loss of some function or other. The verse above tells us that the LORD is in charge and has a purpose for those with less than perfect minds or bodies. That means we have purpose and we can please the LORD. I believe that He was pleased that Juanita and I had so much fun despite the limitations each of us had.

We can, as Moses did, which prompted the LORD to speak the words above, whine and complain about our lack and what He wants us to do or, we can step out and enjoy the blessings we have.

60
LOOK BOTH WAYS
September of 1980

There used to be a thing called "common sense." I have now taken to using the phrase, "Uncommon Sense" because it seems that few people possess the former. There are many things our elders teach us when we are children that are very good. I think, however, that the person I encountered in this instance must have had the phrase, "Look both ways before you cross.", so ingrained in her that she was unable to think for herself.

I was on my way to my mother's house and had gotten to the corner across from her block. I stood at the corner for a moment listening for the traffic. When I heard that it was all clear, I crossed to the other side. As I began walking toward my mother's house, I heard footsteps running toward me. I do not know why, but I knew that the person belonging to those steps was running to meet up with me so, I stopped.

When I turned to face the person she said, "Excuse me but I was watching you cross the street. I noticed that you did not look before you crossed. That is very dangerous." I responded with, "I am blind so there is no reason for me to look both ways. Instead, I listen both ways and, since I have one ear on each side of my head, I do not have to turn my head."

I figured that she hadn't seen my Cane and that my explanation would have caused her to turn and go back to whatever she was doing. It did not. Instead, she said, "Yes, but you should still look both ways." I could only assume that she was so traumatize by seeing someone cross the street without looking that she had not processed the information that I had given her so, I tried again to explain.

I said to her, while waving my hand in front of my face for emphasis, "I cannot see anything so even if I turned my head in the direction of the traffic, it wouldn't do any good. Instead, I listen very carefully before crossing." Unbelievably, her response was, "Yes but you should still look both ways before you cross or you could get hit by a car."

Now I had no idea how to reach this woman so I just thanked her for her concern and turned to go. I had a lot of trouble controlling my laughter. I did not know if she was still standing there watching me and, I did not want to offend her by laughing out loud but, over the years, being quite confident that she was not around, I have on occasion burst out into laughter about the whole situation.

Proverbs 1:5 A wise man will hear, and will increase learning; and a man of understanding shall attain unto wise counsels.

I hope that, when people try to educate me about something I already have formed an opinion on, I will still listen, consider, pray and, if necessary and if the evidence compels me to, I will be able to adopt a new and more informed point of view.

61
DIPLOMACY
September of 1980

It is funny how things work sometimes. Just two weeks after the previous story, "Look Both Ways," this happened.

I was on my way to my mother's house and I had arrived at the corner of the street I needed to cross to get to her home. I was not sure of my angle because the corner was not a corner at all, it was rounded. I was using my cane to figure out the direction and I was feeling to the right.

Just then a woman came up to me, put her hand on my arm, asked if I needed help crossing and before I could answer she said, "Let's go." I attempted to tell her that I did not want to cross that street but she was not listening. Once we got to the other shore, I thanked her and waited for her to leave.

Once I heard her footsteps enter a building I crossed back to the other side and then crossed to the corner I had wanted to get to in the first place. I then walked the quarter of a block to my mother's house, laughing all the way. I do not know for sure but I will take a big chance and assume that she did not have much experience helping the blind and was so proud of the chance to assist someone that she couldn't hear me.

I only had a moment to decide the best course of action. I could have been more forceful and asked her to leave me alone. I thought if I had done that, she would never again try to help anyone. I could have been more assertive and gotten her attention, letting her know that she was making a mistake. She probably would have crossed me the correct way apologizing the whole time and then been too embarrassed to help anyone in the future.

I decided to keep my mouth shut and allow her to feel good about helping and perhaps be less excited the next time which would allow her to listen to her next victim, I mean the next person she wanted to help. I also thought that it was possible that she just had that kind of personality that would cause her to do the same to others that she did to me and I would be doing them an injustice by allowing her to continue on her merry way.

By the time I had considered all these possibilities it was too late to make a decision because she had finished crossing me and had turned to go. Though I had waited until she was out of sight, I half hoped she was watching me from a window and had come to realize that she had made a mistake.

I do not wish to discourage anyone from helping the disabled because, in one way or another, every person on the face of the planet is disabled and we can all use some help once in a while.

Job 29:15 I was eyes to the blind, and feet was I to the lame.

Sorry to use a cliche but, it is the thought that counts. Though she took me the wrong way, she tried to help. What did I lose? A few minutes. What did I gain? A good story and a smile every time I remember it.

62
RICHARD GOES ON VACATION
NOVEMBER OF 1980

While teaching in Hackensack, New Jersey, I developed a relationship with a woman in nearby Lodi which caused me to take the last bus home almost every night. There was a bus that would go from Lodi to North Bergen which I had to catch at five minutes before eleven pm. After taking it for a while, the driver and I began to have conversations that would sometimes need to be continued the next day.

One day, on a Friday, Richard, the bus driver, informed me that he would be going on vacation for the next two weeks. He said that he found out who would be taking over his route and told him all about me. He told him what I looked like, where to pick me up, what time I would be there, where I should sit and where to let me off.

I wished him a wonderful time and, after getting off the bus, I did not think about it again until the next Monday on my way to the bus stop. As I got on the bus, I held out my money and he took it. In those days the drivers had a register which they had to punch the information into. It would spit out a card and, if you were due any change, the driver would have to reach into his pocket for the bills or push buttons on the change holder secured to his belt.

Once our financial transaction was complete, I asked him if there was anyone behind him. With a puzzled sound in his voice he responded, "Nnnooooo." I then took a step to the seat behind him, grabbed the pole, swung myself into position and began to sit down. I was immediately accosted with a barrage of blows to the head with an umbrella. At the same time an old lady began to scream. I do not remember what she was screaming because I was busy trying to escape and apologize at the same time.

I stepped back to the driver and asked him, "I thought you said that there was no one behind you?" He started a sentence with, "I looked in the mir'", but broke it off when he realized who I was. He then said, "Oh, you're that blind guy Richard told me about. I forgot all about you." He then apologized profusely and turned around to explained to the irate woman behind him.

Since I did not really suffer from the blows, we all had a good laugh about it, well, at least the driver and I did. I do not think that the woman was able to recover until after she got off the bus. When Richard came back two weeks later, I did not have to tell him, his co-worker had done that already. He also asked Richard to tell me again how sorry he was.

Luke 17:4 And if he trespass against thee seven times in a day, and seven times in a day turn again to thee, saying, I repent; thou shalt forgive him.

For the first few years of being blind enough to need other's help, I used to get angry when they forgot about me. Then, after surrendering my life to the LORD Jesus Christ, I realized that, since He was in control, He was allowing these things to happen.

I then was able to use the verse above, substituting (them for he). knowing that, if I was not physically hurt because of their forgetfulness, I could laugh about what happened. Since I have never been shy, was class clown in school and love to make others laugh, it became fun for me and caused those that did forget to be at ease.

63
UNICORNS
JUNE OF 1981

My sister Lisa was home from school and had brought a friend with her, Patricia. Trish and I hit it off right away and my sister did not see much of her friend for the rest of the weekend. We spent hours walking and talking and by the end of the weekend we decided to date.

When Summer rolled around it was time for one of our family traditions. Every year we would go to several places, Hershey Park, which is an amusement park in Pennsylvania run by the chocolate company, Jungle Habitat which was a drive-through park full of wild jungle animals, Shepherd's Lake, which is a lake in Ringwood, New Jersey with a beach and Great Adventure, which is not as large as Disney World but just as much fun. We had decided that our first stop should be Great Adventure. Unfortunately, only four of us could go. My mother, my sister Donna, Trish and I.

Usually as you get older you become less daring. Not the case for my mother. On this trip she did not want to go on the sit down, face forward one loop roller coaster. Ten years later she would go with us on a stand up, Super Duper Double Looper going backward after it reached its end going forward.

Since Trish was also not very daring, she and my mom decided to wait for us at the stand by the exit ramp. When we arrived there, we found a game booth. For a dollar you got a large wooden ring and could try to win a stuffed animal worth about fifty dollars.

One of the animals was a Unicorn. Trish loved Unicorns so, I gave the man a dollar and got my ring. I had my mother and sister describe the layout for me. When the man realized that I had very little vision, he must have thought there was no chance. When my mother asked if I could put out my hand to touch the animal so I could get a better idea of its position, he must have really thought I was a pigeon.

Later my mother described the astonished look on his face when she made her request. Once I had scoped out the situation and felt the loop and its weight, I knew how to get my Unicorn. I threw the loop like a frisbee to make it spin around the animal to insure it would not get stuck on any of its parts. Also, I figured that the base that the animal stood on must be barely smaller than the ring.

I knew that if the ring had enough spin on it, it would fit itself around the base. I was right. With an even more astonished look than before he handed the Unicorn to me. My sister then asked if I could try to get one for her. She liked horses better but only slightly so. I held out another dollar for the gentleman and he gave me another ring.

My mother said he had a smirk on his face as if to say, no way is he going to be able to do that again. I asked if I could feel the Unicorn to get my position again and this time, he was not so happy about the idea but, finally he said yes.

I threw the ring just as before and, just as before it circled around the animal a few times and landed on the base. It spun itself into position and dropped around the base. Now the man was mad. He gave me the unicorn and declared that he had to go on break. He closed up shop and left.

My mother and Trish stood there holding the Unicorns while Donna and I went on the roller coaster. There was a long line and it took between a half hour and forty-five minutes before we came down the ramp. When we got to them, they were still standing in front of the booth, still closed. As we walked away, some of our party looked back to see the man re-opening the booth. I wonder if he believed that I was blind?

Ecclesiastes 2:24 There is nothing better for a man, than that he should eat and drink, and that he should make his soul enjoy good in his labour. This also I saw, that it was from the hand of God.

I did not see it at the time; however, I now know that the LORD blessed me with the wisdom and ability to win those animals and gave me that wonderful day.

64
DO CATS HAVE ESP?
September of 1981

I was in college for Special Education. Because of my blindness and my love for little people, I had decided that helping children with less than perfect minds or bodies was what I wanted to do for at least the next fifty years. I had spent the previous few months clepping many classes. CLEP, College Level Examination Program, allowed me to knock two years off my Master's program and begin my first year with fifty-two credits.

I was so happy with the way things went that I went to visit my mother at her home in North Bergen, New Jersey. Walking from Boulevard East up seventy-fifth street to get to her home was only two and a half blocks. Though I knew that area very well, I used my cane because of what happened in the story, "I Did Not Mean to Grab That!" As I walked in the house, my mother said from the living room, "Hello Raymond."

I thought she must have seen me through the window and said so. She just laughed and said, "No, I knew you were on your way five minutes ago." When I asked her how, she explained that she knew because the cats began jumping up on all the furniture. That is when I realized that I was not pushing through any of the dozens of cats that were usually on the floor.

Her animals had come to know that I might accidentally step on their tails or nudge them with my foot. Once I was seated, they felt free to walk around again. The only times they would be on the floor were when I was playing with them using my cane or a laser pointer that made them go crazy. I cannot wait until I get to Heaven and ask the LORD how far away I was when they first heard me.

Job 38:36 Who hath put wisdom in the inward parts? or who hath given understanding to the heart?

Wisdom is not something that GOD gives only to humans. You can claim that there is no GOD if you want. However, all you have to do is look around you to see all the wonderful plants, animals and people around you to realize that, to claim that it is all a great accident is foolishness. Christians and non-believers have the same problem. Where did GOD come from or, where did the material for the big bang come from?

Does it not make more sense to see the design and realize that there is a designer. The only reason people reject the Creator is because things have not gone their way. If there is a GOD, neither you nor I are HIM. Why not ask, "What should I learn from this?" rather than, "Why me?" After all, until you ask HIM what HIS plan is, HE will not tell you.

65
WHAT COLOR WERE THEY?
JULY OF 1982

As my habit was, I was visiting my Baltimore family. I did this around my birthday and Christmas every year. My sisters Margie and Terry wanted to go to High's convenience store to get some snacks. They had just finished the laundry earlier and were each wearing black jeans.

The store was only three and a half blocks away so, I did not think they would be gone long. About thirty minutes later, I saw two people walking toward the house. They were about a block away and, at first, I thought they were my sisters.

It was hard to tell for two reasons. One, I had lost the use of my left eye on March 17, 1978 due to a botched surgery and poor diagnosis. Two, minutes before seeing them, a huge rain began, the kind called, 'cats and dogs'.

So, when I saw that the people walking toward me were wearing white pants, I knew it could not be them. That is, until they got closer and I heard their laughter. I did not want to ask them how and where they changed their pants for all the neighbors to hear so, I waited until they got closer.

Before I asked about their pants, I wanted to know why they were laughing so heartily, and that, I could let the neighbors hear. Their answer surprised me because, they said it was their pants making them so hysterical. They said, "Look at our pants, when we left, they were black."

Now they were close enough for me to ask, "Where and why did you change and, what is so funny about it?" In two-part harmony they said, "We didn't change, these are the same pants." I thought they must have purchased a can of paint from High's and said so.

Because it felt so good on such a hot day, we were doing all this talking in the rain. That is when they started brushing their pants and, they started getting darker. It turns out that my sisters thought that, the more detergent you used, the cleaner your clothing would get.

There was so much soap baked into their jeans by the drier that the pounding of the rain on their clothing made it suds up. Their mother had been telling them to use less powder for a long time. I think this finally convinced them to go easier on the detergent.

Ecclesiastes 1:17 And I gave my heart to know wisdom, and to know madness and folly: I perceived that this also is vexation of spirit.

I feel sorry for Solomon because, any man foolish enough to have a thousand sexual partners that he is financially responsible for has to have lost his mind. That may be why he could not appreciate the wisdom God gave him, the intricacies of madness and the fun that folly can bring.

66
MOTORCYCLE CRASH NUMBER TWO
APRIL OF 1985

At the age of eleven, I started delivering papers for the *Jersey Journal*. Since I went to each customer and asked them exactly where they wanted their paper and put it there every day, I got great tips. Years later, when I was living in Maryland, I got a job with the *Baltimore Sun*.

I loved being outside, riding my bike and making good money for the hours I actually worked. As boys quit their routes, if they were near mine, I would take them. At one point I had three routes with over 100 papers Monday through Friday and over 240 on Saturday and Sunday.

There was no actual paper on Saturday but, since the Sunday paper was so thick, the newspaper split it in two. Even so, each half was about an inch thick. During the week, I had two bags. One on my handle bars and one over my shoulder. That way, I could do my rout in one shot.

With the paper being so thick and having almost 250 of them, I needed a shopping cart. I had found one that was quite rusted. I went to the manager of the store that it belonged to, showed it to him and got permission to keep it since it was too ugly for his customers.

On Saturday and Sunday, I had to get up at four in the morning to catch the bus to get to my first route if it was on the weekend. Otherwise, I took my motorcycle. I do not remember which day of the week it was but, I was using my motor bike.

I had delivered my papers and was on my way home on Cedonia Avenue. I was slowing down next to a park because there was a red light.

Some fool, who was parallel parked at the corner, was just waiting for the light to turn green. When it did, he shot into my lane so fast, he or she sent me across four lanes of traffic. I landed under a tractor-trailer. The poor guy thought he crushed me under his wheels.

The idiot that hit me took off and no one at the scene got the plate of the car. I ended up with a compound broken right clavicle, a broken right pinky, a split right patella, a broken right toe and a concussion. I was in a huge amount of pain and bleeding from several places but did not want to wait for the police since there was nothing they could do.

A good Samaritan turned my motorcycle off, placed it in his truck and drove me home. I had a very hard time getting it up the hill with my shoulder not functioning properly. Once I placed it in my hallway, I walked up to my third-floor apartment.

I sat on the couch, got my wife calmed down, wiped off all the blood, changed my clothing and waited for the pain to subside. After an hour and a half, I called an ambulance because the pain got worse, not better. I have been using a phrase for the last few decades, "uncommon sense."

It seems that there is very little common sense left in this world, myself included. I was stupid for going home rather than waiting for an ambulance at the crash site. The medics that came to my apartment were no smarter than I was though.

Once they diagnosed me with a broken clavicle, rather than let me walk to the vehicle, they insisted on strapping me to a gurney and carrying me down four flights of stairs. Three in the building and one from the apartment complex to the parking lot.

It made me wish I had not called them. I noted that this was the second bike crash. The first was in July of 1968. My mother was taking me to the pool for my asthma. I was on the back of her Honda 350 when she was hit by a taxi. Most people would consider me a fool because, if God healed my eyes, one of the first things I would do would be to get a motorcycle.

Proverbs 26:11 As a dog returneth to his vomit, so a fool returneth to his folly.

I had mentioned my love for motorcycles to a friend who rides horses. She said that she hated bikes and thought I was a fool to want to ride one. I mentioned that people die from horse accidents too.

What I did not know was that about five thousand of the twenty million people who ride motorcycles each year die. About one hundred of the thirty million people who ride horses die each year. That is one in four thousand for bikes and one for every three hundred thousand for horses.

That makes you seventy-five times more likely to die in a motorcycle accident than when riding a horse. I still want a motorcycle, but only if I could see well. She was correct in stating that I was a fool to have been riding one with my greatly impaired vision.

"The reason I refer to this story as crash number two is because the first crash is in the story, "Cliff Hanger." Technically, these are the second and third stories Because I was a passenger in the first crash and only responsible for the second and third crashes. It was July of 1968 and my mother was driving me to the pool in Hoboken, New Jersey as recommended by my doctor to help my asthma.

We were almost there when a taxi hit us. My mother went skidding with her Honda 350 and I flew to the wall that led down to Hoboken, New Jersey. I was hanging over the edge by my arms when a man grabbed me and lifted me to safety. When I looked over the wall to the bottom, I think I must have been in shock because, the only thought I had was, "WOW!"

I recently found out that the wall above the cliff is at least three hundred feet tall. I used to love it when my mother would take me on her bike up and down the road that went up from Hoboken. To me it seemed like a giant ramp for having fun.

67
BILL AND THE PRAYING MANTIS
JULY OF 1985

In another story, "Water Fight," I will explain how I lived in the middle building of an apartment complex. Often, we would have a party that would be going on in two, three or even all four of the third-floor apartments. In one there may be mood music, dim lighting and incense. In a second there would be bright lights and loud music. In the third there would be people playing games and in the fourth there would be a movie going on.

This evening was one of those that utilized all four apartments. By two or three in the morning the parties would usually grow more subdued and everyone would filter into one place. This time it was my place. Bill and I were having a chess game on my coffee table, I should say compact dining table because I did not drink coffee but did frequently eat there.

Bill had left his Newports in his apartment. He got up to get them and a few moments later, I heard him yelling my name. I had no idea what could be wrong and rushed into his living room. He had run into the hall that led to his bed room closing the door most of the way. Once I had entered his living room, he poked his head out to tell me that there was a giant bug on his lamp.

When I asked him why he was hiding behind the door he explained that he hated bugs, especially large ones. When I pointed out that he was hiding behind a louver door and that the bug could get through it with no problem, he ran down the hall and slammed the door to his bed room once he was safely in it. Before the door abruptly shut, he yelled, "Let me know when the bug is gone."

My sight was not good enough to spot a bug so I asked him on which lamp the creature was parked. He did not have many lights in his place and the ones he did have were not too illuminating. He said it was the three teared lamp that stood by the patio door in the living room. I looked for the culprit but could not see it. I called Bill out of his room to come and spot it for me. At first, he did not want to do it but, after assuring him that he would have to spend the rest of his life in his bed room unless he did help me, he came out slowly.

When he got to the louver door, he peeked his head out to look. He said that it was still in the same place on the lamp. Since I still did not see it, I started my hand up the lamp and asked him to tell me when I was getting close. He did not have to tell me because, once I was within a few inches of the offender, it started moving up the lamp and I could finally see it. It was a Praying Mantis.

I knew that there was a one hundred dollar fine in New Jersey for killing one of these but, I had no idea if the same rule applied in Maryland. Even if it did not, I hated the thought of harming one of these Star Trek looking bugs. In my younger days I had caught many of these bugs so, I knew that you had to get them directly behind the head or they would turn around and bite you.

Well, I missed and the seven-inch-long beast began to claw and gnaw on my fingers. I decided to endure the discomfort in order to free my friend from the prospect of being a monk and to help propagate the species. I opened his patio door, walked on to the balcony, closed the door behind me and tried to let it go. I guess it was having too much fun turning my fingers into a pin cushion because, it did not leave at first. After slowly opening my hand and then beginning to shake it, the beast finally flew off my hand.

I went back into Bills living room and announced that the green monster was gone. Slowly he emerged from the hallway while carefully looking around. He asked me why I did not kill it, I think he was afraid it would return for revenge. After explaining my reasons to him we went back to our chess game.

It has always amazed me how a creature, that is, a human, who is thousands of times larger than an insect, can be afraid of it. I suppose if you do not know whether or not they are poisonous, there is some cause for caution. In the same way it has always amazed me how stupid most bugs seem to be. Flying in the face of a being thousands of times larger than itself and coming back for more after being swatted away.

1 Chronicles 16:24 Declare his glory among the heathen; his marvelous works among all nations.

There are those that would look at a Praying Mantas and ask, "I wonder what that evolved from?" Then there are those that would ask, "What in the world did God create that kind of bug for?" Then there are those like me that can appreciate its beauty and wait until we get to Heaven to ask the LORD about it.

68
BILL AND THE LOCUST
JULY OF 1985

I love my friend Bill but sometimes we can be so unobservant. Thus was the case with this story and the previous one. Neither Bill nor I could figure out how such a large bug could have gotten into his apartment, and it would not be the last one.

About two weeks after the Praying Mantis, toward the end of another party, Bill went to his place to retire for the evening. Moments later he came back in a panic. He said that there was a very loud noise coming from his apartment but he could not figure out where it was coming from. I went with him and, upon hearing the noise, determined that it was a smoke alarm.

He and I went to the one in the hall that was in the same spot in every apartment and disabled it. As Murphy would have it, just as we thought we had turned it off by removing the batteries, the sound stopped. I was about to ask him what he was cooking, burning rather, when the noise started up again. I asked him if there was another smoke alarm in the apartment. He said he did not think so.

After looking around the place with the noise starting and stopping, he could not locate another alarm. I decided to do a little detective work. The next time the noise started I listened for its origin. I followed it to the kitchen sure that it was a smoke alarm and that Bill had burned something.

When we arrived in the kitchen the noise was so loud that I thought my ears would cease working at any moment. As much as it hurt, I followed my ears to the sound's intensity. When I pointed to the sound's origin on the kitchen windowsill, Bill headed for the door.

That was when I realized that it was a locust and not a fire alarm. I went to open the screen to flick it out and found that there was no screen. After launching the noise maker into the night, I turned to Bill. to my amazement he confessed that he had known about the missing screen but had forgotten about it.

After explaining that the lack of a bug restraint was the reason he was being so often harassed, we entered one of the vacant apartments and, "borrowed", its kitchen window screen. I think we forgot to return it when bill moved out. I know that the Chinese invented the water torture but it cannot compare to the locust in your kitchen torture.

Proverb 30:27 The locusts have no king, yet go they forth all of them by bands.

I lived the first 41 years of my life on the east coast, New York, New Jersey, Maryland, Pennsylvania, Delaware and was aware of locusts every summer. I used to find it fascinating how what sounded like 50 or more of them in one tree would sound off. Once they stopped, you would hear another set in a tree half way down the block go off.

After almost being deafened by one on a kitchen window sill, I think there were probably only two or three in each tree. I am grateful that I have not had to deal with that problem again.

69
A LITTLE TIPSY
NOVEMBER OF 1985

Bill and I loved to do many things together. We loved to watch Monday Night Football and make fun of the announcers who made many mistakes and sometimes said the dumbest things. We also liked to play chess. I had been a carpenter for a few years and made Bill a chess cabinet. He had a folding chess board and plastic chess pieces.

I went out and found a nicer board that did not fold and filled the bottoms of the pieces with clay to make them heavier. Then I had a piece of glass cut to the size of the board. I inlayed the glass and board a half inch from the top and made drawers on either side for the pieces to lie in order.

We had forty-three games on that set. Bill had won twenty-two and I had won the other twenty-one. I had played chess against many people over the years but had not found an opponent so evenly matched to me.

We were playing one of the forty-three games when we decided we were hungry. After some conversation we agreed upon pizza. They told us that the pizza would arrive in about thirty minutes. By now we knew what that meant, more like forty-five minutes.

One tactic I have employed in my business is to go over-estimates and then deliver sooner than the customer expected. I have come across a few other companies that do the same but, on the whole, most of them try to make it sound like you will have your merchandise soon and, then you end up waiting and becoming frustrated.

Well, I was correct. About forty minutes after hanging up the phone, the delivery boy arrived with our dinner. I had him come in and he stood in the hall. I took the pie from him, handed it to bill who examined it to make sure it was what we had ordered. When Bill assured me that it was, I got out the money to pay Mr. Pizza.

Having been a waiter once, I know how important tips are. I never tip because of the food, I always tip based upon the service. The server usually has nothing to do with the preparation of the meal but, has everything to do with how it is served and how we are taken care of during the meal. The service often has more to do with my enjoyment of the meal than does the quality of the food.

Another weird thing I like to do is to pay the delivery person with a bill that he will have to give me change for. This makes them think that I am probably stingy. I will hold out my hand and wait until they have placed all the change in it. After double checking their calculation, I will say thank you which confirms that I am a tightwad. Finally, I will reach into my pocket and pull out the tip that I had waiting for them all along.

Most of the time the person tries to be pleasant even though they are disappointed that they will not be receiving a tip. Once I place the tip in their hand, even though it might only be a dollar or two, they are now so happy that they are getting anything that they seem as grateful as if I had given them a twenty.

I have had a few people over the years who have gotten so upset at the thought that they were not going to receive a tip that they copped an attitude. Usually, it is not so bad and I give them the tip anyway. Rarely, I have declined giving a tip because the person became downright rude.

I had handed the money to Mr. Pizza and he was counting the change into my hand. After dispensing with the bills, he reached into his pocket and pulled out a handful of change. As he was searching for the correct coins, Bill said, "Don't forget to give him a tip." I immediately grabbed Mr. Pizza's shoulders and tilted him to the right, my right. Mr. Pizza didn't even blink. Because he was now a little off balance, he did drop a few coins.

It seemed to me as if he did not get the joke so, I turned my head toward Bill and asked him, "Is this a big enough tip?" Bill answered, "No, tip him a little more to the right." So I did. After picking up the coins that he dropped and giving me the rest of my change, I gave him a real tip. After he left, Bill told me that Mr. Pizza smiled when I went to tip him a little more to the right.

Luke 10:7 For the labourer is worthy of his hire.

Time for a gripe. As I said above, tips are for a job well done. Why then do many restaurants and other businesses not only include the tip in the bill but tell you the percentage to give? I never accept that, instead, I ask for the manager and ask them to remove the tip from my check.

Though I have to argue sometimes, they always take it off. Then, I usually give the tip that I feel is appropriate directly to the worker.

Gripe two:

I think I can remember when tips were eight percent. I know I can remember when they were 10, then 12, then 15 and now 18 percent. Why is that? If 20 years ago a meal cost $20, the tip would have been $2. That same meal is now $40 so the tip would be $4. Why should it now be $6 or $7.20?

Let's do the math.

Say a weight person spends a total of 10 minutes with you in a one-hour meal, taking your order, fixing problems, getting other items and checking to see that everything is good.

Say that meal for four people is $40.

Say they have six tables to care for.

Say only half the people tip.

That means, he/she earns $12 an hour plus their wage if they are tipped at 10 percent.

Realizing that the example above is extremely conservative, they are making a good living without going to fifteen or eighteen percent.

If everyone tipped at 18 percent, he/she would be making $43.20 plus their wage an hour. I think that is ridiculous.

70
WHAT COLOR IS THIS?
MARCH OF 1986

My friend Bill and I decided to go to dinner at a very good restaurant. He was commiserating a recent break with his girlfriend and I was depressed over finding out that the girl I was interested in was a lesbian. We had been friends for over a year and I had no idea.

We ordered our food and, while waiting, we could not help but overhear the conversation at the table next to us. There were four black men and they were using the "N" word a lot. I hate that word because my godfather is a black man, I dated a black girl and I have a lot of black friends.

It is a double standard that black people can use that word with each other but if a white person uses it, he will be, at least, verbally abused. However, black people can call white people honky all day long and we are expected to accept it without complaint.

Climbing down from my soap box now:

I turned to Bill and said, "Watch this." I then got up, took two steps toward their table and excused myself. When I had their attention I said, "Sorry for interrupting but, since we are only a few feet away and can hear most of what you say, would you mind not using that word?"

When they asked what word, I responded, "The N word." They tittered a little and asked, "What's it to you?" I said, "As a black man, I am offended by that word." After the laughter died down, one of them asked, "What do you mean?"

I said, "I am a black man and that word is insulting." One of the young men said, "I hate to tell you brother, but you as white as rice." I said, "I am not and I can prove it." I asked Bill to come over to the table and, as I rolled my sleeve up a little and pointed at my wrist, I asked, "What color is this?"

When Bill said, "White!" I slapped my forehead and exclaimed, "O my God, they've been lying to me all my life!" The table erupted in laughter and we were invited to eat with them. We had a great meal and became fast friends. It was a wonderful evening.

Genesis 1:27 So God created man in his own image, in the image of God created he him; male and female created he them.

There is only one race, the human race. People may be different colors, have different color eyes and hair, be different shapes and sizes but, we are all human. It is reprehensible to treat others poorly because their skin is not the same as yours.

71
STOP LOOKING AT MY GIRLFRIEND
April of 1986

My friend and the best man at my wedding, Bill, and I decided to go to IHOP. When we got to the door, he started laughing. It took him a little while to calm down enough to let me in on the joke. As we approached the building, we had been discussing irony.

Once he could breathe again, he told me that there was a sign in the window of the door that let customers know that they had braille menus. I did not "see" what was so funny about that until he explained. He told me that the sign was the size of a small poster, the print was bold and in giant letters.

As my brain wrapped itself around what he just said, it became my turn to chuckle. to have only four words take up the space of a two foot by three-foot sign was indeed, something to brighten my day. That reminds me of people that speak louder when they find out that you are deaf or blind.

We went into the restaurant, found a table and, Bill asked me if I wanted a braille menu. I could read braille as I had to learn it in order to go to college. However, I was not proficient because of all the carpentry, masonry, electrical and plumbing I had done over the last ten years.

So, though I declined, when our waitress arrived, my friend thought it would be fun to get a bumpy menu anyway. You should have seen her face when, upon handing the menu to me, Bill took it and began to look at it. The poor girl was confused.

After placing our orders, Bill needed the restroom. During the time he was gone, I almost got into a fight with another customer for flirting with his girl. They were seated across from me and, without knowing it, I was staring at her.

Just before my friend returned, the guy got up, approached me and asked, "What the Hell is your problem?" At first, I did not realize he was talking to me. When I finally woke up to that fact, I said, "Excuse me!" He loudly said, "Stop staring at my girlfriend!" I said, "I cannot possibly be staring at your girlfriend because I am blind."

The man did not believe me. Just then, Bill chimed in, lifted the bumpy menu and said, "My friend is blind, which is why he has a Braille menu." When he still refused to believe us, I pulled out and opened my cane. I also told him to ask the waitress if he did not believe me.

I do not know if he left because his meal was over or if he was just too embarrassed to stay after making such a fool of himself in front of his date. I do know that this happened to me a second time in a different restaurant in New York City when I was with my girlfriend.

Once I went completely blind, I stopped wearing "Ray Charles" glasses. Maybe, if I had been wearing shades, I could have avoided these problems?

Exodus 20: 17 Thou shalt not covet thy neighbour's house, thou shalt not covet thy neighbour's wife, nor his manservant, nor his maidservant, nor his ox, nor his ass, nor any thing that is thy neighbour's.

When I still had eyesight, I loved staring at beautiful women. I did so to appreciate them, not to have designs on them. What causes a man to be so insecure that he feels the need to threaten another man for appreciating his girl's beauty?

Over the decades, many men as well as women have approached me to let me know how beautiful my wife is. Perhaps they feel that I would like to know that since I can no longer see her for myself. I have not once been other than grateful for their comments.

72
WILL THERE BE ANIMALS IN HEAVEN?
JULY OF 1986

Heart has a song about a dog and butterfly. This story is about a dog and a bee. My father had been a Pinkerton for the Baltimore Colts until they left for Annapolis in 1984. In addition, he would work other events and, when I was in the area, he would get me hired on as a security guard at crab feasts.

That experience allowed me to apply for and get a job as a guard for Baltimore Outdoor Storage. I loved the job but had two bad experiences while working there. My asthma was so bad at the time that I had to carry a bottle of epinephrine and syringes everywhere I went because of my severe allergies to stinging insects and all animals with fur or feathers.

I told Bill, the owner of that business, of my plight and how to administer a dose of epinephrine if needed. Two weeks later, I rushed into the office and passed out. Before hitting the rug, I told him that I had been stung so, he knew what to do.

Upon waking up I told him that one of our water hoses had fallen off the curb and, when I replaced it, I had annoyed a bee which took it out on my left arm. Two weeks later, a dog ran up to say hello, touched his or her wet nose to my thigh and, I ended up in the hospital for three weeks.

By the time I had been released, the job was no longer mine. It is very hard for most people to understand or believe that my allergies are that severe. Let me give you an example.

My mother rescued over a thousand cats, over two hundred dogs and animals from a turtle which was thought to be banned in the USA to six ducks that were barred from entering Aruba as she was coming home from there. She lived in New Jersey and I lived in New York.

In order for her to visit my family, she had to shower in the basement, take her clothes out of the drier, dress and immediately leave the house. Still, I ended up suffering for three days after each visit.

Revelation 6:2 And I saw, and behold a white horse: and he that sat on him had a bow; and a crown was given unto him: and he went forth conquering, and to conquer.

The above verse mentions the first of the, "Four horsemen of the apocalypse." What does this have to do with my allergies? I am glad you asked. Despite what many believe, there will be animals in Heaven. This verse proves that, there will at least be horses.

Throughout Isaiah, Revelation and the first chapter of Genesis, we see that animals are important to God. Animals, birds, fish and bugs were all created before man and woman. Therefore, if Adam had not sinned, we would be in Heaven with no death and all those creatures.

When I eventually get my perfect body, I will not be allergic to anything. This may have been a circuitous explanation; however, I have had so many people ask me over the years if there will be animals in Heaven, I thought it was worth the longer walk.

73
WHO WAS DRIVING?
JULY OF 1986

I had gotten married in August of 1981 and after moving around a bit, we ended up in Baltimore, Maryland. My wife wanted to get a car because she was tired of having to wait for the bus whenever we wanted to go somewhere. So we got a car, a Gremlin.

I have been in many accidents in my life and I tend to believe the statistic that most accidents happen close to home. At least this one did. We had just turned left out of our apartment complex's parking lot and drove about twenty feet. There were two cars in front of us and we were all waiting for the red light to change to green.

As the light changed the cars in front began to move and they both went straight ahead. We, however, needed to make a left and just as she began to turn, we were hit on the passenger's side by a van. We were told later that the van was going about sixty miles an hour. After seeing what was left of our car, I believe it.

They had just passed the seat belt law and it was to take effect the next week. I hated seat belts and still do. I think it is ridiculous to legislate common sense. Anyway, I decided that since I was going to have to comply with the law in a few days, I might as well get started now. Despite the skewed numbers by those with special interests, I believe that seat belts cause as much damage as they prevent.

In this case however, I believe that if I had not had my belt on, I would probably not be here to tell you this story. My wife sustained severe bruises to the abdomen and a few bumps and bruises elsewhere. I had my right hand out the door holding on to the frame and lost a one-inch chunk of meat from my ring finger. I also received a bunch of cuts around my right eye when it hit the van.

When we came to and attempted to get out of the car we couldn't because my door was smashed shut and the body was so bent that it prevented the driver's door from opening. Once we got out of the car we tried to assess the situation. My wife told me that the wheels on the left side of the car were at a forty-five-degree angle and that the car was completely on the median except for the two right tires which were at a slight angle as well.

Here comes the funny part. When we received the police report there was almost nothing correct on it. They stated that we proceeded through a light before getting the green arrow to turn left. Up until that time, there was no green arrow at that intersection and we could have not proceeded if the two cars in front of us had not gone first. They said that I was driving. NOT!

They said that there was one passenger, my son. I know that after an accident like that you do not look like yourself but, is it possible that she looked like my son? Funnier still is the fact that, since we were locked in the car because of the damage, the two officers that interviewed us had to have seen where we were sitting. After all, who was blind, me or them?

Psalm 91:5 Thou shalt not be afraid for the terror by night; nor for the arrow that flieth by day; 6 Nor for the pestilence that walketh in darkness; nor for the destruction that wasteth at noonday.

You may say, but you had to have 18 stitches around your eye, you had a fractured skull, you had a concussion and you lost a piece of your finger. All that is true and more. However, the LORD did not and does not promise that we will not have pain, suffering, injury, sickness, disease or tragedy. He has, however, promised to be with us as He brings us through those things.

74
WATER FIGHT
AUGUST OF 1986

This story took place when I was living in an apartment complex in Baltimore, Maryland. Earlier that summer I discovered the hard way that I could not see well enough to play Frisbee any more. I was outside with a few friends on the grounds and we were throwing a Master Frisbee around. Someone threw it to me and as it was on the way, I lost track of it in the air.

One of the dumbest expressions I have ever heard is, "Heads up!" This is usually said when something is on its way to hitting you. If you put your head up, you are likely to get hit in the face. Well, that is exactly what happened. I was about to turn away so as not to get hit in the face when, like an idiot, I obeyed the call to put my head up.

The Frisbee hit me in the upper lip, cutting all the way through to the teeth. I had to have several stitches and decided that it was not worth playing that sport any more. It seems that over the years, as I lost more and more sight, I would only stop doing things after getting injured because I did not see what was coming.

Well, there I was, sitting by myself while everyone else was throwing the flying disk forth and back. I sat there trying to think of something to do and, finally came up with it. I went into my apartment and filled a bunch of balloons with water. I placed them in a bucket and, because I was on the third floor, was able to get on the roof.

Since my apartment was on the back side of the building, I had to walk to the other side with the bucket. I had to be very careful not to be seen. I took up position and began to fire. I had no idea what would happen. In fact, when it was all over, no one seemed to know that I was the culprit that started the whole thing.

After unloading quite a few balloons, everyone scattered. A few minutes later, people started coming out of their buildings with pots, pans, buckets filled with water and arms loaded with water balloons. World war wet was on.

It kept on getting worse and worse and, eventually there was so much water in the halls that they had to be mopped. After unloading my bucket of balloons, I went back into my apartment and got some more. This time I stationed myself outside, waiting for victims to come my way. I did not care how much I got wet, just as long as I could hear that satisfactory groan which let me know that I had gotten the enemy.

After using up all my latex ammo, I decided to get up on the roof with a hose. Unfortunately, the hose was not long enough to get to the front of the apartments. I put the hose up on the roof anyway and placed a bucket up there as well. I would fill the bucket and take it over to the opposite edge. Upon hearing someone come out of the front door, I would let them have it.

Someone who lived in the front saw what I was doing and got the bright idea to hook up a hose and clime on the roof. A few minutes later the war was over and he had won. Since no one was safe from his reach, they all gave up once they were thoroughly soaked. Though we were comrades while the war was still on, as soon as it was over, he got me royally. And I had just about gotten dried off too!

Proverbs 18:24 A man that hath friends must shew himself friendly: and there is a friend that sticketh closer than a brother.

It was a good community because we were all friendly with each other. I could have chosen to stay by myself. If I had, I would not have needed stitches in my upper lip. However, if I had chosen solitude, I would not have had fun that day or made some of the great friends I did.

75
JUST WEIGHT
September of 1986

My first wife's step-father had a bunch of weights that he was not using because he had a bad back. It was the big bulky plastic covered cement kind. Since I was just starting out, it was fine for me. Quickly, however, I needed to get more weight. I did some calculations and decided that purchasing more plastic weight was not the way to go.

I called a few stores in the area and found one that sold steel plates. I got on the bus and was dropped off across the highway from the store. After a little searching I found a way across the highway and got to the store. Once in the store I soon found out that they did not have much in the way of US pound plates. I ended up purchasing four twenty-two-pound plates, four tens, four fives and four three pounders.

This totaled one hundred and sixty pounds in four boxes. Once at the counter I stacked the four boxes and paid for them. I then picked up the plates and walked out of the store. One of the sales people came up to me and asked if they could help me to my car with the boxes. I told them that I did not have a car and was going to take them home on the bus.

I walked to the bus stop and waited for two hours. It was a cold drizzly day and I was tired of just standing there. I picked up the weight and started walking, hoping someone would take pity on me and stop to help. After walking a few miles with a hundred and sixty pounds in my arms I realized that I was not going to make it home. I took the box containing the eighty-eight pounds and placed it on the curb.

I figured that I would take the seventy-two pounds with me and find a phone. I would then call a cab and retrieve the other weight and go home. It was now getting so dark that I could not see where I was going.

I kept walking along the side of the road, making sure to reach out with my right foot once in a while to ensure that I was not drifting into the road.

I finally spotted bright lights ahead. It was a Seven/Eleven. I had been to that convenience store before and knew that there was a phone to the right of the doors. My arms felt like they were going to soon disconnect at the elbows but, I finally made it to the parking lot. There was someone using the phone and, though I was trying to not listen to his half of the conversation, I thought I recognized the voice.

As he hung up and started walking away, he turned to me and said, "I know you." I told him that I thought I knew his voice but could not place him. He then told me that his name was Richard and that he frequently came to the Taco Bell where I worked. Then it clicked.

He asked me what I was doing and why I was out in the dark without my cane. I told him that I did not expect to be out in the dark so I did not bring it. When I told him the rest of the story, he told me that the busses did not run past a certain time on Saturdays. He offered to drive me to pick up the weight I had left, if it was still there and to drive me home. I accepted.

The plates were still there. When we got back to my place, we talked for a while and became fast friends. He even did a little lifting with me once in a while but was not interested in becoming serious. He was more into jogging and walking fast; after all, he was a Mailman.

1 Timothy 4:8 For bodily exercise profiteth little: but godliness is profitable unto all things.

One of the things that has bothered me over the years is how so many people misquote the Bible. I am not speaking of those who refuse to follow the LORD and His Word. I mean those who claim to be Christians and yet, either do not understand the verses they read or purposely use them in wrong ways.

Take the verse, or, I should say, the half verse above. I have had many people over the years try to convince me that lifting weights and doing the treadmill as much as I do is a waste of time. Most of them have used the verse above to buttress their argument.

What the verse above is actually saying is, exercise only helps the body stay fit but being Godly helps you in every area of life.

If I had used more wisdom than I had that day, I would have made sure of the bus schedule or had a friend take me there and back. Do not ask my wife or children if I have learned my lesson from that day. They would probably say no. I, however, would say that I did learn, however slightly.

76
DID YOU LOSE SOMETHING?
MAY OF 1987

I have lived in New York, New Jersey, Pennsylvania, Maryland, Delaware and New Mexico. Of all those states I have found Delaware to be the most aware of the needs of the disabled. The general public as well as agencies seem to pay more attention to the needs of those who are more challenged than the average person.

I had just moved from Maryland to Delaware and gotten a job with McDonald's. I am not sure but I believe it was my first week on the job when this happened. I was getting off the bus in front of the restaurant and had put my cane on the ground, or what I thought was the ground. As I moved forward my cane slipped forward and down.

I had placed my cane in the hole of a sewer and, because I did not have the loop around my wrist, it fell all the way into the sewer. When the bus driver saw what had happened, he got off the bus to see if he could get it for me. He couldn't. This sewer was some kind of access area and went down about nine feet.

The driver then helped me to the back door and I went to work. On my break I called the Department of roads and they said that they would see what they could do. They asked for my address and I figured that if I would ever see my cane again, it would be in a week or so through the mail.

When it was time to go home, I had someone take me to the bus stop. When the driver stopped, I explained what had happened and he did not seem to think it was strange at all. He said that he would let me off at the closest point to my door as he could. When we arrived at my stop, he offered to walk me to the front door but, perhaps because of pride or maybe embarrassment, I declined his offer.

I stepped off the bus and he told me to walk straight ahead. I did and walked right into a tree. Now I know that the bus driver could not have been blind so, all I can figure is that he must have been vertically challenge, (short). He apologized and gave me better directions from that point on and I made it home with no further calamities.

An hour or so later there was a knock on my front door. I was not expecting anyone so I could not imagine who it might be. As I opened the door the man standing there asked, "Mr. Whitehead?" and I said, "Yes?" He held out his hand with my cane in it and said, "Your cane." I took it and shook his hand. I was so surprised that they had gotten to it so quickly and even more surprised that they had delivered it instead of mailing it back to me.

I am now very happy living in New Mexico because I cannot stand the humidity but, if I had to live anywhere else in the country, I think it would be Delaware.

Proverbs 19:22a The desire of a man is his kindness.

Whether you believe that this verse is saying that people do desire to be kind or that people are drawn to those that are kind, the point is that kindness is attractive. It certainly was to me that day and has been since.

77
THE BLIND LEADING THE BLIND
JUNE OF 1987

I had received my license to teach gymnastics and ever since then I have been teaching or training people in some capacity. Once I had joined the Delaware Association for Blind Athletes, I started making connections. One connection I made was with a girl that was attending the University of Delaware.

She lived on campus and was in need of some mobility instruction. I decided to volunteer until her mobility instructor could get there. After helping her to get from place to place I discovered that she was with the Pennsylvania ABA. She was into power lifting but was at a disadvantage since she did not have a trainer nor did she have enough weight to progress.

I told her that I was into power lifting and would be glad to train her. She was also into swimming so I helped her with that as well. I went to her dorm and trained her there for a while but soon ran out of weight.

We started working out at my place and she increased dramatically. Since I was allergic to dogs, she had to leave her dog tied up outside whenever she came to my place. On one of her last trips to my place she decided that she would leave her dog in the dorm.

She decided to rely on my arm for the two-mile walk. I had been up and down that strip so many times that I thought I knew every crack. Well, maybe I did know every crack but I did not know every pole. I guess I must have just missed it with my Cane because she did not miss it with her body.

Boy did I feel awful. Here I was, the blind leading the blind and you think that would have cause me to be mor cautious. She forgave me and fortunately, she was not hurt. We went to my place and lifted and then walked back to her dorm without further incident. I ended up moving back to New York shortly after that but I kept in touch with her for a few years.

I was unable to go to the next regional competition because I could not get hooked up with the New York chapter in time. She was able to go to the next competition and, she broke a world record in her weight class. She had been trying for a few years to increase her lifts but was unable to. I wonder if running her into that telephone pole had anything to do with her success?

Hebrews 11:1 Now faith is the substance of things hoped for, the evidence of things not seen.

In the above verse we have faith, hope and evidence. Kristine had faith that I could help her get stronger to break that elusive record. I hoped that, with all the work we did together, she could get there. The evidence is the gold medal she won.

78
FATAL ATTRACTION
JULY OF 1987

I hate humidity mixed with heat. So why did I spend most of my life on the east coast? Because I did not know that there were places that were substantially less humid. I found this fact out in 1987 when I went to an international track and field meet in Albuquerque, New Mexico. I knew then and there that I would have to live in New Mexico someday.

Why did it take me until 2002 to move there? Well, praise the LORD that he brought a wonderful woman into my life who was born and raised in New Mexico or I may have never made it here. Why did we stay in New York for ten years after we got married? Well, I asked my wife about every six months if she would like to move back home yet. Every time, year after year, she said, "No, I don't think the LORD wants us to move back yet."

At least the "yet" gave me hope that it might happen someday. What the heck does all this have to do with the story? I have no idea. Actually, I just wanted to give you a picture of how much I hated humidity so you could truly understand what is to come next without thinking I had lost my mind.

I loved working in front of a three hundred and sixty-five degree grill all day long. Why, because once you get off work and go outside into ninety degrees with one hundred percent humidity, it feels cool.

There were times that I would get off work, go to Rickles, purchase lumber and carry it home a mile and a half on my back. This tended to have the same type of effect on people as my eating ice cream outside in ten degrees had, it made perception of the weather worse.

One day I decided to go home without the lumber. I was looking forward to lifting weights for an hour and then taking a shower and relaxing. I got to my door, unlocked and opened it. As the door swung open, I felt a breeze go by me. It did not feel like a regular breeze and, there shouldn't have been a breeze anyway since the apartment building was enclosed and the doors were never left open.

I closed the door and turned to walk into the living room. As I did, I realized that someone was there. I backed up and placed my hand on the door knob as I asked, "Who's there?" The response came, "Hi Raymond, I'm Rachael and I have been watching you."

I said, "That's nice" and asked, "but why are you in my apartment?" she said, "Because I wanted to be with you." We had a little more discussion and then I made one of the worst decisions of my life. I decided that she was not much of a threat and invited her to stay. That was like a fly inviting a spider to spin a web around himself.

We talked for a while and then I asked her to leave so I could exercise. She left and I had hoped that was the end of it. Boy was I wrong. She was obviously following me around because she just, "turned up" everywhere I went. She started bringing me clothing to try on that she had gotten on sale. Then she started inviting me to her place to meet her son. The real clincher was when she told me that her son was having trouble and she wanted me to be a father to him.

One day she went to my job and stood in the lobby for hours waiting for me. When someone approached her and asked if they could help her, she replied, "No thank you, I am just waiting for my husband to get off work." When they asked who her husband was, she said, "Raymond Whitehead."

My manager came to me as I was working in the back, and told me that there was a woman waiting for me up front. When they told me that she said I was her husband, I flipped. I went up front and asked her to leave. I told her that if she did not stop bothering me, I would call the police.

Now she would leave me alone, right? Wrong. About three days later she approached me and said that she had bought some underwear and would like me to come to her place and try it on. That was the last straw. I called the police and filed a report. They informed me that they had a file on her already and that her real name was not Rachael.

Now I had a restraining order on her. Did it end there? No! Over a year later I was living in New York and had forgotten all about this bothersome thing. I Was at work and had gotten a phone call. Now, since I was a customer service manager it was not unusual for me to get calls. I picked it up and guess who was on the other line? That's right!

She had the nerve to ask me why I moved away without telling her where I went. Then she told me how hard it was for her to find me. Now I was getting a little concerned. I asked her to please leave me alone and, she did. I never heard from her again.

In 1990 my girlfriend and I moved into an apartment. Months later she got a phone call from someone who claimed to be with the FBI. She was told that I was very dangerous and that she should be careful. Well, she was careful. Without wasting a moment, she and her mother went to our apartment with a man and his truck. They removed everything that belonged to her.

I was not able to find out who the supposed FBI agent was and, though I have no evidence whatsoever, the first person that leaped to mind was Rachael. I actually tried to contact her but was unable to. Unfortunately, the damage had been done and the relationship never completely recovered. I must admit that it was mostly my fault because I did not know how to forgive and forget.

Acts 16:16 And it came to pass, as we went to prayer, a certain damsel possessed with a spirit of divination met us, which brought her masters much gain by soothsaying: 17 The same followed Paul and us, and cried, saying, These men are the servants of the most high God, which shew unto us the way of salvation. 18 And this did she many days. But Paul, being grieved, turned and said to the spirit, I command thee in the name of Jesus Christ to come out of her. And he came out the same hour.

I do not know if the woman following me around had a spirit or spirits that needed to be cast out. I do know that Paul was relieved when she stopped bothering him and I would love to have the power to get people to stop bothering me with words like Paul's.

79
PENNSYLVANIA STATE FAIR
JULY OF 1987

During the first part of 1987 I discovered an organization called The Delaware Association of Blind Athletes. In the Spring I started practicing with them and was invited to go with them to the North East Regional Track and Field Meet. While there, I competed in the one hundred- and two-hundred-meter dashes, goalball, shot put, javelin and discus.

Goal Ball is a very interesting sport. You have three people from each team on the floor, usually a basketball court. Everyone is blindfolded, even if you are totally blind. You have rope covered by tape outlining the court. This is so you can feel the positioning with your feet or hands. You have a ball the size of a basketball with holes in it.

There are bells in the ball. The object is to roll the ball across the field and get it passed the other team members into their goal. to stop the ball, you have to throw your body to the ground and lay in its path.

I do not remember if we won a metal or not in Goal Ball but I had fun. I won metals in the shot, javelin and discus but, I had not run in so long that if I could have seen I would have been embarrassed at how poorly I ran. I was walking with someone to get to the dining hall as we passed a building where something was going on.

When I asked him what was happening, he told me that there was a weight lifting competition. He then looked at me and asked, "You look like you are strong, why don't you enter the competition?" I was not sure about entering but decided to go into the building to check it out. As we entered, someone approached me and asked if I wanted to compete. On a whim I said yes.

I weighed one hundred and sixty-four pounds at the time and ended up winning first place in my weight class. On the bus ride back to the hotel I met Carol Ann. She was a runner from the Pennsylvania team. We started dating. She invited me to the Pennsylvania State Fair and I accepted. She was completely blind in both eyes from a gunshot. She not only had no vision but, I found out later that she could not smell or taste either.

Her older sister was married and had a son about four or five years old. We all decided to go to the Fair together. As we were walking through the fair behind her sister and brother-in-law, we passed by a group of teen girls sitting by a tree. As Carol Ann's brother-in-law was leading the way he said to the girls, "Excuse me, we have two blind people coming through."

I could not believe my ears when, as we passed by, I heard one of them say, "I can't believe they let blind people in here!" She said it in a voice that was meant for her friends and not for us but, I have very good hearing and was able to catch every word. I stopped, turned in the direction of the remark and said, "Really, well I can't believe that they let stupid young girls in here!"

After her nasty remark a few of them began to snicker at how humorous she was but, the snickering ceased at my reply. As I turned back to Carol Ann and our party continued on, she asked me what had just happened. It was a good thing we had kept walking because, after telling her what had just transpired, she was so mad that I am sure she would have gotten into a fist fight with someone. She kept asking to go back but, since no one had actually seen the offenders, we assured her that it would be a wasted trip. She stopped asking but, she was mad on and off for the rest of the day.

Proverbs 18:7 A fool's mouth is his destruction, and his lips are the snare of his soul.

Though there was much more I wanted to say to those ignorant girls, I had the wisdom to keep my comment short. If they did not get embarrassed enough after what I said to be more circumspect in the future, their mouths would get them in trouble at some point.

80
LIGHTS OUT
September of 1987

I started working for McDonalds in Newark, Delaware in June of 1987. The first thing they had me doing was making salads. Sadly, the only reason I was hired was because the owners were greedy and the Commission for the Blind in Delaware (CFTB) offered an incentive program.

The CFTB offered to pay half the wage of any blind person they would hire for six months. They also would pay for any equipment that blind person needed in order to do their job. The owners only hired me to get the half-free labor for six months. I was told by the manager that they fully intended to fire me after that.

I fooled them though. I started making the salads. Chicken, chef and vegetable. There might have been a fourth one but, I cannot remember. I do know that, according to the person training me, they only sold about 72 salads a day. By the time I had been there a week, the salad sales had doubled.

By the time I had been there two weeks, the sales had tripled and the tiny girl who was training me was able to graduate to doing the window. Window is just another word for register. It was a good thing that she left, because her salads did not look appetizing.

Once I became proficient at the salads, they trained me to do the fry racks. Each rack held twelve baskets which were filled with frozen fries. Once I got good at that, I added condensing the trash to my duties. Then I added filling the shake machine with the chocolate, vanilla and strawberry mixes.

If you hire me to work, that is what I am going to do. Unfortunately, most of the people I worked with were teens or those in their early twenties. The work ethic of those youngsters was sadly lacking. Most of them would use any excuse to stop working. Bathroom breaks, cigarette breaks or just plain hiding were the most common tactics.

I, on the other hand, tried to keep as busy as possible because I found that the day goes much faster that way. So, I added another responsibility to my list. I began to stock the mini freezers with the hamburger meat, the quarter pounder meat, the hash browns and fish filet patties as well as the pies.

Once I mastered all that, I still found time to keep the burger stations filled. Making sure the containers with the catsup, mustard, regular onions, Quarter onions, lettuce, Special Sauce, cheese and buns for all stations from getting too low.

When the owner saw how much work I was doing, he changed his mind about letting me go. In fact, the manager gave me a raise that caused me to be earning more than all but the managers. When I asked him why, he said that I was worth any three teen-agers.

The only person I ever saw work consistently faster than I was a young man named Steve. He could make you dizzy watching him handle the hamburger grill. I did not even want to try doing what he was. Instead, they trained me on the Quarter grill.

I was trained to do five on a turn with two under the clam. That meant that you put down five burgers on the grill, hit the button, seer the meat, season it with the salt and pepper mix, place another two patties on the grill, place the clam over it and hit the other button.

The clam cooked the meat on top while the bottom was also cooking on the grill. In the middle of this, you had to place the bun tops on a tray, place the tray in the toaster, place the bottoms on a huge spatula, scoot them in the top of the toaster and pull the handle down.

Then you flipped the burgers over, took the two out from under the clam, placed those two on the bull nose to keep hot, turned around and dressed the buns. Once they were toasted, placed the meat on the buns, put the bottoms on the meat and placed them on the shelf to be packed.

If someone wanted something special, it was called a letter. Those receipts were usually given to the grill master. However, since I was too blind to read them, the shift manager had to tell me what they were.

After doing all that, I had to scrape my grill to get it ready for the next round.

There were times that we got so busy that I was required to do ten on a turn in addition to the clam. Talk about crazy. When it got that busy, a shift manager would usually come over to do the buns for you. That is because you would have to lay down another ten burgers after flipping the first ten. Even Steve could not keep up with that.

One day, I was doing five on a turn with two under the clam when the building was hit by lightning. We did not know that the loud noise we all heard was the restaurant being hit by 1.21 gigawatts of electricity. I heard a few of the girls scream and noticed a lot of commotion afterward.

After putting my five Quarter Pounders I realized that people were laughing around me. It turns out that all of the electricity had gone out but, since I could not see enough to notice that the lights went out, I kept working.

It was a topic of conversation for the next few weeks as many of my co-workers approached me to confirm what had happened. After that incident, the General Manager gave me more training. I learned how to do everything in the store except window and drinks.

In fact, in the two-and-a-half years I worked there, hardly a week went by that I did not have overtime. When I asked my boss about it, he told me that they rarely gave overtime but that since I was worth three teen agers, paying me time-and-a-half was actually like only paying me half a wage.

Genesis 4: 7 *If thou doest well, shalt thou not be accepted? and if thou doest not well, sin lieth at the door. And unto thee shall be his desire, and thou shalt rule over him.*

I know that the word "sin" is no longer accepted in our culture. I still think it is a great word. If someone is paying me to do a job, and I drag my feet or do anything less than my best, it is a sin. After all, if I am paying someone to do something for me, I expect them to do their best.

81
THE BLIND LEADING THE BLIND, AGAIN?
SEPTEMBER OF 1987

Because of the aforementioned gunshot wound, Carolann had to go through a lot of rehab and surgery. It happened while she was in high school. By the time she had recovered completely, she was passed high school age. Even so, she wanted to go back to school and get her diploma. I admit it, I robbed the cradle. When we first met, it did not occur to me to ask her age.

I had always been told that there were two things you did not ask women, their age and their weight. It probably would have been a lot longer before I found out her age except for the fact that she mentioned that she had to return to school soon. When I asked her what college she was attending, she told me the whole story.

I expressed to her that it was a unique situation and that I gave her a lot of credit for going through the process rather than getting a GED. She then asked me if I would like to visit her school. I said that I would and she went about making the arrangements.

Her principal agreed to allow me to go with her to all her classes. He informed all her teachers and I prepared to walk into an institution that I had not seen the likes of for a decade. When I arrived, I was surprised at how well received I was. Having been a professor seemed to clear the way and, no one made any mention of the age difference.

Carolann's school was very proud of the accommodations they had made for her. It turned out that there were quite a few students with special needs. We were in her science class and the bell had just sounded for the end of class. We went to the front of the class to speak with her teacher for a minute while the other students vacated. Once the class was clear, Carolann said that we had to go or we would be late for her next class.

We departed, made a left, walked halfway down the hall and after a few steps she turned right. She stuck her hand out and found her locker. After opening it and exchanging books, we closed it and were on our way again. We arrived at an intersection and turned right. We started walking and she told me to go faster. I started walking faster and she said to go faster still. We broke into a trot.

I think a moment is about fifteen seconds because it is between a second and a minute. A moment later she blurted out, "Watch out for the..." She did not get to finish her sentence because just at that moment, she ran into the support column between the open doors. Her glasses flew off and one of the other students retrieved them for us. After making sure Carolann was okay, the student was off to her class, lest she be late too.

I felt bad because, until that moment, Carolann did not realize how limited my vision was. She had assumed that I would be able to see the doors and stop in time. Since she was completely blind it was hard for her to understand how I could see so much better in some conditions and so much worse in others. I guess we both learned a lesson that day, after all, we were in school.

I have been trying, since 1972, to explain how you can have enough sight to play some games and ride a bike but not to have enough vision to drive a car. I have come up with many different ways, tools, demonstrations and have even gotten a few people to allow me to temporarily compromise their vision enough to help them understand.

For the most part, it has not helped the inquisitors. I do believe, however, that it has made me a better teacher.

Luke 19:5 And when Jesus came to the place, he looked up, and saw him, and said unto him, Zacchaeus, make haste, and come down; for today I must abide at thy house. 6 And he made haste, and came down, and received him joyfully.

As the above two verses point out, sometimes it is warranted to be in a hurry. Trying to get to class on time by running through a high school while one of you is completely blind and the other is more than legally blind is not one of those times.

In my own defense though, she could have told me that there would be an obstacle up ahead.

82
ORGANIZATION
September of 1987

The only job I did not do at McDonald's was window. The only job I hated was gopher. We had one fridge next to the salad station which was a holding fridge and was about six feet by eight feet. We had another fridge outside the back door which was about the size of a large bed room. We had a freezer which, if the compressor had been turned off, could have made a nice sized studio apartment. We had a room outside that was for foam clam shells and cups which was about six feet by twenty feet. There was a dry stock room downstairs which was about six hundred square feet.

Not one of those rooms was organized and we were constantly throwing out expired food or supplies. I went to the manager and asked him for permission to rearrange the freezer. After explaining that it would make things easier to find, thereby wasting less time locating items and that it would prevent items from expiring, thereby saving money, he agreed.

I had the whole thing mapped out in my head so, it did not take long for me to get it done. I started at two in the morning and by the time we were ready to open for business, it was done. I had gone home and printed out a list of products in alphabetical order on the left of the sheet with a locator letter and a map on the right side of the sheet. That way, anyone trying to find anything could look at the map, which I had taped to the freezer door, and find it in less than thirty seconds.

My boss was so pleased that it took no effort at all to get him to let me do the same to the fridge outside. After that, he let me do the same to the dry room, (the six hundred square feet of stock that did not need refrigeration). That one took a lot longer to do because the shelves needed to be broken down and reconfigured. Now every door had a list of items within and a map to help you find it. After that, he put me in charge of all the stock rooms and the truck crew.

My boss told me that I probably saved the company about twenty thousand dollars in all the months I worked there, with the exception of a week of vacation, not one item expired. Also, because everything was so easy to find, almost nothing got damaged because no one had to move things around to look for what they needed. Before that we were throwing dozens of cups away every day because they would get squashed.

When my boss asked me how I was able to do all this when I could not see very well. I told him that it was precisely because I could not see well that this had to be done. People were so careless in putting things where ever they could fit them that it was a mess. It was because I was doing so many jobs that I realized what a waste of time it was to spend five minutes looking for something only to have to send one of the shift managers to find it.

It got so bad that until I rearranged each room I would not bother to go in and look for anything. If I had a nickel for every time I heard a manager ask where someone was and the reply was, "They went to look for..." I don't think I could lift the piggy bank.

Ecclesiastes 1: 13 And I gave my heart to seek and search out by wisdom concerning all things that are done under heaven: this sore travail hath God given to the sons of man to be exercised therewith.

I have always been a problem solver and an inventor. I now know that these gifts came from the LORD though I had no idea at the time. Though I used to wish I could profit from my fixes and inventions, I was glad to make things better for everyone.

83
OH NO YOU DON'T!
October of 1987

There was a girl at McDonald's all the guys seemed to like. If she looked as cute as she sounded and acted, I can understand why. She was married and so I never made a pass at her but, it seemed that having a husband was not a deterrent to many others.

One day I was on my break and, after eating I still had some time left. I was headed up the stairs from the "crew room" when I came upon two co-workers at the top of the stairs talking about something. I got into the conversation and one of them asked me a question.

My step-father is Italian. One day as he was talking and using his hands my mother and I decided to see if he could still talk if we tied his hands behind his back. I do not know if he was just humoring us or, perhaps he was just stunned that we would actually do something like that but, he did not say another word until we loosed his hands.

Perhaps I got it from him but in any case, I was talking with my hands. Just at the moment I had spread my hands wide, Laura came through the door. My left hand was only inches from her chest. She jumped back just in time and said, "Oh no you don't."

I tried to convince her that I had no idea she was coming through the door and that I would never grab someone like that anyway. She did not seem to believe me and, from that moment on she seemed to be overly cautious around me.

Song Of Solomon 1: 13 A bundle of myrrh is my well-beloved unto me; he shall lie all night betwixt my breasts.

Breasts are wonderful for many reasons. They are beautiful to look at. They can feed and nourish babies. They are wonderful to fondle and, resting your head on them is very comforting. However, if those breasts are not attached to the woman you love, you should leave them alone as Proverbs 5:20 suggests.

84
STAND BACK
December of 1987

I wanted my girlfriend to meet my sisters and brother in Baltimore so, we planned the trip. There was a very important piece of information that I had forgotten to give her and only remembered it as the taxi drove up.

I turned to her and said, "I need to tell you something that you have to promise to listen to." She agreed and I told her that, "When we get out of the car, I will place you somewhere safe and step away from you a few feet. You need to promise to stay where I place you."

She agreed, I walked her to the curb behind the car, paid the driver and, as he drove away, I stepped five feet to her right. When the car was less than twenty feet away, I heard the front door slam and, my sister Terry ran down the front stairs screaming my name.

She ran down the walkway, jumped down the two stairs to the sidewalk, jumped off the curb, ran across the street and leaped into my arms. During the entire fifty feet run, she yelled my nickname, Ray, Ray. In a stunned voice, Carolann asked, "What was that?"

What was that? Terry bomb! My sisters Margie and Terry are eight and eleven years younger than I. When they were very little, and they could not say Raymond very well so, it morphed into Ray, Ray. Though I am over sixty at the finishing of this book, they still use the nickname, and I love it.

After a few minutes of hugging my sister, I walked her over to Carolann and introduced them. In another story I mention that my girlfriend was completely blind. After they met, I mentioned to CJ, "Now you know why I wanted you to stand away from me."

I have experienced many family situations where there are bitter sibling relationships. I am so blessed that my brother and five sisters still love me and each other.

Proverbs: 15: 23 A man hath joy by the answer of his mouth: and a word spoken in due season, how good is it!

One of the things I love about my sister Terry is her exuberance. Whether it is her hug, her smile, her laughter, her words or the way she says them. We are all capable of a bad attitude or cross words but, even if she says something less than positive, like an Etch A Sketch, all the wonderful things about her erases the tainted stuff rather quickly.

85
USHER
DECEMBER OF 1987

My upstairs neighbor, Rob Schweppi, found out that I lifted weights. He told me that he lifted too and would like to work out together. At first, we worked out together three times a week. He was engaged and, as the wedding got closer, we could only manage once a week. Even so, we became good friends.

A couple of months before, "The Big Day," he asked me if I would be one of his ushers. I was not sure at first if it was a good idea but, after his future bride, Anita, assured me that she wanted me to be part of their wedding as well, I agreed.

The night before we all went to the church to practice. I counted the rows, memorized who was supposed to sit in the front three pews and counted every conceivable combination of steps I could think of. I was ready. Both Rob and Anita told me that the most important thing to remember was to have fun.

I took them up on it. I had a great time. When it was time to get to work, I stood in the back of the church and waited for someone to approach. As I heard someone in front of me, I would greet them and ask if they were on the bride's side or the Groom's side.

I soon realized that the people were being screened before being sent to me so, I ended up with everyone from the same side, I do not remember which one it was though. If the person was male, I would tell him to follow me and I would turn and escort him to a seat.

If the person was female, I would hold out my arm for her to hold on to and I would escort her to a seat. Since I knew how many people could comfortably fit in each pew and I kept count of how many people I put in each row, I thought I had it made.

Once everyone was seated and the wedding was about to start, I took my place in the front pew. The wedding was wonderful and I was very happy for my friends. After the wedding we went to the home of the parents of, I believe it was the bride.

They had someone video tape the wedding and, after a small reception, they put the video on. I was still in the kitchen talking with someone. I heard a lot of laughter coming from the TV room. Since it was a wedding video, I expected to hear a lot of Ooos and Ahhhs, not laughing.

I asked the person who I was speaking with to take me into the other room. Once there I asked what was so funny. In approximately twelve-part harmony I heard, "You!" I asked them to explain and this is what they told me. You did a great job of ushering people to their seats Raymond.

The only problem is that most of the people were pointing to where they would like to sit and you just ignored them. After depositing them in the pew they would give you a puzzled look and then go to where it was they wanted to sit in the first place.

With the people moving around so much I did not know that the pews that I thought were empty were actually filling up. I would try to place people in a pew that had no space and they would turn around and find their own seat. Later on, most of the people found out that I was blind and we all had a good laugh.

I would have asked for a copy of the video but, if I could not see them pointing up close and in person, well, you get the point.

Proverbs 17:22 A merry heart doeth good like a medicine: but a broken spirit drieth the bones.

Because one of my foremost goals in life since grammar school has been to make people laugh, I am glad that I was able to accomplish it without even trying. I am also glad that we got to know each other well enough that they Were comfortable in telling me that I was the butt of the joke. None of them were self-conscious about my blindness being the cause of their laughter and I cannot describe how wonderful that made me feel.

86
HOW TO MAKE PEOPLE COLD
JANUARY OF 1988

I have severe asthma. While in Newark, Delaware I discovered a respiratory specialist named Doctor Seltzer. Though he dealt primarily with children, he agreed to see me because of my history. I guess he felt it would be a challenge. He was an absolutely wonderful doctor who helped me greatly.

In order to get to his office, I had to pass a store called "TCBY." I had not heard of them and just out of curiosity, I stopped in one day. For those of you who may not know, as I did not know at the time, TCBY stands for, "The Country's Best Yogurt." I fell in love with their "Frozen White Chocolate Mousse."

You would receive ten dollars worth of McMoney each week if you did not miss any days and if you showed up on time. Since you got paid every two weeks, you would get twenty dollars if the afore mentioned conditions were met. I did not fail to get my twenty dollars worth every pay period.

While working for McDonald's I developed a pattern. I would get my pay, purchase thirty-five boxes of chocolate chip cookies with my McMoney, walk to my doctor's office, give him the cookies to give to his good patience, get my treatment and go to TCBY.

I would then walk down the main street which had a peculiar name, "Main Street," until I got to the Good Will Store. I would then do some shopping and go home. If I had purchased something I would go straight home but, if I had made no purchase I would stop at TCBY and get another cone.

As the weather got colder, the cone would last longer. One day I did not finish my cone by the time I had reached Good Will so, I kept walking. Guess what I discovered, an ice cream store named, "Steve's Ice Cream."

I went in and made friends with the owner. I asked him if he had lime sherbert. He did not. I would stop in from time to time and ask for lime sherbert. Still, he did not make any. I told friends about his place and had them start asking for lime sherbert as well.

After several weeks of being told no, I asked him why he did not make any. He said that it would not sell. I told him that if he made it and it did not sell, I would purchase whatever was left. One day I walked in and there it stood, a five-gallon bucket for lime sherbet.

I say for, because it was empty. When I asked Steve about it, he said that he had made it a few days ago, knowing that I would be stopping in and, he sold out. I wished I could have seen his face as he tried to explain how surprised he was that any of it sold, let alone sold out.

When I went in the next week, he had made more telling me that he had no idea that it would be so popular. Now my pattern changed. I would take a walk every day after work. I would get a TCBY and eat it on the way to my friend's place.

I would talk for a while and then leave with a lime sherbert cone I would eat it on the way to TCBY where I would get another White Chocolate Moose and eat it on the way home. One day I was walking down the street when I figuratively bumped into a friend.

I was eating a cone on my way to Steve's when I heard someone behind me. I stopped to see if they would pass me but, they stopped as well. When I started walking again, so did they. I became annoyed so yelled, "I do not know who you are but I do not like being followed and I am carrying a large knife."

I heard the person laugh and was about to pull my knife out of its sheath when I realized who it was. My friend Richard had not only been following me, he had been observing the people around me.

He started walking with me toward Steve's place. When I got my lime sherbet, he started walking toward a table. When I told him that I wanted to eat it while walking he said, "Its only ten degrees outside."

I told him that I liked eating ice cream in the cold because it does not melt. He said, "This I've got to see", and followed me outside. As we were walking back to TCBY, I asked him why he had been following me.

He said that when he saw me, he could not believe his eyes.

He said that, as he was going to approach me, he saw someone look at me, raise their coat collar and appear to shiver. He said that the person seemed to get colder just watching me eat my frozen yogurt outside, in ten degrees, with snow on the ground.

He then decided to keep watching others watch me to see if their responses were the same. They were. He then told me that he was going to stay with me in order to give me a running commentary on people's reactions to my insane behavior.

Naturally, when we approached TCBY, I told him that I was stopping in for another WCM cone. He just smiled and shook his head.

Genesis 3:8a And they heard the voice of the LORD God walking in the garden in the cool of the day.

Since there is nothing in the Bible about frozen yogurt or ice cream, I thought that I would just point out that God likes cool weather too.

87
TO MCDONALD'S, AND FAST
April of 1988

Because there were no busses running at the crazy hours I worked, I would walk. There was almost no one on the road and there were many times I would walk the mile to work without a car passing in either direction.

I was supposed to be to work at four o'clock on this morning because I had to clean the fry vats, mop the floor and clean the shake machine. I do not remember why but I was running late and those things had to be done early so we could open.

I had been a bicycle mechanic for several years and still loved to work on bikes. A friend had brought his bike over for me to fix and I had a way to get to work more quickly. I got my cane and the bike and out the door I went. Since I had walked this strip so many times, I figured that I would be able to make it with no problem.

I crossed the highway, faced the correct direction, got on the bike and started to ride. I tried to run the cane in front of me but that just hurt my hand and wrist because of all the jolts. Also, it almost caused me to fall off the bike once. Then I got the bright idea to run the cane along the curb behind me. That worked really well.

There were a few times when coming to an intersection got a little tricky. One time I hit the curb so hard after crossing one street that I did fall off the bike. I did arrive to work on time and, I did not cause any damage to my friend's bike.

You should have heard the questions and comments when people saw the bike in the back hall and they found out that I had ridden it. Before losing my sight enough to make it impossible to ride, I used to average twenty-five miles a day. I have now found a friend that has a tandem and we go for a ride about once a week.

His wife says that I am the bravest man she knows, to get on the back of that bike with her husband. There are a few things I miss since becoming completely blind. Bikinis, motorcycles and my twenty-one-speed bike.

I read about a young man in California who had both eyes removed and, from a very young age, uses echo location. According to the story, he can ride his bike in traffic. I considered taking classes from him but, with the severe tinnitus, I am not sure it would be worth the effort and cost.

Job 12: 11 Doth not the ear try words? and the mouth taste his meat?

Yes, the ear does try sounds and, if it can distinguish among the half million words in the English language, maybe I can still learn to navigate like a bat. After all, I do prefer to tell people that I am as blind as one rather than using a politically correct term.

While we are on the subject of the ear discerning sounds, let us visit a misnomer. Blind people cannot hear any better because of their lack of vision. Our hearing does not improve. What does get better is our ability to use what we hear because we have to.

If you are sighted, you do not have to rely on the sounds around you to navigate because you can see the car moving, you can view the cyclist coming toward you, you can ocularly notice the person skate boarding across your path and you can spy the dog being walked near you so you are able to avoid getting tangled in its leash.

88
TAKE MY MONEY, PLEASE!
MAY OF 1988

After working for McDonald's for nine months I was offered a job with Taco Bell. I really liked my work at the Golden Arches and I am not ashamed to say it. I was getting paid very well because I could do everything in the store except window.

I had been offered the opportunity to learn to do the registers, but I turned it down because there were too many buttons to have to learn.

I could work all the breakfast grills, make all the different burgers, make pies, nuggets, fish sandwiches, fries, take apart and clean the shake and sundae machines, clean the fry vats, make salads, do all the prep work for every area and even compress the trash smaller than anyone else.

I would make sure there were enough salads, fill all the fry vats and then go around the whole pit making sure everything was as full as it could be. It was wonderful to have so much stress relieved by having everything ready before the lunch rush. Then the only yelling you would hear was for special orders.

I must admit that moving to Taco Bell was a mistake for me. I did it because they offered me more money and because it was only one block away from my apartment. I mistakenly thought that the work would be similar. Other than mopping the floor, there was nothing about the two places that was alike.

Well, I did the same thing there that I had done at McDonald's, I organized everything. That was not hard to do since all of TB's supplies would have fit into the larger of the two refrigerators at McD's. Even so, it was a fun place to work. Once I mastered the making of all the different foods, I was moved to window.

This was not as daunting a task as it would have been at McD's because the menu selection was much smaller and the keypad they used had texture to it. I could still see up close in bright light enough to make out the different bill denominations.

It was a little difficult at times because some of the non-regulars, not knowing that I could not see them, held the money out to me anywhere but in my outstretched hand. There were many times when a regular customer, standing in line behind a new one, would tell the new comer that they had to put the money in my hand because I was blind.

Man oh man, the conversations that would start. After a while I was asked to take over the drive through. That task included taking the orders, making sure the orders were filled properly, making the drinks for my customers as well as the customers up front and, taking the money at the drive-up window.

This was worse than doing the inside window. At first, I would get everything ready, open the windows and stretch my hand just inches from the sill. That did not work because I found out the hard way that many people pulled up too far away to get the money into my hand without difficulty.

One time a woman got so frustrated with me that she actually got out of her car to give me the money. I felt so bad when my supervisor told me what had happened that I knew I had to come up with another approach. I decided that I would stick my hand out much further from then on.

That is until I almost punched a customer in the face. Now what was I going to do? I decided to combine the two. Now when I opened the window, I would quickly put my hand a few inches from the sill and slowly keep extending it until the money found its way to me.

That was not the solution either. I finally had it, almost. I would open the window and greet the customer with more than just their total. I would ask them a question. Once they answered I could judge about how far they were from the window and thus, how far I had to stick out my paw.

This worked really well for two reasons. First, because by this time, many of the customers were getting used to me and somehow found out or figured out that I could not see. Second, because most people answered me and I was a good judge of where the sound was coming from.

It did not always work however. There is always someone who either did not hear you or, thought it was a rhetorical question. I eventually came up with the solution for these customers as well. I would tell them that I was blind and needed them to place the money in my hand. Now why didn't I think of that in the first place.

Job 23:8 Behold, I go forward, but he is not there; and backward, but I cannot perceive him:

It took me a while of going forth and back, not only physically, but in my thoughts, to come up with a combination of solutions that worked for me and, almost all my customers.

89
YOUR LICENSE, PLEASE
AUGUST OF 1988

By now I was a shift manager and was usually closing the store. That was the case this day. Two other shift managers were closing with me. It was about two o'clock in the morning and we were headed to the car. Like me, one of the other two lived nearby, Tammy.

The other, Jodi, lived about a mile away. Tammy and I were planning to walk but, Jodi said, "Just let me throw this garbage out and I will give you a lift home. Tammy then walked me over to the car and we stood there waiting. As Jody approached the car she asked from the passenger's side, "Hey Raymond, do you want to drive?"

I turned slightly to face her and said, "Yes." She threw the keys to me and they hit me square in the chest. I reached out to find the car and when I did, I realized why she had asked me that. I was standing in front of the driver's door. I love a good joke and so I wanted to see how far they would let me go with this.

I unlocked and opened the door, then got in. At any moment I expected Jody to say she was just kidding. Not yet. I closed the door, put the key in the ignition and started it up. Still nothing. I grabbed the shifter, put it in reverse and started backing up. Finally, a response, but not the one I was expecting.

Jodi, who was sitting in the front passenger seat, started giving me directions. I Stopped, went forward and serpentine out of the parking lot onto the street. She said that I was too far left in the driveway and ended up in the incoming lane. Since it was after two in the morning, I did not think it was a big deal because no one would be coming in at that time.

220

Tammy's apartment was across the street and the driveway entrance was a little down the road. Since Jody was using terms like, "a little more" or "a little less," it was much harder to navigate than it was with my friend on the bicycles in, "Beep, Beep, Five Degrees Left."

After swerving forth and back over the double yellow, we finally arrived at her driveway. Since it was a one-way driveway, it was much narrower than was the driveway at Taco Bell. After some navigational corrections, we were in. I drove up the parking lot, did not hit anything and arrived at Tammy's front door.

We sat and talked for a while. When Tammy got out to go into her apartment, I expected Jody to want to switch but, she did not say anything so, I started her up and continued our journey. Since Tammy's parking lot was a horse shoe, I did not have to turn around.

I made a right and started down the drive toward the street. When I was about halfway there, I heard screaming. I kept driving until I realized that the screaming was getting closer and was coming from behind the vehicle. Then I recognized the voice, it was Tammy, and she was yelling my name.

I stopped, rolled down my window and waited for her to catch up. When she got to the car, she told me that there was a policeman at the end of the driveway, parked in the street. We all started laughing and I audibly pondered the following scenario.

If I had kept on driving, with my track record of swerving over the double yellow, the officer would have stopped us. I can just imagine the conversation. May I have your license sir? I don't have one officer. Why not? Because I am blind and they wouldn't let me have one.

I am sure that he would have arrested me immediately for driving while intoxicated. Fortunately for us, Tammy saw the danger and stopped us. We talked for a few more minutes to make it look less obvious and, before taking off again, Jodi and I switched places.

She drove me the block home and the officer did not follow. I'm not sure why, but Jodi never let me drive her car again. That is okay though because other people did.

Ezekiel 33:5 He heard the sound of the trumpet, and took not warning; his blood shall be upon him. But he that taketh warning shall deliver his soul.

Tammy's yell was not like a trumpet, but it was a warning. Because I heeded her caution, she did save my soul.

Definitions:

Body, The physical part of you that includes flesh, blood and bone.

Spirit, The part of you that God said He would make in His image and, until it is seared, intuitively knows right from wrong.

Soul, The mind, will and emotions.

Lest you think I am suggesting that Tammy did more than temporarily protect me, I will explain. If I had been arrested, which I will be in the future, I would have suffered greatly, as I will in 2000 and 2011. So, I am grateful that she stopped me for continuing on my foolish trek.

90
THE SURVEYOR
SEPTEMBER OF 1988

I had gone to a meeting in an area of town that I was not familiar with. Upon leaving the meeting I asked someone where I could find a bus stop. They gave me directions and I followed them. I waited for a while and since no one had come along I could not find out if I was waiting in the correct place.

I knew that the bus ran every half hour but, it seemed that it had been longer than that. I turned my body in the direction of the oncoming traffic and squatted down while holding my cane in front of me. A minute or so later I heard to women walking up the street.

They were talking when one of them said, "Hey, I think we are in the way." As they got closer, I stood up and asked them if I was standing at the bus stop. They looked around and did not see a bus stop. I told them that I was blind and I needed to find a bus stop.

One of them apologized for being in my way and asked, "How can you be a surveyor if you are blind?" I told her that I was not a surveyor. The other one asked, "Then why do you have that stick in your hand?" When I explained that it was my cane, they both felt a little embarrassed.

One of them exclaimed, "Oh, we thought you were surveying this property and that we were in your way." I never did find out the color of their hair. They said that they were both physical therapists and that they were going to a meeting.

They said that the meeting would only take about forty-five minutes after which they would be happy to drive me home. Since I did not seem to have any other decent option, I went with them. The meeting lasted more than forty-five minutes because the speaker was late.

Once he showed up, I discovered that the theme for the evening was, prosthetics. It was actually interesting. Afterward they walked me to their car and they drove me home. We exchanged phone numbers and kept in touch for a while.

We got together and each time there was someone new to meet, and each time I was greeted with the same phrase, "You must be the blind surveyor. I guess they had told everyone they knew about the incident.

Ezekiel 40: 3 And he brought me thither, and, behold, there was a man, whose appearance was like the appearance of brass, with a line of flax in his hand, and a measuring reed; and he stood in the gate.

Psalm 23: 4 Yea, though I walk through the valley of the shadow of death, I will fear no evil: for thou art with me; thy rod and thy staff they comfort me.

It does not matter where I am going, I never get afraid. First, because I know that God is in control and, only what he wants to happen to me will happen. Second, most people are helpful when they come across someone in a wheelchair or using a cane. Third, I perceive all of the weird things as an adventure and am excited for their possibilities.

91
CONFOUNDING THE MIME
MARCH OF 1989

My friend Richard, the one in the story, "How to Make People Cold," and I took a trip to Atlantic City, New Jersey. We walked into a casino where there seemed to be a great deal of commotion in the lobby. As we drew nearer, Richard asked me to put away my cane. I thought it was because there were so many people that he was concerned I might trip someone.

I folded my cane and put it in my back left pocket. Once it was away, Richard crept us closer and closer to the action. People were intermittently laughing. When we finally stopped it seemed as if we were part of a very large circle of people. Also, it seemed as if there was someone in front of me.

Since the person I assumed was in front of me did not speak, and Richard did not tell me that anyone was there, I did not say anything. I just stood there waiting for something to happen. As I waited, I turned my head one way and then another in case I might catch a glimpse of anything through the little peripheral vision I had left which might give me a clue as to where we were.

As I moved my head around it seemed as if the person that may or may not be in front of me moved around as well. Still there were spots of laughter here and there. Finally, Richard spoke. He said, "He's blind," to the person in front of me.

The person responded, "Oh, I didn't know." At that moment Richard yelled, "Gotchya." The whole place erupted in laughter. It turns out that the person in front of me was a Mime. He had a sign out that said, 'You can't make me talk but I can make you laugh." It seems that my quick-witted friend saw the sign and contrived his plan to thwart the Mime using me without my knowledge.

Ecclesiastes 3:1 To every thing there is a season, and a time to every purpose under the heaven: 7 A time to rend, and a time to sew; a time to keep silence, and a time to speak;

Without knowing it, I heeded the time to keep quiet. I started being the class clown in sixth grade because I love to make people laugh. Though I had nothing to do with the situation, I loved that I was used as a prop to make an entire room of people laugh.

92
WHO'S BLIND, ANYWAY?
MARCH OF 1989

After leaving the Mime, we went into the main lobby of the casino. This time I figured out what he was up to. He asked me for my cane and glasses. He put the glasses on, opened the cane and had me walk a little in front of him. He held onto my arm as if I was guiding him when he was actually steering me.

We walked up and down the main thoroughfare for a while. It is obvious that he wanted people to think that he was blind and that I was leading him around. I could not figure out why though. After a while he returned my accouterments to me and I asked him what in the world he was doing.

He said that he would watch for people that would look at his face. Then, as we approached them, he would stare right into their eyes while tapping the cane. He would keep eye contact with them as we passed each other. He registered the expression of each person as they first looked at him.

Then he would watch their expression change as they thought he was looking at them and again when they realized that he could see them. He said that some people freaked out so much that they walked into other people or even walls.

I must admit that I wish I could have seen their faces too. I used to be a people watcher as well. This however was not watching, this was manipulating.

Mark 15:39 *And when the centurion, which stood over against him, saw that he so cried out, and gave up the ghost, he said, Truly this man was the Son of God.*

There are a lot of things to stare at in this world. Paintings, sculptures and beautifully proportioned women to name a few. I used to go to the mall and just sit and watch people. I would study their walks, shoes, clothing and facial expressions.

Now though, as the centurion did, I try to keep my focus on Jesus. I find myself in a lot less trouble that way.

93
HEART ATTACK
MARCH OF 1989

I was at my friend Steve's ice cream place with Richard. There were two young ladies at the table next to us. Richard and I were making observations and cracking jokes. The girls started laughing with us or perhaps, at us. In either case, we asked if we could join them at their table. They agreed.

One of the girls, Andrea, and I started to date. She would come to my place once in a while and I would go to her dorm at the University occasionally. We were at her dorm when we decided that it was time for me to go. She was tired and really did not want to drive so, I said I would. She jokingly said, "Okay."

When we got to the car I asked her for the keys. I got in the car, started her up and began to back up. Unlike Jodi, she said that was enough and we should switch places. I convinced her that I could do it since I had already had practice besides, it was so late that no one would be on the roads anyway.

She finally agreed and we started off. Just as in Jodi's car, there were a lot of curves to negotiate so, it went slow at first. I was correct about the traffic, we only encountered one car on the whole two-mile trip. We were driving down a road that was lit with crime lights because it was a car dealership.

As I was listening to Andrea's directions the one car we encountered pulled up next to us on the left. Andrea was paying such close attention to where our car was headed so she would be able to accurately guide me that she did not notice our company at first.

In the course of time however, she looked up and almost passed out. You could tell that she wanted to go ballistic but was restraining herself so as not to attract the attention of the people in the other car.

Who were the people in the other car? Police officers. I have had much emergency training in the past and one thing I have not yet done in a situation is panic. I did not want to start now so I asked her to let me know when the officer looked our way. When she did, I turned to the left and waved to them. Then I let up on the throttle ever so slightly and allowed them to get ahead of us.

They sped up and took off. When they were out of sight Andrea screamed, "stop the car!" So I did. We exchanged places and she drove to my apartment. It took her a long time to get over the incident, especially the fact that I waved to them.

She never let me drive her car again. You know, there seems to be a pattern developing.

Romans 13:3 For rulers are not a terror to good works, but to the evil. Wilt thou then not be afraid of the power? do that which is good, and thou shalt have praise of the same:

Unfortunately, I was not yet afraid of those in authority. I did grow to have more respect for the police, fire department and all those who serve our country in uniform and caused my family to appreciate them as well.

94
EVERYBODY LIMBO
April of 1989

I was, as they say, between jobs. I had been a vegetarian now for about two years. Many people who knew me did not believe it though, because they would see me at McDonald's or Berger King a lot. That was because I loved McD's, French fries and BK's Vegi Whopper. I could not, or rather did not want to, show my face at McD's because I had been fired for stealing.

As I had explained before, I was in charge of the stock at McD's. I had been on vacation and when I returned, I found out that two cases of cheese, forty pounds each, had expired. I went to my manager and asked if I could have the cheese to give out to the poor and elderly. I had often asked in the past to be able to take some of what we threw away and bless someone with it. He refused every time and he refused to allow me to have the cheese as well.

Well, I took the cheese out to the dumpster and put it on the side. When I left for home that evening, I went to the dumpster and took one of the cases with me. I gave most of it away and, somehow, someone found out about it and reported me. When my boss called me on the carpet, I told him what I had done.

He fired me for stealing their garbage. Since at the time you had to sue for unemployment benefits, I did. I had to go before a judge and when I told him the story, he denied my benefits. He agreed that I stole from the company and, if you are fired for steeling, you cannot collect benefits.

But I digress. Richard was not a vegi and liked BK so, we went there a lot. We became friendly with the manager and workers. We even became known to some of the regular customers for our comedy. I decided to apply for a job there and told them what happened with McD's and they hired me anyway.

Before getting the job, we used to hang out by the front door. It was a warm evening and Richard and I were standing on either side of the front door. As people came in, we greeted them. Then, I got the idea. I asked Richard to let me know when the next customers were just a few feet away. When he said, "Now!" I lifted my cane tip up and to my left in front of Richard.

I then said, "Everybody limbo." There were a lot more fun-loving people than I thought there were going to be. The majority of them actually did limbo into the restaurant. The manager later told me that it seemed to increase business.

Proverbs 3:13 Happy is the man that findeth wisdom, and the man that getteth understanding.

We understood that people wanted to smile and needed something to be happy about. We had the wisdom to do something about it. That made everyone happy.

95
SPEAK UP, I CAN'T SEE YOU!
SEPTEMBER OF 1989

I went to a white table cloth restaurant with my girlfriend and her family. Andrea read the menu to me and I decided what I wanted to order. The waitress came by and started taking our orders. She very properly asked Andrea's mother first, then Andrea, then her father and her brother.

Then she turned to Andrea and asked, "And what would he like?" Because we had this conversation before, she deferred to me by telling the waitress, "I don't know, why don't you ask him?" The waitress turned to me and in a louder voice than she had been speaking in before asked, "What would you like sir?"

I could not help myself. I am naturally a practical joker and always like a good laugh. Normally I can look right at you when you are speaking to me. In fact, since I am able to do that, I have had a lot of people not believe that I am blind.

For some reason it seems to be disconcerting to others. And still more want to test the ability by moving around while talking to see if I can follow them. I did not look right into her face even though I could have. I figured it would have a better effect if I was looking in her general direction but missing the mark.

I raised my voice a little and then said, "You will have to speak up because I am blind." She then started her sentence over again in an even louder voice. By the third word she realized what had just happened. As I busted out in laughter, closely followed by the others at my table, she began to apologize profusely.

I assured her that she was forgiven, that she need not apologize anymore and that I just wanted her to learn something that might help her in the future. Many years ago I had "seen" the movie, "Hear No Evil, See No Evil." If you have not seen it, I do not recommend it because of the bad language.

Anyway, there is a scene where a blind man and a deaf man meet. When the blind man realized that the other man is deaf, he starts speaking louder. If someone is hard of hearing, speaking louder might help. As for the deaf, speaking louder might be a hindrance.

It certainly will not affect their ears but, increasing your volume can change your cadence and the shapes your lips make. If the person reads lips, in effect, you are blurring their view. The blind are definitely not helped when you speak louder, because we generally do not want that kind of attention focused on us.

This was not the first, nor will it be the last time this happened. So, the next time you are out with a blind or deaf person, watch and listen to the way people change their communication style around them.

Leviticus 19:14 Thou shalt not curse the deaf, nor put a stumbling block before the blind, but shalt fear thy God: I am the LORD.

As the above verse suggests, those of us with disabilities are not looking for special treatment, nor are we wanting people to make things harder for us. As I have said to many people over the years, everyone is dealing with something, it is just easier to recognize what blind people are working around.

96
THE WOLF SPIDER
SEPTEMBER OF 1989

I had just moved back to New York and was living in the finished basement of my girlfriend's parents' home. The foundation of their home was shifting due to the fact that the builder was a crook and cut many corners. This shifting allowed small creatures to explore new territory.

Most of the creatures were spiders. When I was young, I was in the Boy Scouts. We used to go camping every month. I had not formulated an opinion about bugs until I started camping. After many camping trips I decided that, as long as they stayed out of my cranial orifices, eyes, ears, nose and mouth, bugs were okay.

My girlfriend however did not share my opinion when it came to spiders. It was sometimes humorous to see her reaction when she discovered that a spider was in the same room with her. Her brother was much worse. I believe he is the only arachnophobe I have ever met.

One time we were on a road trip. Somehow a spider about a quarter of an inch in diameter got on the dash board of the car. It started climbing up the windshield directly in front of him. As soon as he spotted it, he opened the door and attempted to jump out of the car.

It took a lot of effort and many hands to keep him from his intent. We were going about eighty-five miles an hour when he tried to jettison. Until that moment I had no idea how serious and paralyzing some phobias could be.

Thus, when I discovered a spider in my room on the ceiling, I was unsure what to do about it. I was in my room and had turned my head in just the right way. My eyes landed on a spot on the ceiling about eight feet away. It seemed that there was a dark spot on the ceiling.

As I approached, I discovered that it was a wolf spider. The body was larger than a silver dollar and from tip to tip his or her leg span was about nine inches. I did not want to alarm anyone so, I asked my girlfriend if she had an empty bucket. She asked what I needed it for and I told her that she did not want to know.

Well, I guess that gave it away because she asked, "Do you need it to catch a spider?" When I responded in the affirmative, she said that she wanted to see it. I decided that I had better get the bucket and a piece of cardboard before showing it to her because, once she saw it, I figured she would run out the door and I might not hear from her again for a while.

Once I obtained the spider removal kit, I took her to see it. It was still there and when she saw it, I thought I would lose the use of my right arm for life because of the way she gripped it. I was unaware that she had that much strength in her hands.

She said, "Hurry up and get it out of here, if my brother sees it, he will never sleep in this house again." I started toward the arachnid and she bolted for the door. I hate harming any of God's creatures so, I wanted to take it slowly so as not to pin any of the spiders' legs with the rim of the container.

Once I had it against the sealing, I slipped the cardboard slowly between the two in order to encourage Wolfie to drop. I do not know how Robert found out but, he did. He came running down the stairs asking what was in the bucket.

I knew he would figure it out as soon as I said, "You don't want to know." Since I did not know what else to say, I let the words fly. I had just discovered how to make him into a world class sprinter. I am probably off in my calculations but, it seemed that he ran about thirty meters in three seconds.

I walked across the street to a wooded area and took the cardboard off the bucket. I then turned it over to gently pour the creature into the grass. My girlfriend was about thirty feet away and I asked her if it had dropped out yet. She said that it was still in the bucket.

As I turned it over to peer inside, I realized that it had spun a web already and was holding on to it. I turned it over again and gave it a gentle shake. I could actually feel the weight of the spider and hear it land in the grass. My girlfriend's brother yelled from the next block, "Is it gone yet?"

When I responded in the affirmative, he began slowly and cautiously retracing his steps. I will not know for sure until I get to heaven but, I do not think that I caused any damage to Wolfie. Since I have lost my vision, I have not liked to handle bugs. I have always thought that it was because I did not want to harm them. I wonder now if that is completely true.

Proverb 30:24 and 28
24 *There be four things which are little upon the earth, but they are exceeding wise:*
28 *The spider taketh hold with her hands, and is in kings' palaces.*

My spider had hold of the ceiling which was in a very nice house though it was not a palace. It also took hold of the container which was not much more than trash. He or she was wise enough to know that its world was moving and it needed security so, it did what it could.

97
TAXI PLEASE
NOVEMBER OF 1989

I had just finished an appointment and was waiting for a taxi. I heard a car stop in front of me so, I walked toward it. I reached for the handle and opened the door. I started to move toward the seat when I heard a woman's voice say, "Thank you?"

When I realized that someone was getting out of the vehicle, I thought that worked out well for the driver. Drop one customer off and immediately pick up another.

I could be wrong but, it seems to me that all handles on car doors were in the same basic place both on the inside and outside. That is until the early nineties. That is when some cruel joker decided that a handle on the inside could be anywhere on the door.

If that was not bad enough, now they can be shaped like a hook, a circle, an oval and, they can be sticking out or recessed in the door. There have been times it has taken me ten, twenty or even thirty seconds to find the stupid release. Thank God that all handles on the outside of car doors are generally in the same place.

They have not left those alone either. Now you can pull down, forward, backward or just straight out. I hated the changes at first. Now however, I love the handles that pull straight out. I did not realize why the woman sounded confused until I started to get in the car.

I will get off my soap box now and finish the story. As I started to sit down, the driver asked, "Can I help you?" When I started to tell him my destination, he responded in a quizzical tone, "I was just dropping off my wife." It took me a second to realize that I had opened the door of a personal car and not a taxi.

I hate feeling stupid. Fortunately, the feeling only lasted a minute because the taxi had arrived. Naturally, my first thought was, 'Why could you have not shown up two minutes ago?"

Psalm 71:1 In thee, O LORD, do I put my trust: let me never be put to confusion.

What I did not know until a year and a half after this incident was that God is in control of every quark, nutrio, atom and molecule of everything we can see, hear, taste, touch or smell. Once I finally realized that, there was no longer a reason to be frustrated, angry or embarrassed about what happens to me.

I am not saying that I have it down yet, but, more often than not, I do. Even when I fail in the moment, upon reflection, I see the bigger picture.

98
SHEER STUPIDITY
APRIL OF 1990

Though I did not start lifting weights until the end of 1996, I had known that you should never do any heavy lifting without a spot. I did try to keep to this rule but, sometimes it was difficult to resist pushing myself when I was alone. During the three years I was living in northern Delaware I had only one serious partner.

Rob was stronger than I was and would push me beyond what I could have ever done on my own. Unfortunately for me but wonderful for him, he was getting ready to get married. Though we tried to lift together three times a week, we only averaged about once a week.

As I got stronger, I became more daring when I was lifting on my own. Stupid would be more accurate a description. There were a few times that I had pushed myself too far and had to let the weight sit on my chest for a while as I tried to figure out how I was going to get out from under it.

The first time I rolled it down my body until I could sit up. It was a hundred and ninety pounds. Once I got it to my stomach I thought I was going to suffocate because, though I had a very strong abdomen, it was not strong enough to lift that much weight.

After that I decided to leave the cuffs off the ends so that if I had to, I could tilt the bar and let some of the weight fall off one side at a time. Once light enough, I could then lift it to the rack. Well, that was not a great idea either. The next time the weight got stuck on my chest I tried it.

I had two hundred and eight pounds on the bar. Two twenty-five-pound plates on each side followed by two twenty-two-pound plates on each side and then one ten pounder on each side. When I realized that I could not rack it, I dropped it to my chest fully confident that I would be able to get out of it this time.

I rested for a moment and then tilted the bar to the left. After shaking it enough to have the ten-pound plate fall off, I decided to let one of the twenty-twos fall off as well. As the larger plate fell off, the bar shot up toward my right with such force that I thought one of the plates would fly off into my stereo unit.

It didn't. Even though nothing got damaged, the excitement was such that it discouraged me from trying that again. After finishing my routine, I sat there thinking of a safer way to lift alone. The only two things that were really dangerous to do by yourself were the squat and the bench press.

Since I did not have a squat rack, I could only work with the amount of weight I could lift up and over my head. Though I could squat with almost three hundred pounds, I could only throw about a hundred and fifty over my head. That was not dangerous.

However, since I could bench almost as much as I could squat, and was more likely to push myself in the bench, that was dangerous. I finally came up with the solution. I got a couple of heavy-duty pipe clamps and attached them to the bench bar.

I got two lengths of two-thousand-pound test chain. I drilled holes at the top of the bench rack and inserted carriage bolts into the holes. I attached the chains to the bolts and to the brackets. The bar was now at a height that was just above my throat when I was laying down and when it had over two hundred pounds on it.

The next time I lifted I pushed myself to exhaustion purposely. When I got the point that I could not lift it to the pins I got nervous. Though I had tried it out with more weight than I ever hoped to lift, I couldn't help thinking, 'What if the chain breaks, what if the bracket breaks, or, what if the bolts break?

Obviously, none of the above happened because I am writing this story.

There were many times that I had to rely on my new neck saving device. Each time I was less and less nervous but, the fear of disaster never went away completely. I had taken the chains off the bench when I moved to New York and had not replaced them yet.

I intended to do it but, since my girlfriend was in the apartment I decided to lift without the chains. Big mistake. Since beginning to lift in 1986, I had entered many lifting competitions and won first place in my weight class in every one I competed in.

I had not won the overall title and was trying hard to get it. I was feeling very strong and thought that I would be able to do it this year. Since there would be another competition soon, I was pushing myself very hard. My girlfriend was sitting on the couch watching a TV show.

The way I worked out at the time was in a reverse pyramid. I would do ten reps with a weight, add ten pounds to that weight and to eight reps, add ten pounds and do six, add ten and do four and finally add ten and do two reps.

I started out with one hundred and eighty-six pounds and did my ten. By the time I got to the two hundred and twenty-six pounds for the two reps, I was exhausted. I had to struggle tremendously to get the second rep up. As I got it most of the way up, I started moving it back toward the pins.

Since I could not see well enough to see the pins, I did not know that I was too far back with the bar. I hit the bottom of the pins and the bar shot back down. It was headed for my forehead and I tried to move it to my chest but, it was moving too fast and I had no strength left.

Before the bar landed in my mouth I yelled to get Andrea's attention. She realized that something was wrong and jumped off the couch. When she got to me, she straddled my chest and helped me lift the bar out of my mouth onto my chest.

She then took some weight off one side of the bar and then the other until I could lift it to the pins. The bar had landed on my upper lip and pushed my front teeth in. My mouth was closed but the weight of the bar forced my mouth open.

As the bar rolled down into my mouth it pushed my bottom lip against my teeth so hard that they pierced through my lip. I quickly threw on some clothing and put an undershirt against my mouth. I had Andrea drive me to the hospital where they told me that my teeth had gone completely through my lip.

They had to put eighteen stitches on the inside of my lip and fifteen on the outside. I went to the dentist the next day. He told me that the teeth were pushed so far back that he thought they would not be able to recover. He pulled the teeth back into place but was so sure that they would die and fall out that he did not even suggest I wear a retainer to keep them in place.

I am so happy to say that he was wrong. I went back to him two months later and he said that he could not believe that the teeth were still in place. He took x-rays and said that the teeth had not even cracked. He said that you could not even tell by comparing the current x-rays with previous ones that the teeth had even been moved.

Needless to say, that I put the chains back on the bar and never again did any heavy lifting without them or a spot. Because of the accident I did not go to the next competition. Though I still lift weights to keep in shape, I never again competed.

Jeremiah 17:14 Heal me, O LORD, and I shall be healed; save me, and I shall be saved: for thou art my praise.

Doctors and dentists may "heal" you but, it does not always stay. If God heals you, another physician will never be needed. That is because, two thousand years after Luke was a doctor, medical professionals are still practicing. God does not need practice.

99
THE BODY SLIDE
July of 1990

I had moved back to New York during the Summer of 1989. My mother has lived in the same house since 1976. Now, instead of being four or five hours away, I was only forty-five minutes to an hour away. Now my mother and step-father were able to come and visit frequently.

During one of those visits my mom told me about a place called, "Action Park." In the winter there were snow rides and, in the summer, there were water rides. Since my current girlfriend was not into that kind of thing, my mother and I decided to go by ourselves.

I had spoken with my sisters Donna and Lisa about their experiences at the park. Lisa was more game but, Donna was almost as daring as I. She told me about the time that she had made her own bikini bathing suit and then had gone with Lisa and my mother to Action Park.

There was one ride that interested me most. Donna said that she had gotten to the top of the one-hundred-foot body slide. As she went down, the pressure of the water snapped both pieces of her suit. I guess this is a common occurrence because there were people ready with cameras as she stood up not knowing that her coverings had left her.

She told me that the reason she was temporarily unaware of her nakedness was because she was focused on the enema she had just received from the ride. Donna told me to make sure to keep my legs crossed and my butt cheeks as tight as possible.

Just as there were perverts ready with cameras, there were women nearby with towels and one of them helped my sister. There was a fifty-foot body slide next to the large one. My mother and I had gone on a few rides and were making our way to the body slides.

When we arrived there, we found that the line for the fifty-foot slide was extremely long. The line for the one-hundred-foot slide was almost non-existent. I tried in vain to get my mom to go on the larger one but she refused.

We walked together to the smaller slide and, she then put my hand on the railing and told me to just follow it up to the top. I did. Once at the top I could tell that there were very few people there. I heard one boy in the far-right corner trying to convince his girlfriend that, even though he was not going to go down the slide, he was not afraid.

There were two or three more people up there but, it seemed that they were not in line. I slowly walked toward the noise of the water. I heard a woman's voice ask, "Do you want to go down the slide?" I was not sure if she was talking to me so I asked, "Are you talking to me?" When she said yes, I said, "Yes, but I'm blind so I will need your help."

At first, she did not believe that I was blind but, after an explanation of how I got there, she took my hand and positioned me in the water. There was a large trench with water rapidly flowing over the top. She turned me in the direction of the flow and told me to sit down and reach out in front of me for the bar.

She said that I was to hold the bar until she told me to let go. Then I was supposed to release my hold on the bar and lay down. I did as she said and, what a thrill. My sister was not the only one who gave me advice on avoiding having my colon power washed. Though I tried, it was no use. The pressure of the water seemed to cause the waist band of my suit to rise above my ears.

My mother was still waiting on the extremely long line for the fifty-footer so, I decided to try to get on the larger one again. With the help of some people that seemed to realize that I was blind, I managed to get back to the larger floom. When I got to the top again, believe it or not, the brave young man who would not go down the floom was still there.

The ride mistress came over, took my hand and led me back over to the ride. I decided that this time I was going to make the ride a little more thrilling. When she said let go this time, I did not just let go, I pulled on the bar thinking it would cause me to go faster. Boy was I wrong.

Instead, it launched me out from the slide board a few inches and I was free falling straight down one hundred feet. It does not take more than two seconds to fall that far. From the time I realized I had left the slide board until I forcefully reconnected with it, I had about one hour of thoughts cross my mind.

As I heard the crowd gasp, the uppermost thought in my mind was how much it was going to hurt to be snapped in half by the guard rail. Needless to say, I remain in one piece. I reconnected with the slide board with a jerk and, finished my ride.

Can you guess what I did next? That's right, I went around and got on the ride again. This was to be the third and my last ride because, as I approached the bar, I heard my mother's scream influenced by the Doppler Effect. The ride mistress had obviously seen or had been told what I had done.

As she held my hand to lead me to the water, with a smile in her voice she said, "I guess you won't do that again!"

2 Samuel 23: 15 And David longed, and said, Oh that one would give me drink of the water of the well of Bethlehem, which is by the gate!

I know what is like to want water from a specific place. I do not think a summer has gone by in the last three decades that I do not wish I could revisit that park. Also, whenever my wife and I go away, the first thing we each want is a drink of our water because it goes through four filters before hitting our lips.

Water is perhaps the most miraculous substance in the Universe. If water did not float after freezing, all of our oceans, rivers and lakes would be solid ice and the world would be uninhabitable. Did you know that the word, "universe," means one spoken sentence? And that is how God created everything.

100
TOTALLY TUBULAR
July of 1990

The second ride we went on was the body tube. I do not know what the name of it really was but, that seems close enough. You had to walk up flights of stairs to what looked like the side of a hill. Two tubes were sticking out of the hill and water was flowing through them both.

There was a man hosting this ride and he had a water gun. Every once in a while, he would squirt the people in line. As we approached our turn, my mother told him that I was blind and she needed to guide me to my spot. He told us to sit down and we did. The water was so cold you would have thought it had just melted off an iceburg.

He told us that something was wrong and we had to wait for a little while. As we waited, my mother and I talked a little. One of the things she said was, "I hope you realize how much I love you because I wouldn't go on this ride for anyone else." Truth be known, if there had been anyone else with us, she wouldn't have gone then either.

When the man finally gave the go ahead, we both let go of the bar at the same time. It was less than a ten second ride but, it was great. The whole time I could hear my mother scream. Did I mention that she is claustrophobic? Well, she is. The funny part about her scream was that it was muted because we were underground.

As soon as we both flew out of the other end, her scream was amplified tenfold. It was only amplified for less than a second though because, we were about ten feet in the air and soon after, ten feet under water. I came up quickly and my mother came up a moment later. I asked her which way to go and she verbally guided me.

Someone on the dock thought something was wrong so they asked my mother if I was okay. She said yes, he's just blind. Their response, "He's what!" I think my mother got as much of a kick out of their reactions as I did from the rides.

1 John 4: 18 *There is no fear in love; but perfect love casteth out fear: because fear hath torment. He that feareth is not made perfect in love.*

As Franklin D. Roosevelt said, "Courage is not the absence of fear, but rather the assessment that something else is more important than fear." I am so blessed that my mother thought that giving me a great day was more important than her fear of tight spaces.

101
T BAR
JULY OF 1990

The last ride we went on was the Tarzan swing. Again, you had to go up many steps to get to it. There were two swings side by side. They were at the edge of a platform which was about twenty feet above the water.

It was such a long line and such a hot day that, by the time we had our turn we were completely dry. As we approached the launch pad, my mother was explaining every detail to me. Once I thought I had the whole picture in my mind, she switched to describing the people jumping off.

Once in a while someone would have a good long swing out to the center of the water hole before letting go. Most of the time however, they would not get far before dropping. Occasionally there was a person who could not hold their own weight and, upon jumping off they would go straight down and splash like a boat anchor.

My mother said that she would probably be in the last category. When it was finally my turn, she told me to walk straight ahead for a few feet and turn to the left. The Mistress of the ride had a hook that she would retrieve the T-bar with for the next victim.

Hook girl was involved in a conversation so she did not notice my mother giving me directions. She told me to take a step forward and to put out my right hand. I had my hand out and the girl pulled the T-bar to within six inches of my hand. She then let go and the bar went swinging out over the water.

According to my mother, she turned and looked at me as if to ask, 'What, are you a moron?" My mom then told the woman that I was blind and that she would have to place the bar in my hand. My mother said that the look of shock on the woman's face made her wish she had a camera.

The Mistress retrieved the bar and placed it in my hand and watched with disbelief as I swung out. As I swung, I waited for the momentum to slow down so that I knew when to let go. As I released my grip, I curled into a ball and did a flip. I came out of the tuck and dove straight into the water.

When I came up, most of the people were clapping. Because the platform was in the shape of a horse shoe, I received my applause in surround sound. Only the people close enough to hear my mother knew that I was blind. That is, until she started shouting directions to me so that I could swim to the dock.

When I got there, I sat on the edge until my mother could get there. Soon I heard her scream quickly followed by a splash. After she got up on the dock, I took her arm and we walked off.

1 Corinthians 10:31 Whether therefore ye eat, or drink, or whatsoever ye do, do all to the glory of God.

Now that I know that He gave me the talents and abilities I possess, I give Him all the applause I received that day, and every day. I Heard a few people talking about us as we walked past a little crowd, it made me smile to freak people out and hear their amazement afterwards.

102
RAYMOND THE JUNIOR WHITEHEAD
DECEMBER OF 1990

Before reading the following story, I want you to know that, even though I do not celebrate Santa or any of the other nonsense that has grown up around Christmas, I do have a sense of humor. Most of the people that know me have heard me state that Santa and Satan have the same exact letters and you should think about what that means.

Rather than explain those truths to our children, we want to tell them about a fat stranger that comes down our chimney without getting soot on his clothing and leaves presents for them. Would it not be better to tell our children that the gifts are from us because of our love for them? When we spend years lying to them about Santa, the Easter Bunny, the Tooth Fairy and others, why are we surprised that they no longer believe us when they hit their teen years?

While at work, just before Christmas, someone jokingly said that my cane was like the reindeer's nose. That got me to thinking and I came up with this song. You sing it to, "Rudolph the Red Nosed Reindeer."

My mobility instructor had just received a cane from Canada for me. It had a red plastic area on the handle about eight inches from the top. Inside the plastic was a halogen light. The light was operated by a switch in the handle and, when turned on, would flash.

Raymond the Junior Whitehead
Had a very shiny cane
and if you ever saw it
you would think he was insane
All of the other workers

used to laugh and call him names
they never let poor Raymond
in on any office games
Then one foggy Christmas Eve
the bus driver said
Raymond with your cane so bright
won't you drive the bus tonight
then all the bus passengers
shouted out his name with fear
Raymond the Junior Whitehead
won't you please get out of here

This is the fourth time my cane was used for something other than guiding me. The others were in the stories, "Queer Cue, Everybody Limbo," and "Late For Lifting." There have been other times but I have not written stories about those yet.

It makes me sad to know that most people ignore the Holy Spirit telling us that the Father gave his Son Jesus so we could not only be forgiven, but so we can also have an abundant life.

Isaiah 9:2 The people that walked in darkness have seen a great light: they that dwell in the land of the shadow of death, upon them hath the light shined.

I use this verse here because it is a double entendre. First, because it is about the Birth of Jesus. Second, because many of the people that saw my flashing cane marveled.

103
GUARD RAIL
JANUARY OF 1991

I was working as the Customer Service Manager for a gourmet cake and pastry company. The two people working for me decided to quit at the same time because of the general manager. He was a real tyrant and gave the women an especially hard time. Both of my reps were women. Larry, the manager, tried giving me a hard time too but, after telling him off twice, he tried to avoid me at all costs.

Because I was not able to do all the work myself, I hired a temp and pulled someone from another department to get the work done. Raj, the temp, was a young man who had just graduated from college and did not yet want to get tied down to a nine-to-five. He chose to work for a temp agency so that he would be able to take time off after completing an assignment.

Though he did take a few weeks off when one of my reps returned, only because Larry was fired by headquarters, he ended up working for me as a temp for over a year and a half. He noticed that I was in great shape and wanted to know what I did to stay that way. When I told him that I lifted weights, he decided to give it a try. He was a runner and thought that putting on a little muscle would help his wind.

I found out later that he smoked occasionally and drank more often. Over the years I have needled him about these two vices but, he still continued. He would complain about his limitations but would only give them up for a week or two before each marathon.

I invited him to lift with me and he accepted. We lifted for several weeks together. I now understand why my Russian gymnastic instructor was so hard on me. I have discovered that, though they may complain, the people that I have lifted with like to be pushed. Thus it was with Raj.

Sometimes you had to begin pushing before you even got to the gym. In this case, my apartment. We were lifting three days a week and this was one of those days. It started to snow heavenly and Raj thought that the lift would be canceled. As the snow got heavier, we began to send people home early lest they get stuck in the snow.

I decided to close my department early and Raj and I left. I was planning on taking the bus home but, as Raj began weedling out of lifting I came up with an even better idea. I played on his sympathy and convinced him to give me a ride home. Once we were in the car and on our way, I said, "Well, since you will be at my place, I guess we can lift after all."

I think that of all the people I have trained over the years, Raj needed the most encouragement. Actually, he needed to be kicked in the pants quite often. He responded with, "I do not have my exercise clothes." I suggested that he could borrow something of mine but, seeing that there was no way out, he decided to stop at his place on the way and get his clothing.

Once we were finally on our way from his place there was a lot more snow on the roads. Not being a cautious driver, he was going a little faster than he should have been. As he headed into a curve to the left, he started losing control of the vehicle. Not being able to see anything but bright white outside, I braced myself for impact.

Raj began loudly saying to himself, 'Pump the breaks, steer into the skit, pump the breaks, turn into the skid." He said these two phrases over and over until we came to a full stop. We ended off the road, half on the shoulder and half on what would have been the dirt if it had not been covered by so much snow. After sitting still for a while to regain his composure he said, "You should be glad you are blind."

I asked him what he meant by that and he explained that at one point the car had come within inches of the guard rail and that he was sure that we would hit it. He also told me that we were all over the road and if there had been any other cars around, we would have certainly have come in contact with them. He pulled back onto the road once his heart returned to a more normal beet and we arrived safely at my place and lifted together.

Isaiah 55:10 For as the rain cometh down, and the snow from heaven, and returneth not thither, but watereth the earth, and maketh it bring forth and bud, that it may give seed to the sower, and bread to the eater:

As of 2023, I have been living in Santa Fe, New Mexico for 21 years. It is almost shocking to me how people complain about the rain. We have been in a drought condition for most of those years and you would think that people would appreciate the moisture.

As the above verse tells us, without the rain and snow, we would not have much vegetation. Some like fruits, others like veggies and still others like flowers. None of those things would be possible if not for the precipitation. Even meat eaters would suffer as cattle need at least grass to survive.

So, let's learn to appreciate the weather in all of the four seasons that God has given to us.

104
AGAINST THE LAW
April of 1991

By this time, I had been asked by hundreds of people what legally blind meant. I used to go over the definition and the resulting restrictions. However, I was so tired of the answer that I decided to change my answer.

Instead, I started telling people that it meant that I could not be arrested because I could not see well. Maybe you would and maybe you would not be surprised at how many people accepted that answer.

What it really means is that the vision in their good eye with corrective lenses cannot be greater than 20/200. Or, the better eye has less than 20 degrees of vision with correction. Healthy eyes have 20/20 and 155 degrees horizontally and 135 degrees vertically.

That means a legally blind person has less than 10 percent of the visual acuity and about 14 percent of the visual field. Or, as I used to explain to people that asked, What can you see?" it is like looking through an ice cube with a McDonald's straw.

Over the years, as I have been teaching, discussing or debating with people, many have said to me, "You see better than I do." If I had to choose between regaining my sight or having spiritual vision, there would be no contest.

If I live to 120-years-old, I will have been blind for over 100 of those years. That sounds like a lot but, it is nothing compared to eternity. Also, the LORD has allowed me to lead many people to Him and, had it not been for my infirmity, I may not have been so successful.

Paul, the apostle, was blind and look what God accomplished through him.

2 Corinthians 12:7 And lest I should be exalted above measure through the abundance of the revelations, there was given to me a thorn in the flesh, the messenger of Satan to buffet me, lest I should be exalted above measure. 8 For this thing I besought the Lord thrice, that it might depart from me. 9 And he said unto me, My grace is sufficient for thee: for my strength is made perfect in weakness. Most gladly therefore will I rather glory in my infirmities, that the power of Christ may rest upon me. 10 Therefore I take pleasure in infirmities, in reproaches, in necessities, in persecutions, in distresses for Christ's sake: for when I am weak, then am I strong.

When I stop fighting against my weaknesses, as of 2023 I have twenty-three medical conditions, it is beautiful to watch what the LORD does through them.

105
LATE FOR LIFTING
MAY OF 1991

I had been living in Delaware and had just moved back to New York. I got a job as a Customer Service Rep. Toward the end of September. Nine months later I was promoted to Customer Service Manager. The previous Manager left the company to get married and the other rep retired.

We promoted the receptionist to a position as a rep and hired a temp to fill in the other position until we could get a replacement. His name was Rahjeev. Raj was working as a temp until he could figure out what he wanted to do with the degree he had just earned. As we talked, we discovered that we had many of the same interests.

Raj started coming over to my place to train. He was a runner but felt he needed to build up his muscles so, I began training him in weight lifting. There are many good reasons to have a partner when you are lifting. One of them is to have someone kick you in the but when you do not feel like working out.

Since I had a Russian Gymnastic instructor when I was young and impressionable, pushing yourself was drilled into me. I rarely had to be pushed to workout but, it was great having a partner for safety reasons.

We had just gotten off work and were supposed to go to my place to work out. Raj needed a little persuasion to go through with it but, after a while he agreed. We were both hungry but Raj had less control of his appetite. As we were driving to my place, we got stuck behind someone who was either lost or sightseeing.

I have always known that there are maximum speed limits but, I did not know until now that there were minimums, generally fifteen MPH lower than the max. Raj started complaining about the driver in front of us and I began to be irritated as well because they were well under the minimum.

When I moved into the new apartment, I had arranged for my Mobility Instructor to come out and help me with the logistics. Seeing that I had to cross a highway in order to catch the bus to work, and knowing that I would have to walk along that highway in the dark sometimes, she ordered a special cane for me which I mentioned in a previous story.

While stewing about the car in front of us, I came up with a great idea. I turned my cane on and held it over the roof of the car. Miraculously, the car in front of us pulled to the side. We passed them and got home much sooner than we otherwise would have. Since it was not as large or bright as a Police light nor did it flash as fast, I did not think it would work but, it did.

I was just trying to be funny, and as my wife sometimes says, "Keep trying." I thought that the only thing that would happen was Raj would laugh a little and I would put my cane away. I never did that again because I did not want to get arrested for impersonating a police officer.

Romans 5:3 And not only so, but we glory in tribulations also: knowing that tribulation worketh patience.

Patience has never been one of my strengths. In fact, as I write these stories, my computer is speaking so fast that even after thirty-one-years together, my bride cannot understand what is being said. Over the years I have had many customers come into my office as I was listening to something. More than once they have said, "Wow, I didn't know you understood Chinese!"

On every device I own that allows you to increase the speed, I have revved it up so that most people cannot understand what is being said. Whether it is my computer, cell phone, talking book player or even my Alexa devices, I cannot listen slowly.

106
HOW JOVANNA AND I MET
JUNE 8, 1991

It was Friday, June 7th, 1991. I had just moved into a new apartment six days earlier. I was working as a Customer Service Manager for Vie De France Bakery Yamazaki, Inc., a gourmet cake, pie, pastry and bread bakery.

The girl that I was dating usually drove me to work and to our apartment again but, since she and I were going our separate ways, I was getting rides from my coworkers. This day I was not able to get a lift, so I had to take the bus home, something I had not planned for.

I had contacted the Commission for the Blind to have a Mobility instructor come out and help me learn how to get from home to job and vice versa. The appointment was set for the middle of June, so I figured I could just cop rides until then.

I called the bus company and got the information I needed. I then walked nine minutes to the bus stop. When I got on the bus, I told the bus driver that I was blind, I was wearing dark sunglasses and I held out my cane as evidence.

I told him that this was the first time I was getting off at my stop and asked him if he knew it. He said no and I tried to explain it to him. Having no success, a passenger walked up and described it to the driver. He then, in a not too convincing voice, said that he knew where it was.

In addition to blindness, I have a few other minor problems, one of which is the following. If I am not actively involved in something my metabolism shuts down and I fall asleep. Before I knew it, I was waking up. Concerned that I had missed my stop, I asked the bus driver if we had gotten there yet.

He said, "Hey, I forgot all about you." At that point we had passed my stop by one block and instead of stopping to let me off the driver told me to sit down and he would let me off in a better place. When he finally stopped to let me off, I asked him where we were.

He could not tell me where we were because he spoke less English than I spoke Spanish. He was kind enough to "point the way." When I once again explained to him that I couldn't see and, could he please tell me where to go. He began to point the way again.

The girl that was sitting next to me on the bus started to laugh so hard I thought she would fall off her seat. I got off the bus in frustration hoping to find someone on the street that could be a little more helpful than the driver was. I wandered around for about an hour and not one person crossed my path.

It was getting dark and I knew it would be impossible to cross the highway unless I was to get there soon. I looked across the street and saw what I thought was a neon beer sign. I carefully crossed the road and found myself in a deli, not a bar.

When I gave a short synopsis of my plight to the person behind the counter, she gave me directions to the highway but didn't know the road I was looking for, "Lincoln Place." I started to walk slowly up the street.

I didn't know the street was rounded and I didn't know there were trees in huge cement blocks in the middle of the sidewalk. Since I couldn't see more than three or four feet in front of me, I had to walk slowly. As I would spot one of these cement squares, I would slow down and walk around it.

I had traversed two or three of these when I heard a car pull up next to me. I didn't hear any voices so I just kept walking. About 90 seconds later the same car pulled up next to me. I heard the window of the passenger's side start to descend. A voice that I did not recognize came from the car.

In heavily accented Brooklynese I heard "Yo, you need some help?" I went to the car and explained to the women what had happened to me.

They said they didn't know where my street was but they would be happy to give me a lift home if they could find it.

Less than three blocks later, and at high speed, the driver said, "Oh my God, there it is." Slowing down as little as she had to while still keeping the car on all four wheels, she made the turn and got me home in one peace. It turns out I was lost for an hour less than four blocks from my apartment.

They got me to my driveway and we sat there talking for about 15 minutes. It turns out that they had been watching me. They did not notice the folded cane in my hand and thought I was tripping on acid. They thought I was afraid of the trees. When I reflected on the scene from their point of view, I can understand their reluctance to pick me up at first.

They invited me to a picnic the next day and in order to avoid sitting in the car any longer because I had to go to the bathroom, I accepted. I intended to come up with an excuse to not have to go. I thought, from the way they were talking, they were part of a cult like Jehovah witnesses or Mormons or something.

When they asked me if I wanted to pray with them, I knew I was in trouble. They called me that night to confirm the details but I had forgotten to come up with an excuse to bow out and I did not want to lie so, I agreed to go. I asked them to call me that evening to confirm the details.

I thought that would give me a few hours to figure out some reason I could not go with them. I made dinner, cleaned up the dishes and started preparing for my Saturday house cleaning routine when the phone rang. I had forgotten to come up with a reason to not go so, I agreed but asked them to call in the morning in case something came up.

I got up Saturday morning, made breakfast, cleaned the house and prepared my laundry. When they called me late Saturday morning I had again forgotten to come up with a reason. I did not want to lie just in case they really did know God. They said they would be at my place about twelve o'clock.

When they got to my place they were running twenty minutes late. When I got in the car there was a young lady in the seat next to me. We were introduced but I had never heard her name before so, I promptly forgot it.

When we arrived at the picnic I was surprised to find that the people there were very nice and not at all what I thought they would be. I sat at a table on the back balcony. to my right and almost in front of me was Jovanna, the same woman that was in the car.

We struck up a conversation during which I asked her where she worked. She said "I work for a bakery that used to be in Katonah." Since I also worked for a bakery that used to be in Katonah and didn't think there could be more than one, I asked her if she worked for Vie De France.

She answered yes and asked me how I knew that. I told her that I worked for them too, as the Customer Service Manager. She responded with "No you don't." It turned out that we worked for the same company for two years and had not met.

Though we had not met she did see me once without knowing it. It was Halloween 1989. I had just begun working for the company two months earlier. My boss, Judy, wanted everyone to dress up for the occasion. She decided to cross dress and wanted me to do the same.

I wore a pair of women's white sneakers, black paisley stockings, a dress just above the knee, makeup, earrings and a wig. She was dressed like a man with the tale of her shirt sticking out of her pants zipper. Judy decided that we should go for a tour of the bakery.

That is when Jovanna saw me, thank GOD no one told her that woman would be her husband someday or she would have quit her job and gone back to New Mexico that very moment.

After the picnic the ladies dropped me off and invited me to church and another outing. I accepted without reservation this time and fully intended to go.

We arrived at Jack and Gina's home after church. We were early so Ann Marie, the girl with the Brooklyn accent, decided to go for a walk. I asked if I could go along and we asked Jovanna to come with us. We got to the end of the driveway when Ann Marie remembered that her reason for wanting to go for a walk was still in Heather's, the maniac driver's, car.

When she tried to get the little red and white box Heather coaxed her into the car and took her for a ride. Jovanna and I went on the walk by ourselves. She started telling me about her life. She stopped in the middle and said, "I don't know why I am telling you all of this."

We were on our way back when Ann Marie was dropped off to

finish the walk with us. They each took turns guiding me and each ran me into 1 tree. We, the Crazy Christian Crowd, spent the next couple of weeks hanging out together, doing our laundry and dining together.

Then Jovanna went home to New Mexico for one and a half weeks to visit her parents. I was very touched when she called to wish me a happy birthday. I found that while she was gone, I missed her. Just one week earlier I had thought to myself, "She's pretty and sweet but she's too good for me."

Little did I know that the Lord had told her on the plane ride home that I would be her husband. A few weeks later we, the CCC, were going to a Carmin concert in Southern, New Jersey. Richard was driving, I was sitting front passenger and Jovanna was in the middle. there were five others in the car with us.

Jovanna looked very tired and was nodding off. I thought of asking her if she would like to put her head on my shoulder to rest. Then I thought she might slap me for being fresh. I decided it would be worth the risk. When I asked her, she said yes in a grateful voice. The instant her head touched my shoulder the LORD said, "This is your wife."

When we got into the concert hall I needed to go to the bathroom. Jovanna took me to the restroom area. We were on our way back to our seats when she said she needed to talk to me. We told each other that we had feelings for the other and would like to start courting.

We prayed together in those seats and then she kissed me, that was a most wonderful feeling. We walked back to our seats holding hands and, Praise the Lord, the rest is history.

Proverbs 18:22 Whoso findeth a wife findeth a good thing, and obtaineth favour of the LORD.

This is so true that I used it in my vows.

107
THIS IS MY SWEETHEART
AUGUST 17, 1991

My beautiful wife and I met for the first time on June 8 of 1991 and, though I was interested, she was not. She was extraordinarily beautiful in spirit, soul and body so, I did not pursue her because I knew she was too good for me. Until I decided to follow the LORD, there was no way she would accept my attentions anyway.

Jovanna was kind and helpful but, so was everyone else in her church. I did not know that she had any interest until the day I gave my life to Jesus the Christ. As I walked out of the house with the pastor, she jumped out of the hammock she was lying in with her friend Ann Marie.

Unfortunately for Ann Marie, she hit the ground. Fortunately for me, Jovanna gave me a flying tackle hug because she knew Whom I had just committed to. That was the best hug I have ever received. I thought she was just happy for me and had no idea that she was interested in me.

About August 10, we decided to court. Laugh if you want but, I love being old fashioned. I knew that my mother needed to meet this Angel so, I arranged for my parents to visit Ossining, New York from North Bergen, New Jersey on August 17.

I was born in Manhattan just as my mother Barbara was. If you did not already know, New Yorkers have attitude. My mother had more than most. In fact, she had so much that, when our daughter was about two years old, she said, "Daddy, Grandma scary!"

My mom was also quite physical with me. If she did not like what you said or did, she would let everyone but me know verbally. With me, she would add something pugilistic like a smack or a punch in the arm. I have to be honest, I liked it.

My mother and step-dad Tony show up to my apartment where Jovanna is timidly anticipating their arrival. Perhaps I gave my beloved too much information but, I did not want her to pass out from lack of preparation when my mom came in like a bull from Pamplona.

I forget why but, my step-father was still outside when my mom came in. So, I introduced the ladies by saying to my fiancé, "Sweetheart, this is my mom, Barbara." "Mom, this is, (pregnant pause)…my Sweetheart" I now know why people use familiar terms of endearment, I forgot her name!

My mother promptly smacked me in the left arm and called me stupid. Embarrassing moments are so good for us because they keep us more humble than we would otherwise be. My bride to be then introduced herself and, by the time my dad came in, I had her name on my brain again.

James 4:10 Humble yourselves in the sight of the Lord, and he shall lift you up.

I have been known to point out that Albert Einstein and I shared two things, we each had an IQ over 160 and we each failed the second grade. That may not seem humble but it is said tongue-in-cheek. I have also been known to say that, "No matter how much you know, you had to learn it. So, there is no sense in being stuck up about it."

108
THAT RINGS A BELL
September of 1991

I first want to say that I have the most wonderful wife in the world. We have been married just over eleven years as I am writing this in the Summer of 2003. You know that it must be true love after all the things she has run me into. It started even before we were married and I now know that it was a sign of things to come.

We were newly engaged and beginning to plan our wedding. We had a lot of help from people in our church with some of the specifics but, we did all the coordinating ourselves. We made our own cake, arranged the music, hired the harpist and designed the layout of the church.

All this after what happened so you know that it was true love. We were walking out of the grocery store hand in hand. I was carrying one heavy bag. The store had a large overhang where they had the shopping carts. The overhang allowed their shopping carts to stay out of the weather and allowed people to wait for cars without getting soaked if it was raining.

The overhang was held up by eye beams. My wife to be, Jovanna, ran me into one of the beams and, many of the people around us instantly knew what had happened. Probably because they saw me holding my head and they saw Jovanna looking mortified.

I would like to think, however, that they heard the same bell I heard the instant my head made contact with the solid immobile object. In either case, a worker from inside the store came running out and, after talking briefly with my beloved ran back into the store.

By this time I had a bump on my forehead that was the size of an egg cut in half the long way, and it was bleeding. The man came running back out of the store with a five-pound bag of ice in his hands. I thought he was going to open it, produce a paper towel or napkin, place a few cubes in it and hand it to me.

Instead, he came over to me and slapped the entire bag on my forehead. This did not help the dizziness I was having nor did it help the pain in my head. He was trying to help though so, I thanked him, picked up our bag and stumbled off with my Fiancé to the car.

Once there I produced a bandanna, opened the bag of ice, took out a few cubes, placed them in the bandanna and placed the bandanna on my wound. I then poured the rest of the cubes on the ground and put the plastic bag they came in into the trash.

My bride to be suffered from peoples comments longer than I suffered from the headache. If I had a dollar for each time, she apologized for running me into something, we could take a trip to Tahiti.

Jeremiah 30:17 For I will restore health unto thee, and I will heal thee of thy wounds, saith the LORD; because they called thee an Outcast, saying, This is Zion, whom no man seeketh after.

It is amazing to me that anyone would believe in evolution and billions of years. There are at least a dozen scientific evidences I could give for my belief in God. I will just use one here. Healing. The fact that our bodies can heal themselves from broken bones, torn flesh, sicknesses, diseases and blood loss is testament to the love of God for his creatures.

109
SOME FRIENDS!
APRIL OF 1992

It was Thursday the twenty-third, just two days before my wedding. Jovanna's parents, sisters and brother had all arrived in New York and were going to take her shopping for the big day. My brother and best friend had arrived on Wednesday and had stayed at my place.

I had arisen to make breakfast, vegetable and cheese omelets. After breakfast we were sitting around talking about the arrangements when the phone rang. Jovanna was calling to let me know that her family had arrived at her apartment and they would be leaving shortly for my place.

Since we lived only nine tenths of a mile apart, I figured they would be to my place in less than fifteen minutes. Since they had not shown, I wondered what could be taking so long. At the half hour mark I became concerned and called her apartment. There was no answer.

I decided that with three sisters a brother and her parents there, they probably all took bathroom breaks and had just departed. If they had indeed left just before the phone rang it should take less than five minutes to arrive at my door.

Ten minutes after I hung up the phone without reaching them, they had still not arrived. It was at that point that my brother and my best friend colluded to tease me and try to make me nervous. We heard a siren in the distance and Bill said, "Maybe they got into a wreck."

My brother said, "Maybe her family decided that you were not good enough for her daughter and are not coming." Bill then chimed in with, "Well I guess we can tell him now Dan. Jovanna's family decided that they did not want her to marry you so they went to her apartment, packed up all her stuff and are taking her back to New Mexico."

They both made many more remarks designed to needle me but I can only remember the ones above. At the forty-five-minute mark the phone rang. Before I could pick it up Bill said, "That's Jovanna calling you from the airport to let you know that the wedding is off."

Actually, it was Jovanna. She had called to apologize that they were so late and to let me know that they would be here in a few minutes. I cannot remember which one said it but one of them said, "She just called to throw you off the trail so that you would not be able to reach her before the plane takes off."

About ten minutes later I heard a car pull up in my driveway. Bill suggested that it was someone coming to give me the bad news of Jovanna's decision to call off the wedding. Actually, it was Jovanna and her family. They were finally here.

They all came in, introductions were made and, Bill and Dan proceeded to regale Jovanna's family with their torturous remarks. It turns out that as they were driving to our place, her mother wanted to stop somewhere to pick up something for the wedding.

Ephesians 5:4 Neither filthiness, nor foolish talking, nor jesting, which are not convenient: but rather giving of thanks.

This verse is focused on the harm that this kind of communication can cause if that is its intention. Neither my brother or Bill were trying to hurt me, they were just having fun, and so did I.

110
NICE TEETH
April of 1992

Once we got married, my wife felt comfortable in sharing her utensils with me. I wonder how many people over the years had thought my wife was a dentist? I wonder how many thought she was a doctor? I wonder how many people looked at me and felt sympathy for my wife because I was obviously nuts.

If you knew me you would know that one of my favorites sayings is, "You are what you eat, which is why I eat so many bananas, crackers and nuts." But that is because of the weird or crazy things I say and do on purpose. It is a totally different thing when what someone else makes you look goofy.

In the eleven years we have been married, there has been a decidedly lopsided habit she has. Jovanna will almost never taste anything I ask her to. Sometimes she will say that she will taste it later because she is full.

Now I am not suggesting that she is untruthful, I am sure she means to taste it later. The problem is I always forget to ask for her definition of later. On the other hand, she will frequently ask me to taste things.

Sometimes she just wants me to enjoy the culinary delight she is experiencing. Sometimes she wants to know what is lacking in the dish and, sometimes she wants me to identify some flavor in her food. Whatever the reason, that infamous Murphy always seems to be around.

As soon as she asks me to taste something, sounding like she has it ready to deposit into my mouth, I will open up like a B52 hanger. Then, inevitably, some morsel will slip off her fork or fall out of her spoon and she will have to retrieve it. Not being privy to this happening, I just sit there with my mouth open.

I often wonder if an insect or bird will fly in to investigate or if a spider sees me and thinks, 'Hey, that would be a great place to build a web.' Eventually she will place the food ladened utensil in my orifice and I will give her the response she needs.

I have asked her to please let me know when she is ready because I will no longer sit there looking like a baby bird waiting for its mother to regurgitate a worm into its mouth. You would think this would solve the problem, wouldn't you?

Well, it solved one problem but because of that blasted Murphy guy, it created another problem. She will tell me that she would like me to try something. Then she will immediately tell me to wait. Good so far because my mouth is still closed. Then she will tell me that she is ready.

I open my mouth and she says something like, "Whoops, wait a minute." Now I close my mouth again and wait. She again gives me the green light and I open. If it takes more than a second after that, I will close again and ask what the matter is. When she is finely truly ready, I will open again.

Now I have the food, chew analyze, swallow and report. The problem is that I looked like a moron sitting there opening and closing my mouth several times. My children have not been able to intercede for me in this one. What is the solution?

Stop tasting her food? Stop going out to eat with her? I wish I could find Murphy and pay him off to leave me alone at the dinner table.

1 Timothy 6:8 And having food and raiment let us be therewith content.

Sometimes I need to be reminded of how blessed I am. With the thousands of fruits, vegetables, nuts, grains and beans there are to eat and the millions of recipes that can result from their combinations, sitting there with my mouth open for a few seconds is really not much of a hardship.

111
DO THE FDA AND DOA CARE?
JULY OF 1992

At this time, I had a food product that I was selling to many individuals. Some of them encouraged me to get it in stores. I began trying and soon found out that you have to pay a kickback if you want your products in any of the chain stores.

I decided to go with local mom and pop stores instead. to make sure I was not going to get in trouble, I contacted the FDA to find out what the requirements were for the product I had, "Raymond's Gourmet Garlic Butter."

When I asked the man at the FDA what the regulations were for my product, he began to tell me about the size of the label as regards the size of the container, the position of the label, the font size and color of the printing compared to the background color of the label and how many types of labels I needed to have.

I stopped him and asked, "What about the ingredients? to which he responded, "We don't care what is in it as long as it is labeled properly," I asked, "So, as long as I label it properly, I can have nuclear waste in my product"?

He responded, "Technically, That's right"! He then asked me how much of the product I intended to sell. When I described my hopes, he told me that they had no jurisdiction over my business until I sold over one hundred thousand units a year.

Through a little more research, I later found out that, if I did not apply for a license, they would not have any say in my business, no matter how much I sold. Then he asked me what the product was. When I told him, he said that I would have to contact the Department of Agriculture.

I did. When I asked them for their requirements, he asked what my product was. When I gave him the name of my product, he asked, "How much butter is in it?" When I told him, "A little less than half," he said, "then you cannot use butter in the title."

When I asked why, I was told that it had to have more than eighty five percent butter fat in order to use the word butter. When I asked him, "What about Peanut butter, butternut squash, buttermilk, Butterfinger, butter brickle, I can't believe it's not butter, Butterscotch, buttered almond, butter pecan, buttered rum, apple butter and butterflies.

Are you going to tell God that he has to change the name of one of His creations?" He responded, "Well, actually we have no jurisdiction over the use of the word butter. It's just that dairy farmers like us to discourage people from using the word without eighty-five percent of it being butter fat."

I thanked him, hung up and, for ten years, I sold my product all over Westchester County and North. A few weeks after that phone call, I received a letter from the Department of Agriculture (DOA) reminding me that I had no right to use the word butter in my product's name.

I wrote back to them and gave them the following list with the note, "If you can get all those responsible for the below items to take the word butter out of their names, I will do the same. Until then, the name of my product will remain, "Raymond's Gourmet Garlic Butter."

I never received a response from them and I had my product in forty-seven stores for over ten years. I was about to strike a deal with a chain in Manhattan which had thirteen stores when the LORD called us to New Mexico.

Dear Department Of Agriculture:

Here is the list of items that need to remove butter from their names. When this happens, I will change the name of my product.
Peanut butter, 0% butter fat
butternut squash, 0% butter fat
buttermilk, up to 1.5% butter fat
Butterfinger, 0% butter fat

butter brickle, less than 80% butter fat
I can't believe it's not butter, 0% butter fat
Butterscotch, averages less than 80% butter fat
buttered almond, 0% butter fat
butter pecan, 0% butter fat
buttered rum, less than 80% butter fat
apple butter, 0% butter fat
butterfly, 0% butter fat

Mark 11:22 And Jesus answering saith unto them, Have faith in God.

    I am so glad that my faith is in God and not in the institutions erected by man. Though those organizations may have been started with good intentions and goals, they have been corrupted. How can we trust a government entity that cares more about labels that the food behind those labels?
    How can we trust a group that tells us that the food necessary for good health changes every few years? How can we trust people that are willing to lie so that dairy farmers will be appeased? I would rather trust in Jesus whose message has been the same since creation than to believe the messages of man that change with every whim.

112
SO YOU WOULD SEE ME
SEPTEMBER OF 1992

The church my wife and I had been attending had gone from a non-denominational to a Pentecostal to a health and wealth church rather quickly. Since they were now preaching that all Christians are owed healing and prosperity, my ears perked up.

I started to do everything I could to get healed. I went to special meetings, went up for altar calls, prayed specific prayers and tried to believe. I was becoming angry and depressed because after months of doing what I was told, I was still blind.

We had a very dynamic music ministry and I was in charge of the twenty-four-channel sound board. We had drums, congas, flute, saxophone, keyboards, piano and many good vocals. We had a mid-week service on Wednesday evenings.

On this particular evening, I was so angry that I was considering ending my life. I figured that, if you have faith, you would be healed. It is impossible to please God without faith. Being a math professor, I put two and two together and had the answer.

You need faith to please God and to be healed and since I was not healed, I did not please God and should get out of His way. So, I got the sound to where it needed to be and left the building.

I went to the parking lot and, bouncing off the cars as I tried to pace up and down between two rows of vehicles, I yelled, screamed and cursed at God. After about twenty minutes, I finally came to the end of myself and said, "I gave my life to you so, do whatever you want with it."

That is when the LORD spoke to me and said, "I took your eyes so you would see me." I had the talent to become a professional football player. If that had happened, I would have been so involved with the money, drugs, booze and sex that I would have never darkened the door of a church.

I may have enjoyed it for a while but, I never would have been happy or fulfilled. God took my eyesight to keep me from destroying my life here, and the possibility of eternal life later.

John 5:14 Afterward Jesus findeth him in the temple, and said unto him, Behold, thou art made whole: sin no more, lest a worse thing come unto thee.

Sadly, most ministers no longer preach the whole Gospel. God has His reasons for causing hardship, grief and tragedy in our lives. Most Christians do not want to accept that spankings are part of being His child.

113
WRONG SHOULDER!
MARCH OF 1993

Because I find it easier to follow someone if I have my hand on their shoulder many people have commented that they can see how in love I am with my wife. Personally, I would much rather be holding her hand but, since that is not a very good way for her to guide me, I don't hold her hand unless we are in wide open spaces.

I also do not like holding people's upper arm. For some reason most people seem to think that when they offer their upper arm to me, they have to hold it way out in space, like a chicken on a hot day trying to cool off. Even if the person does keep the arm down by their side in a regular posture, they are usually thrown off balance unless they are accustomed to guiding the blind.

Also, when going up or down a stair or moving right or left in traffic, most people use their arm as if I was a marionette attached to their appendage by strings. The most uncomfortable situation is when someone grabs you by the hand and leads you around like a child.

This is made worse only if the person in question is a man with large hands. It is not so bad when a woman grabs my hand, in fact, it is a nice physical touch. I have taken to asking men if I can borrow their elbow because it is easier for me to follow.

Once in a while though, the person is not really listening to you and drags you to your destination as quickly as they can. I have found that holding on to the shoulder gives me much more information than any other way. I am able to remain one step behind them and can better detect when a step is coming and in which direction we are going.

It is much harder for them to move their torso than their arm so you are rarely misdirected by the motion of their body. Since there are many places where very minor adjustments are needed to get through a crowd, it is much easier to pick up on those nuances via the shoulder as well.

The last benefit I can think of at this moment is that holding on to the shoulder puts you a half a person to the side. This gives those who are coming at you less of a target to hit. Since I was a gymnast, I have fairly good balance. Since I played a lot of football, I have a good center of gravity.

Since I have been lifting weights for the last decade and a half, I am not small. All those things added together have caused many people to walk into me and bounce off. Some of them going as far as, or should I say as low as, landing on their but. Once in a while the person bouncing off me would be a high testosterone male who wanted to pick a fight.

Their hormones were usually calmed by my wife's explanation, all except once. We were in a crowd and a half drunk, very loud and very large man bumped into me. He did not say anything but, since we were all traveling in the same direction, I braced myself in case of another contact.

It came. This time, instead of being thrown off step, I was ready. He bounced off me. He got so upset that he grabbed me and threw me up against a vending machine asking what my problem was. I was told later that he had cocked his fist to flatten my face until my wife screamed, "Don't hit him, he's blind."

This piece of information sobered him up enough to look at my dark glasses and the folded cane in my hand. He straightened out my clothing, pulled me away from the machine and apologized profusely. His female companion added her regrets as well.

I thought about giving him a piece of my mind but decided that he had suffered enough embarrassment at the witness of the dozens of people around us that I just let it go. Where was I going with all of this, well, I'll tell you. One day my wife and I were in a store.

She was looking at some clothing. I listened to her comments for a while as she perused the rack in front of us. Then I heard her say, "Okay, we can go." At that I lifted my right hand and placed it on the shoulder in front of me. I felt her body stiffen and I felt her begin to turn around.

At that moment I felt a hand grab my wrist, lift my hand from off her shoulder and place it on another shoulder about two feet away. As this was happening, I heard my wife's voice say, "I'm sorry, my husband is blind." When I heard the response coming from where my hand had just been placed, I understood what had happened.

As I replayed the tape in my head, I realized that my wife's voice had not come from in front of me but off to the side. I had placed my hand on the shoulder of a strange woman. You could hear the nervous tension in her voice as she said, "Oh, that's all right." I have often thought that it would be interesting to hear the thoughts of some of my victims.

1 Corinthians 7:1 Now concerning the things whereof ye wrote unto me: It is good for a man not to touch a woman.

I have suddenly laid hands on many people, all of them by accident. At that, moment, it was anywhere from slightly to extremely embarrassing. Now, however, I can laugh at those situations. I hope those that were touched by me can also see the humor years later.

Though I have accidentally touched many women on places that should only be touched by a lover, it was always in public, no one got hurt and, let us face it, they make great stories and learning experiences.

114
ELIZABETH'S BIRTH
JUNE 15, 1993

At eight minutes to seven in the morning of June 15, 1993 my wife woke me up and said, "I don't know if I am having contractions or an upset stomach." I asked her what it felt like and decided they were contractions, so I started timing them.

The second contraction was at seven o'clock and lasted for forty seconds. The Lamaze instructor said the procedure would last one minute so I thought they could be false labor pains. I kept timing them anyway. The third pain was eight minutes later, the fourth was seven minutes after that, the fifth was five minutes after that, the sixth three minutes after that. They stayed at three minutes for a while so I called the doctor's answering service. The doctor, Dr. Karp, called back exactly three minutes later, approximately 7:32, and told us to come into his office at 8:15.

I don't remember how I knew, but I knew that our friend Paula had taken the day off so I called her to see if she would be able to drive us to the hospital. The answering machine picked up the first time and I left a message. I called back after Jovanna's next contraction and Paula answered the phone this time. She sounded like she had just gotten to sleep ten minutes earlier and was not going to become cognitive for at least an hour. I asked her if she might be able to do us a favor. Her reply assured me that she had not yet been disturbed by this phone call and would probably not remember a thing. When I asked her if she might be able to drive us to the hospital if we needed to go her response was so fast and perky you would thing she had just gotten a cardiac needle full of adrenalin chloride. She said yes, of course and would be to our house at 8:00.

We continued practicing the Lamaze until we arrived at the doctor's office, a half block up the street from our house. Jovanna was examined by the doctor. and we were told she was three centimeters and we had three options.

Go home and do nothing (not likely).

Go to the hospital and hope it wouldn't take all day.

Go for a walk to possibly induce labor even further.

We decided to go for a walk.

It was a nice cool morning so the four of us started out, Paula was with us. We walked for about an hour and ten minutes and were one block from home when a bird messed up Jovanna's hair and shirt. The contractions had been coming every three minutes give or take five seconds and lasting one minute. Jovanna decided to go home to wash her hair. All the while stopping to time, and breathe. Once her hair was clean, curled and blown dry I called the doctor to tell him about the times. He said come back in and we'll see. The second time he examined her she was, "fully five centimeters." It was five minutes until ten o'clock and the doctor asked us what we would like to do. We decided to go to the hospital and he thought that was a good decision. He said we should have the baby by dinner and that he would be to the hospital in about an hour.

We arrived at the hospital at 10:30, we each signed our names once and went into the birthing room. I thought that was too easy so I went out to the desk to find out where the other forms were that would have to be signed. There were none. I would have fainted but my wife needed me so I went back to her. We put down our bags, got out the bottled water we brought with us, got "mommy to be" into a gown and onto the bed.

The contractions were coming on harder and more frequently now. Jovanna said she felt like she needed to have a bowel movement and that it was very uncomfortable. I asked the nurse if she could check and she said "You just got here. It will be a while." I yelled, "I need a doctor, now!" It was 10:50 when she did check and she said, "O my, she's fully dilated, I'll be right back." I found out later that she had gone to see if the doctor was on his way. He was still in his office until the nurse told him the situation, then he was in his car driving 70 miles an hour to get to the hospital, four miles away.

The nurse came back with the staff doctor and when she said, "This baby is ready to come out now," Paula left the room. I knew enough that I could have delivered my daughter by myself but, without the Lamaze classes I would have been completely useless to my wife. I was helping her with massage, relaxation and breathing for about 25 minutes. At this point she had pushed about six times. Finally, our doctor rushed in, threw on a gown, washed his hands, looked at Jovanna and said "Jovanna, you're not supposed to do it this fast." He sat down. My wife pushed two more times and I held my daughter's head as she came out. She stopped pushing so they could suction her nose, mouth and throat, and when that was done, she pushed once more and Elizabeth Joy Whitehead was born at 11:20 am on June 15, 1993.

My wife and I held each other and cried because of the gift the Lord had just given us.

Elizabeth was given to me about three minutes later. I held my daughter for a few minutes while the doctor finished stitching up her mother. She looked into my eyes and I handed her to her mother. She looked into her mother's eyes, closed her own and fell asleep.

My wife didn't have an episiotomy, or an epidural. They barely had time to put the I.V. line in. The doctor said she had a small tear and that it was clean and it was where he would have done the incision anyway.

Ten minutes after the delivery Jovanna asked the doctor if she could go home now. He said that he had no problem with that but the baby would need to stay the night until the pediatrician could give her a clean bill of health. Thirty minutes after the delivery Mommy was up taking a shower.

During our Lamaze classes we were told of the complications that could happen with the baby and a few things to be aware of.

Some of the things that were told to us were:
    misshaped head, maybe like a banana
    yellow color because of jaundice
    blue color because of the need for a transfusion
    red color because of blood pooling
    bowed legs because of the position in the womb

None of these came to pass. She was perfect and pink and only cried for ten seconds when they were removing mucous from her nose.

Elizabeth Joy Whitehead, June 15, 1993: 6lb. 12oz., 21inches, dark brown hair, black eyes.

Sometimes when a person or group of people has to struggle to get another group to treat them fairly, they end up with a persecution complex. Once I started losing my sight, I had to struggle to be treated fairly. I never wanted any special rights or treatment, I just wanted the right to try and not to be shut out just because someone else could not envision how I would accomplish the task.

I thought that I was being ill treated during our hospital stay because of some of their rules. In retrospect I realize that I still had some persecution complex molecules floating around in me. When the doctor said I could not deliver my own baby, I thought he figured I would drop her. When they would not allow us to go home right away, I thought it was because they figured I was not capable of taking care of my wife and new child. When they gave me a hard time about staying with my wife all night, I figured they thought they would have to look after me as well. When they gave us a hard time about keeping Elizabeth in the room with us over night, it seemed that they did not trust me.

Well, I know the truth now. Hospitals think that any child in their care belongs to them until they decide that they will let you take the baby home. This and many other reasons prompted my wife to opt for a home birth for our next child. I had wanted to do that for our first but, Jovanna was not yet comfortable with that idea and since she had to do the carrying and most of the work, she should get to choose the place.

I am now over my persecution complex and, though there are still plenty of people that are ignorant of the needs of the disable or uncomfortable interacting with us, I now use it as an opportunity to educate and remove barriers.

1 Timothy 2:15 Notwithstanding she shall be saved in childbearing, if they continue in faith and charity and holiness with sobriety.

Since I began studying medicine at the age of fourteen, studied chiropractic's and massage for two years as an apprentice and began learning all I could about diet and exercise starting at twenty-six, I would love to say that I was responsible for the quick delivery.

I had a friend named Cia who rode horseback until the day before her 30-minute labor. I found out how important exercise is and how it was so contrary to the doctors prescribing bed rest until after the birth. Because of these things, I put Jovanna on a walking regiment the moment we found out we were pregnant.

Though these are all good things, God is ultimately in control.

115
THAT'LL LEARN YA DERN YA
October of 1994

When I was a teen, I was above average in height and I could jump with the best of them. These two attributes gave me an idea one day. While walking down the street with my family, I began to skip. As I approached the corner, I got close to the STOP sign.

I made one final leap, got my head as close to the sign as possible and hit it with my hand. I then fell to the ground holding my head and everyone came rushing to my side. When I got up unharmed, I thought I had just gone through the gauntlet because of all the slaps and punches I received due to my prank.

I would do this trick each time there was a new victim nearby. I would do it over and over again just to amuse myself. I would also do this stunt whenever there was a new person walking with us or if I was with friends that did not know the trick. Over the years I got varied reactions depending upon how attentive the victim was.

That was the one thing you could not control, how well they were watching you. Once I had lost a sufficient amount of sight to make it impossible to do the trick anymore, I forgot about it. That is until I moved to Thirty-Four Lincoln Place.

The apartment was over a two-car garage. There were thirteen steps, eight up, one to the left and four more up. There was an overhang that was just low enough that if you were not careful you could bang your head on. Every once in a while, I would have someone over that did not know about my trick.

As they were leaving, I would go ahead of them down the stairs making it look like I was being a good host. As I quickly descended the stairs I would smack my hand on the overhang, fall back and slide down the stairs. As with the trick with the sign, most people fell for it, and as with the sign, I did not know where they were looking when I executed the gag.

Even though I tried to make it look like an accident by holding my hand to my head after slapping the wall, some did not buy it. One person that did buy it was my wife. I married the most wonderful woman in the world in April of 1992. Sometime after that I decided to play the gag on her.

She was so sweet and caring that I felt guilty after doing it because she was so concerned. I guess that she had become hypersensitive since the incident in the story, "That Rings a Bell." Well, a few months later I tried the trick on my friend Raj. He fell for it but, by now my lovely bride knew what was up.

She did not give me away but she did let the victims know a little sooner than I would have that I was okay. I kept practicing my deception, even when I was alone. One day my wife and I were headed out the door. I decided to practice my trick. This time I miscalculated and actually hit my head on the overhang.

As I slid down the stairs, I held my head and groaned in pain. Have you ever heard the story of the boy who cried wolf? Well, my bride had. She thought I was just playing again. That is until she got to the bottom of the stairs and saw the mark on my forehead. You know, I do not think I ever tried that gag again. As my father would say, "That'll learn ya dern ya."

Proverbs 10:23 It is as sport to a fool to do mischief: but a man of understanding hath wisdom.

Yes, I have been called a fool more than once and by more than one person. In this instance, I would agree. However, once the headache went away, I was able to put the slight discomfort on one side of a scale and the fun others had at my expense, once they learned I was not harmed on the other side.

There was no contest. I love making people laugh which is why I was class clown from third grade through college. My wife has even said that it was my sense of humor that attracted her to me. So, I will keep on, as my wife sometimes says, "Trying to be funny."

116
JOSHUA'S BIRTH
MAY 18 OF 1995

My wife was about two months pregnant when we found out that our next child was on the way. That gave us about seven months to prepare but I have to say that we did not do much in the way of preparation until the day before my son arrived.

The LORD is so good and here is one of His goodnesses toward us. As they say, a child can come two weeks earlier or later than the "due date." We were only about twenty-five percent ready on the sixteenth. We needed to do laundry so that we would have towels, wash cloths and clothing to dress our new child in, and we didn't have anything cleaned yet.

We had at least ten receiving blankets still in the packages and finally washed them on the seventeenth. That day we needed to switch the tables on the sides of the bed because Jovanna and I were going to switch sides to make nursing easier for her and to make the basinet more accessible.

I needed to go through my daughter's toys and pack the ones she didn't use so there would be enough room in the living room to have the birth. We had to pack a bag for her so she could go with our friends for the day. There were many other things we did at the last minute but, I'm sure you get the picture.

If these things had not been done it would have been very difficult and somewhat dangerous for my wife and the coming baby. What was mentioned above plus much more was done the day before or while Jovanna was in labor.

I was selling a gourmet garlic butter and had a lot of work to do to fill some orders. When the product was done I had to do some work on my computer. When that was done I had to go down to my garage to box the orders going out the next day. When I was done with that I listened to my Bible until I started dozing off.

I went to the bathroom and as I was headed to bed my wife was entering the bathroom. She said that she felt funny and after talking with her for a minute, we decided that she was okay and I went to bed. It was five minutes before one in the morning.

At one o'clock Jovanna called to me from the bathroom saying that she was bleeding a little. She wanted me to call the midwife, so I did. After talking with her for a few minutes they decided to wait a while to see what would happen. Jovanna had me hang the phone up and told me to go back to bed. It was quarter after one.

At one sixteen she called me back to the bathroom and said that she thought she was having contractions. She told me to lay down while she called the midwife again. Though I had been exhausted when I first climbed into bed, I now was unable to think of sleep while I listened to Jovanna's half of the conversation.

At the conclusion of the conversation at twenty after one, I realized that I had better get up and start making the final preparations. Since our first child came in only four and a half hours, and the second one is usually quicker, I knew that I did not have a lot of time to play with.

Since I had never felt it necessary to be quiet around children that are trying to sleep, Elizabeth had no problem sleeping with a lot of noise around her. Even after the lights started going on in the apartment, two phone consultations and our conversations, she was still sound asleep.

I put water to boil, got the receiving blankets and washed clothing out, took the coffee table down to the garage, got out the blanket and blue pads, got out the birthing kit, turned the heat up to eighty-five degrees and got Elizabeth's bottles ready.

In between getting her own clothing ready and getting Elizabeth's clothing ready, my wife would go to the bathroom. At one fifty-five we called our friend who said she would come over and take Elizabeth for the day. Her husband answered the phone and after telling him that we needed his wife to come over now, he asked, "Is this real?" After assuring him that it was indeed the real thing, he said that his wife would be right over.

Jovanna had been in the bathroom and was headed into the living room to lie on the blanket I had prepared for her when she did a one-eighty. She went back into the bathroom thinking that she had to have a bowel movement and that is when I realized that she was in active labor. The same thing had happened with our daughter's birth.

She called to me from the bathroom, "Sweetheart, the baby is coming!" I have to give her a lot of credit for not panicking. Though there was an urgency in her voice I found out later that it was only because she did not want to have our baby in the toilet.

I walked into the bathroom and looked between her legs and saw a dark spot. Thinking that it might be the baby's head, I put my hand there to catch it. That is when I realized that it was the sack filling with fluid. I picked up my wife and carried her into the living room. I placed her on the blanket and reached between her legs again. It was two thirteen.

In my earlier preparations I had unlocked the front door so our friend could just come in. As she knocked and opened the door, I took the sack between my fingers and tore it open. Our friend was walking up the stairs. As I put my fingers inside, I felt my child's head coming out.

The baby was face up and since I was told in Lamaze class that the child should be born face down or sideways, I placed my finger under the arm to twist the child around at the same time telling my wife to push. That was the first and only push. My son shot out like a cannon ball just as our friend walked into the living room to see it. It was two-fourteen.

I flipped him over and cleaned out his nose and mouth and he started to breathe. There wasn't much crying, just wonderful baby noises. I placed him on mommy's chest and covered them both. Our friend was a great help in making mommy comfortable and getting me the things we needed.

Since Elizabeth was still sleeping, we decided to let her sleep and have our friend come back late morning to take her for the day. The midwives showed up about forty minutes after the delivery. I clamped off the cord and cut it. Then I helped my wife pass the placenta.

One of the midwives said it was one of the healthiest placentas she had ever seen. When she asked us if we wanted to save it, we asked what for. I was surprised to learn the things people do with it. Some plant a new tree with it and some even eat it. No thanks.

Jovanna wanted me to call our mothers so, I called her's first.

Then I called my mother at work. When she got on the phone I said, "congratulations grandma." She let out a shriek and then asked me what it was so I said, "It's a baby." She said, "I know that, you fool, is it a boy or girl?" When I told her I didn't know, she repeated that to her co-workers. They all had a good laugh after their initial gasp of disbelief. I told her that whatever sex my child was, he or she was going to be that forever and there was no sense in making the baby uncomfortable so we could find out something that was not that important.

We spent the 20-30 minutes after the delivery praising and thanking the Lord because he answered our prayers. Other than the usual prayers for a healthy baby and a quick, easy and painless delivery, I prayed that the Lord would let me deliver my child. It wasn't until almost an hour later that I found out that my prayers for a boy had also been answered.

While the midwives were cleaning the kitchen sink getting ready for Joshua's first bath, one of them turned to me and said, "So, you got your wish after all." When Jovanna probed into the meaning of that statement she found out that the midwives and I had planned all along that, even if they had made it there in time, I was going to, "catch the baby," instead of them.

I do not know which was more of a shock to my wife, finding out our conspiracy or finding out that I had prayed for noisy children. I guess I had forgotten to share both of those with her.

My wife was so amazing through the whole thing but it wasn't until after the birth that I found out why. Try to imagine, if you can, being in the following situation. You are minutes from giving birth, your midwives are not going to make it in time, your husband is blind and has never delivered a baby before. Do you think you would have just cause to be slightly nervous? The Lord had spoken to Jovanna in a dream the night before, telling her that the midwives would not be there and that she would give birth at home.

Joshua Daniel Whitehead, May 18th 1995 at 1:14 am, 9lbs 4oz and 21 inches.

1 Samuel 1: 27 For this child I prayed; and the LORD hath given me my petition which I asked of him:

117
FIVE LOAVES AND TWO FISH
JULY OF 1995

After church one day a friend, Benjamin, and I decided to do what we could for the homeless people living in and around Central Park in New York City. We would gather blankets, clothing, food and Bibles. Then, on Wednesday evening after dinner, he and I would go down to the city. He drove.

Once we got there, we would shlep our stuff around looking for people in need. I thought we would spend most of our time looking around to find someone to bless if we found anyone at all. Boy what an education I received. It was much easier to find homeless people than I would have imagined.

It seemed that those who were on the outskirts of the park, on benches or steps, and were alone did not want our help. Those that were in groups inside the park graciously accepted our help. We would let them go through the clothing we had. Then we would give them the food we had.

Finally, we would talk to them about Heaven and Hell and where they were going. As I said before, it was an eye opener. Pardon the pun. I knew my family was poor growing up but, thankfully we did not have to live on the streets. When it was time to go, I asked the men, there were almost never any homeless women to be found, what they would like the next time we came.

It has always been sad for me to know that the majority of Christians are fat, dumb and lazy and are happy being so. The true followers of Jesus Christ should be doing much more for the lost, hurt and dying of this world than they are. Rather than live up to the great commission, we have allowed the government to take over our responsibilities and to kick God out of public life.

When Jesus came to Earth he provided the needs of the people before preaching the truth. It is a lot easier to listen when you are fed and clothed and healed. It was not easy and it was not convenient but, we knew that the LORD wanted us to be there for the homeless.

One Wednesday evening I was a bit discouraged and really did not want to go but, I knew it was the LORD's will so, I went. When Benjamin arrived, he had several bags of donated clothing and a box. This cheered me up a little and we went to find the men. They were so happy to see us and especially with so many bags.

We were told by the donator that all of the clothing was men's garments. We did not even think to check. When the men started to go through the bags, we realized that we had almost nothing they could use. It was almost completely women's clothing. We gave them the food we had and talked for a while. They were so gracious even in their disappointment.

When we got up to leave, several of them offered to help us carry the bags back to our car. We accepted the help of one of the men because it was a long distance and we figured he could handle it. The only reason, or so I thought, that we accepted the one man's help was because he insisted so vehemently.

Once we loaded the car back up, I turned to the gentleman and asked what I could bring for him next week. He said that he could really use some socks. I had just gotten some socks as a gift and, since I had taken a shower before heading for the city, I sheepishly offered him mine. I told him that they were very nearly clean since I had showered only a few hours ago.

He accepted the gift and I got back in the car with my feet in my sneakers, no socks. Normally I hate the feeling of any footwear against my peds without having socks on but, this night, it was a wonderful feeling because it was a slight sacrifice that blessed someone else.

My wife had left the bakery that we had both been working for and was now working for a pastry place in Nyack. Her boss would let her take home food that they were not going to be able to sell the next day and allow me to give it to the homeless. It was a tremendous treat for the men to have such fine gourmet desserts and we enjoyed their pleasure.

Normally my wife would have a large bag for us but on this particular night, all she had was a small bag of bread. She told me that she had left it in the car and I retrieve it when Benjamin picked me up.

He felt like going to the store to get some more things for the men since we had such slim pickings and the general manager of the Chilmark had asked us to stop by before going to the city each week. We had been in that store a few weeks earlier purchasing stuff for the homeless. Somehow, he found out and began putting things aside for us to take.

When we arrived, the manager had been called away on an emergency and had not been able to leave anything for us. When we realized that there was not much we could get because neither of us had much money. As we were about to leave, we saw a sign for tuna on sale. We had only enough money to purchase two cans so, we did and then we drove to the City.

Upon arriving I mentioned to Benjamin that it probably was not wise to have purchased food in cans since they probably did not have an opener. We took them anyway, with the bread, and sought our friends. We were unable to find them that night so we looked for other people to bless.

We found a group of men under a bridge and when we asked them if any of them had a can opener, I was surprise to find out that many of them did. We handed them the cans and as we pulled out the bread, we discovered that there were five loaves. I immediately thought of the story where Jesus broke the five loaves and two fish and was very excited.

We stayed with them and though we did not bless the bread and give it to any disciples, it turned out to be enough for the men present to be satiated. On the drive home I was brought to tears by the symbolism of what had just happened. I wish I could have seen their faces each time we blessed homeless people. I was, however, able to hear the gratefulness in their voices.

I have been given the opportunity to bless many people since then but, I do not think that anything can come close to what my friend and I did for a few months for a few men in Central Park.

Luke 12:28 If then God so clothe the grass, which is to day in the field, and tomorrow is cast into the oven; how much more will he clothe you, O ye of little faith?

One of the greatest lessons I gained during that time was the faith of those we thought we were ministering to. It turns out that they gave me much more than I gave them.

118
IS ANYONE AWAKE?
NOVEMBER OF 1995

Since June 15th, 1992 I have tried to work from home. By the second half of 1995 it was becoming difficult to make ends meet with the little amount of work I could muster up. I applied for a job as a telemarketer and was accepted. Within weeks I became one of the top three telemarketers in the company.

Every morning we would have a meeting in the lunch room that would take about forty-five minutes, and then we would be off and dialing. Though I have had telemarketing jobs in the past that targeted Joe citizen, this job was exclusively to business owners. Because of my lack of vision, the company had to make a few alterations, but nothing that cost them a dime.

Because I had to have a special computer with a giant screen, I had to have a desk that was exclusively mine. Most of the desks in the office were used by at least two people each week. Because of the lighting situation I needed, I ended up at the desk outside the supervisor's office since that was the most dimly lighted area.

There were a few people that worked full time but most of my co-workers were part time. Within a few weeks I had made many contacts and a few friends. One morning, about half an hour after my first phone call, my boss came up to me to tell me that she was ready for the meeting. She was standing on my right perpendicular to me and made the announcement as I hung up the phone.

I got up and went into the lunch room. It was a wide-open space with six tables and a bunch of chairs. The room was very bright and there were no other items in the room except the telemarketers. After a forty-five-minute meeting we were dismissed and all went back to our desks, passing each other in the room and in the hall.

A few minutes later one of my co-workers came to me asking a question. Several minutes later another one came asking another question. They had both stood in the same place as my boss, but no one said a word about my strange attire.

When I was a child, it was difficult for my mother to break me of the habit of wiping my mouth on my sleeves. As gross as it may sound, I also used to wipe my nose on my sleeves. Well, I was finally broken of these habits. Sometimes people thought that I had continued doing it but, what I was actually doing was using my sleeve to scratch my face or ear.

I had such an itch moments after the second co-worker left my side. As I lifted my shoulder to scratch my cheek, I felt something strange. I reached up to find a burping towel. I left it there and walked into my boss' office. When she got off the phone I asked her, pointing to the towel, what is this?

She said that it looked like a towel. I then asked if she had seen it on my shoulder while I was sitting at my desk or in the meeting. She replied in the affirmative. I asked why she did not tell me and she gave me an answer that infuriates me, "I don't know." I then walked to the desks of each of the co-workers that had come questioning me and asked them the same questions.

It must have been a conspiracy because they each gave me the same answer my boss had. I then asked them that if my zipper had been down would they have told me. They said probably. I went back to my desk, removed the towel and folded it. After placing it in my brief case I went back to work.

I had been holding my son before leaving for work and had the burping towel on my right shoulder to prevent messing up my shirt with slobber or other projectiles. When I arrived home, I told my beloved what had happened and we both had a good laugh.

When I went to work the next morning, it was almost as if I had been caught in a time warp. My boss came up to me at my desk, other workers came up to me, we went into our meeting and later, I discovered a towel on my shoulder again. I felt a little stupid at first but decided that these people needed an education. I went into my boss' office again and again received the same answer. I went to my co-workers and, if I could see well enough I am sure that I would have gotten blank stares.

I just walked away shaking my head and folding the towel. For some reason, over the next few weeks I found myself checking my shoulders and my zipper enough to have been considered compulsive.

Isaiah 42:20 Seeing many things, but thou observest not; opening the ears, but he heareth not.

Many of us go through life seeing things but not really paying attention to them or to what they might mean. If something different happens to me once, I try to pay attention to what it might indicate. If it happens twice or more, I feel like I have been jolted awake.

119
BLIND AS A BAT
MARCH OF 1996

Because of the nature of the telemarketing business, you need a trainer. Many come through the revolving door but few stay. It is the trainer's job to make the task seem as easy as possible. Thus E.J., our trainer, would bring people to hear my shpiel. I was told that it was because I was one of the top three telemarketers in the company.

I believe that was part of it but, I think that the fact that I was also mostly blind had something to do with it. I do not think that anyone ever said it but I do believe that it was a subliminal message that, 'If he can do it, you can do it too'. I think it was a great motivator.

There was at least one person that listened to me, took the job and, became pretty good at it. I was able to hear her on the phone and it used to make me laugh because she didn't use anything she could have heard from me. She stuck to the script using a monotone and, if the person on the other end interrupted her, she would go back to the beginning of the sentence and start over.

For her it was like a wrestling match and I think that many of her appointments were granted her in the spirit of surrender. Either give this girl an appointment or I will never get off the phone.

E.J had brought someone to my desk to listen to me. I needed to take a bathroom break at that very moment. Since she had been placed directly to my right, I had difficulty getting past her. I guess that is why the next day, E.J. placed the person a little further back. She then mentioned to the person my visual limitation by using political correctness. In a lower than conversational voice she said, "He's visually challenged."

I went to E.J. later and asked her to not be so P.C. She agreed and the day went on with no further incident. The next day she brought another candidate to my desk. She placed this one about six inches further back than the last one and said in a quieter voice than last time, "He's visually challenged." I grumbled, "E J," and she apologized while sheepishly retreating.

The next day I was subjected to another trainee. This one was placed even further back and given the same instructions. in a whisper that even I would probably not have heard if I had not known what was coming, E.J. repeated her P.C. warning.

That was it! I had all I could stand so, in a voice loud enough for everyone in the office to hear I said, "E.J., I'm not visually CHALLENGED, I'M BLIND AS A BAT!" to my delight the whole office erupted in laughter and she never used that phrase again.

Acts 24:16 And herein do I exercise myself, to have always a conscience void of offence toward God, and toward men.

Obviously, E. J. did not heed the advice in this verse. However, rather than get upset about her ignoring me, I chose to make light of it and brought everyone around us a moment of happiness.

120
WHEN LET GO DOES NOT MEAN, "LET GO!"
April of 1996

I love comparing myself to others if they are famous. For instance, Albert Einstein and I failed the second grade twice. Jack Lalanne and I were both so sick until the age of 12 that we spent a lot of time in bed recovering from asthma and wishing we could be out there with the other youngsters playing.

Jack and I also got so sick-and-tired of being sick-and-tired that we started exercising to build strength and stamina. On his 70th birthday, he pulled 70 people in 70 boats over one mile in Long Beach Harbor. I do not know if I could do that but, who knows as I am only 63 as I write this.

Friends of ours were moving from an apartment that had a flight of stairs to the second floor that had no twists or turns. There must have been twenty or more stairs. We had taken many things down that flight of stairs including a dryer.

When it came time to move the washing machine down, I chose the bottom as I had already moved over seventy-five families. There were some unforeseen challenges ahead though. The first of which is the fact that a washer holds several gallons of water in it when it is supposedly empty.

The second is that it is much heavier than a dryer because it needs a larger motor and stronger parts as it tries to move thirty gallons of water filled with clothing in circles. The third problem had nothing to do with the machine itself. It concerned the man it belonged to.

Olivier was born and raised in France so was unfamiliar with some of the colloquialisms around the moving trade in the United States of America. By this time, I had moved five pianos, dozens of large pieces of furniture, over a dozen convertible couches and hundreds of boxes.

I had moved people in cars, vans, pickup trucks, moving vans and even twice using a forty-five-foot tractor trailer. The moves ran the gamut from not one thing packed because of the space they were going to have in the trailer to people that were packed, organized and ready before I arrived.

I bet you can guess which I prefer. Well, my friend and his family were packed and ready. However, I was not ready for him. We got the washer to the top of the steps, decided that I would take the bottom because I lifted weights and got myself in position.

We scooted the machine to the edge of the first step, tilted it backward, moved the feet over the precipice of the first step and leaned it back far enough to begin sliding down the stairs on its smooth side.

It was all going great until I made the mistake of telling Olivier to let go. Now, in the jargon used by those of us that move a lot of friends and family, let go does not mean take your hands off, nor does it mean to release ninety-five percent of the restraint you have been holding the machine back with.

It means that you can now allow the item to gently and slowly begin its descent. What did my friend do? He took his hands off the washer and because it was so heavy and I was not expecting that much weight, I had to run backward as fast as possible while not allowing the machine to run me over.

I did not get hurt and the washer did not even get a scratch. However, it did take a few minutes to catch my breath and allow my heart to calm down. Since the machine and I arrived at the bottom with no damage to either, I did think it was funny.

Moments later, however, I did want to fall on the floor in a fit of laughter as my friend asked me, "Why did you run down the stairs so fast?"

Psalms 17:5 Hold up my goings in thy paths, that my footsteps slip not.

One of the things that I rarely forgot to do before starting any move was to pray. Yes, I had experience, yes, I had strength and yes, I had speed. All those things were important and played a small part in my safety. However, the most important thing I had was a Father in Heaven caring for my needs.

121
BE THAT WAY
APRIL OF 1996

This is somewhat like the story "Uncommon Sense." My wife and I were attending a church in the Greenberg area of Westchester County, New York. The church was very sound when I first started attending and for about a year and a half after I surrendered my life to the LORD Jesus Christ.

    I had, as far as I could remember, always been a pessimist. I had developed a philosophy around pessimism that proved it was a good thing. You see, if you are an optimist and something goes wrong, you have a letdown. If it goes right, well, you figured it would so it is not a surprise nor is it as unpleasant.

    On the other hand, if you think something will go wrong and it does, you are prepared for it. If it goes right, it is a great surprise. Because of this attitude I was constantly on the lookout for the pastor to preach something wrong.

    One day it happened. I decided to write a letter questioning the teaching and give it to the pastor. I was waiting to hand it to him the following Thursday evening after service when his wife approached me. After exchanging pleasantries, I asked her if she would give the letter to him for me.

    She said she would and asked if she should read it as well. I told her that she could if she wanted. The following Sunday I asked her if she had read and delivered it. She said that she had read it but was not going to give it to her husband because she thought it would hurt him. When I explained that all I wanted was to have something he taught cleared up through the Bible, she still refused.

Months went by and things got worse. The church turned into a faith movement, health and wealth church. After another year and a half of not getting anywhere I left to find another church. Once I did my wife joined me. Since we had been in that church for about five years, everyone knew me and most of the time you did not shake hands, you hugged.

Now that we were in a new place, no one knew us and many people began to get insulted by my behavior. They would come up to me and as they introduced themselves, they would put out their hand. I would just stand there and not flinch. They would then cop an attitude and walk away. I guess many of those people were related to the bus driver in the story, "How I met Jovanna."

Though I was standing there with dark glasses on and a white cane in my hand, they just could not figure out that I could not see their hand. At one point I took to extending my hand to everyone I was introduced to. That did not work, instead, it led to more embarrassing moments. Most of the time when my hand was not grasped, it would just hang out there waving in the breeze or I would poke someone.

Whenever my wife was near, she would grab me by the wrist and place my hand in the one offered by the here to fore, stranger. There was one person who took a perverse delight in watching me struggle with this and observing the reactions of the person in front of me. After they walked away, he would approach them and explain that the reason I did not offer my hand was that I was blind and did not see theirs. He would then come over to me and with a twinkle in his voice, tell me what had just happened.

Even when people realized that my blindness would prevent me from knowing that they had proffered their hand, they did not know how to get around it. Maybe two percent of the people I have met have been creative enough to do something about it. One man said, "I want to shake your hand." That was not at all ambiguous.

A few people just reached down to my hand, dangling at my side, placed theirs in it and shook. Still others would say, "I have my hand out." Again, not hard to understand. But, for some reason I will, every once in a while, come across someone that does not realize that sticking their hand out a few inches from a blind man's belly will do no good.

Isaiah 26:11 LORD, when thy hand is lifted up, they will not see: but they shall see, and be ashamed for their envy at the people; yea, the fire of thine enemies shall devour them.

First, the above verse says that they will not see. That is, they choose to not see. The verse follows with the understanding that, though they do not want to recognize God, in the end, they will and will not be happy about it.

Second, the people that are not noticing that I am blind are just unobservant and are misunderstanding the circumstance.

Third, if the LORD is being ignored on purpose, who am I to get offended when people ignore my blindness accidentally?

122
CATCH ME IF YOU CAN
JUNE 28, 1996

At the time of this story, my daughter Elizabeth was three years old. She loved to run around everywhere but her favorite place to run around in was the grocery store. The isles were long and there were lots of them. Also, since my wife and I did not like to shop in crowds, we would try to go at off times.

Elizabeth had been lost for about ten minutes in a warehouse store once and, though she did not seem much effected by the experience, she also did not like to be far from us. When we finally found her on that terrible day when my heart was in my throat, she was not even upset.

It was a few months before Elizabeth's birthday. We were shopping at Sam's Club. Jovanna wanted to go a few isles away to look for something. Elizabeth asked if she could go with Mommy a moment after my wife started walking away. I took her out of the cart and let her down to catch up with Mommy.

About five minutes later my wife came back and as she approached me, she asked, "Where is Elizabeth?" When I told her that I had let Elizabeth down to catch up with her she told me that she hadn't seen her since she left her with me in the basket.

Though we were Christians and believed in God's provision and protection, there was no stopping all the horrible scenarios from crossing our minds or, at least my mind. Jovanna went to the courtesy counter to have them be on the lookout and to make an announcement. A few minutes later a woman found her playing in one of the isles and brought her to us.

What a relief it was to have her back again unharmed. It was the worst feeling I had ever had because all I could do was stand there and wait. Since I could only see shadows by this time, I could not even go from isle to isle calling her name.

Now, a few months later, she likes to run down the aisle and run back to us jumping into our arms. She had done this a few times and then we put her in the basket. Not in the seat part but in the grocery part, where she could play with the food we were going to purchase.

I usually just hung on to the basket while my wife pulled it along. Once it got too heavy for her to pull, I would push it while she steered. I always had an awful feeling that she would forget to tell me to stop and I would run over her ankle. I know how painful it can be to have someone run into you with a full basket as it has happened to me many times.

I was not paying attention because Jovanna did not have any questions for me to answer. We were in one isle for a long time and Elizabeth asked Mommy if she could get down. I heard the question but I did not here the answer. Since she asked her mother, I assumed that Jovanna took her out. A few moments later I saw a little figure running toward me.

I figured that Jovanna had let Elizabeth down and that she had resumed her game of vaulting into my arms. I moved a little away from the basket, bent down a little and put my arms out toward the figure approaching me. Suddenly it stopped moving, turned and ran in the other direction. For a split second I thought Elizabeth had decided to play a new game. Then I heard my wife say, "That wasn't our daughter."

I guess my brain was not working too fast that day because I had not processed what my wife had just said. Then I heard my daughter's voice coming from within the basket and realized what was said and what had just happened. I fully expected to get arrested for attempted kidnapping at any moment, but I did not.

Psalms 127:3 Lo, children are an heritage of the LORD: and the fruit of the womb is his reward.

Children are such a blessing if you raise them properly. Unfortunately, most people seem to regard their offspring as a burden. Though we have had some difficult times over the years, I would not have wanted to be without them. Thank you LORD for blessing me with three of them.

123
THAT LAST STEP WAS A DOOZY
JULY OF 1996

By this time I had been in my church for five years and had helped over thirty-eight families move. That's right, a blind man moving heavy boxes and furniture. I love physical work. Anyway, it was now my turn.

The pastor made an announcement the Sunday before that, since I had helped move so many people in our church, he expected to see the whole church come out to help my family. Well, that did not happen but, we did have five people come to help.

Fortunately, our move was not very hard because it was only two houses to the right. We were moving from a one bedroom one bath apartment of about five hundred square feet to a three bedroom three and a half bath house of about four thousand square feet.

Granted that in order to make the mortgage payments we had to rent the three bedrooms out but, that was not a problem because the basement was finished with its own full bath. In addition, we had a lot of great experiences hosting students from all over the world from a few weeks to nine months at a time.

They would come to learn English as a second language. When we moved into the house there was a wall unit in the garage that a friend of the owners found at the side of the road and stored in the garage. She was going to take it but had changed her mind. There was another wall unit in the basement.

My wife wanted the one in the basement moved to one of the bed rooms. She also wanted the one in the garage to go into the living room. From the garage to the living room was not a problem. We did that ourselves and my sweetheart was very pleased with the way it looked.

The one from the basement to the second floor was more of a challenge. We had to take it out through the back patio sliding glass doors, through the back yard, up two cement steps and along the side of the house which sloped upward.

My dearest friend at the time, Frank, agreed to help me move it from the basement to the garage where I could have someone else help me move it to the second floor later if I decided to not take it apart and do it piece by piece myself.

We had only been in the house a short time so, I did not have a chance to get the lay of the land. Frank and I navigated the basement, patio, yard, steps, and were on our way along the side of the house when something startling happened. I was walking backward and Frank was walking forward, giving me directions.

I thought it would be a little easier for me if I looped my left arm through the unit and turned to face the same direction as Frank, I started to turn around and I found myself falling. I had no idea what was happening when all of a sudden I was on my back with the wall unit on my chest.

It turns out that between my house and the neighbor to the right there was a four-foot wall shored up with railroad ties. I did not know that was there and frank could not see how close to it I was with the wall unit in his face. I did not get hurt but it did feel like I had just received a quart of espresso through an IV.

Actually, I only use the espresso metaphor to help you understand how you would have felt. Caffeine makes me go to sleep, just another facet of my weirdness. The wall unit became a little looser but, there was no damage to it. We did finally get it into the house.

We lived in that house for six years and five days and I never fell off that wall again. A few others did though which made me feel better about my "trip."

Deuteronomy 22:8 When thou buildest a new house, then thou shalt make a battlement for thy roof, that thou bring not blood upon thine house, if any man fall from thence.

Here in Santa Fe, New Mexico, most of the homes have flat roofs and have a parapet, two and a half feet high to keep people from falling off the roof. Battlement sounds military to me but is the same idea. Too bad that the builder did not make a railing along the railroad ties.

124
SORRY IS NOT ENOUGH
April of 1998

Our church had instituted a program before Easter for all the children. The main focus was prayer. We had a list of all the youngsters that came to our services or that attended our mid-week program for the neighborhood called, "Kid's Club."

It allowed the parents to have a safe, free and fun place for their children to be for a couple hours on Wednesdays after dinner. That way they could go out on a date or just have peace for a while. The stated purpose of the Easter program was to pray for the children at least once a week.

If you were so moved, you could send small gifts like stickers or notes of encouragement to them as well. The program was voluntary and most of our adults chose at least one child. Our son was getting something every week but, our daughter had not received anything.

The program was coming to an end and, all the children were asked to come to our Easter service where their "Prayer Buddy" would be revealed. I was an elder in our church and was having an elder/deacon meeting at our home. Almost everyone was present and I was talking with my wife in the kitchen doorway.

She said that something had arrived for Joshua that day and I made a very foolish comment just as someone was passing by. The comment was, "Joshua's buddy is doing a great job but, I wonder what is wrong with Elizabeth's buddy?"

We had our meeting and, when It was done, my wife told me that the person that was passing as I made my rude comment was Elizabeth's buddy. I felt bad and was about to call her to apologize when I realized that my comment was in front of people so, my apology needed to be in front of those same people.

At our service that Sunday, when it was time for the offering, I walked up to our pastor, handed him my check, turned to the congregation and explained what I had done. I then asked Elizabeth's buddy to come forward. I apologized, asked for forgiveness and received it.

When my children were young, I made it a point to have them face the person they had wronged, look into their eyes, say they were sorry and ask for a pardon. How could I do less?

Matthew 5:23 Therefore if thou bring thy gift to the altar, and there rememberest that thy brother hath ought against thee; 24 Leave there thy gift before the altar, and go thy way; first be reconciled to thy brother, and then come and offer thy gift.

I handed the pastor my tithe check because he represented the altar. Elizabeth's buddy had something against me as I hurt her feelings because I had forgotten that the main thrust of the program was prayer and she had been faithful to that.

After receiving her forgiveness, I took my check from the pastor and placed it in the basket. Please do not misunderstand the following. Many in our church came to me after the service and during the next week to thank me for what I did and how I did it.

They all basically said that they more fully understood that scripture because of it. All I did was carry out God's instructions to the best of my ability. He allowed me to screw up because He knew that I would obey his Word. Because of that obedience, many were blessed.

125
FLUSHING THE MANUAL
JUNE OF 1998

In 1996, the church we had been attending for the last four-and-a-half years had gone from nondenominational to Pentecostal to health and wealth in that short time. When I started to realize that much of what was being preached did not match the Bible, I confronted the pastor. After three months of meeting every Saturday, he cut me off because I refused to submit to his crazy teachings.

I started meeting with the elders until he told them to not meet with me either. We ended up going to a Christian Missionary Alliance church which was only two blocks from our home. That was wonderful because I loved to walk to church with my children.

After a year in Grace Alliance church, I was asked to serve as a deacon. A year later I was put up as an elder but was not appointed by the membership. The following year, I was. At the time of this story, there was going to be a leadership conference in Philadelphia which our pastor wanted to attend. He wanted his two elders to go with him.

As we walked in, we were each given an agenda which was about 30 pages and was about letter sized. Because I had to have one hand on my cane and the other on the shoulder of the person guiding me, I stuffed the book in my belt behind my shirt. Before going to our seats, I decided to visit the bathroom.

I had forgotten that the book was hiding under my shirt so, when I pulled my pants down to use the bathroom, it slipped into the toilet without my realizing it. Now, many people have made fun of me because I sit down to pee, "like a girl."

I had been completely blind now for two years and did not like making a mess. So, rather than possibly missing the water, hitting the toilet seat or even getting my pant leg wet, I sat down. Well, I had one of the largest bowel movements ever because of the long car ride. When I tried to flush the toilet, it would not flush.

I was afraid that I had clogged the throne so, I asked my pastor to check it for me. When he did, he let me know that the book had been causing the blockage and, once removed, the toilet worked fine. I had no book though and they had no spares. Since I could not read it anyway, it was not a great loss.

I was going to take it home and have my wife read it to me though. The rest of the conference went well except for having to share a bed with someone other than my beautiful bride. I lost the coin toss so had to sleep with my pastor.

Matthew 15:17 Do not ye yet understand, that whatsoever entereth in at the mouth goeth into the belly, and is cast out into the draught?

Though the Romans did have toilets back then, they were reserved for the wealthy and certainly not Jews. Today, because of all the medications we consume, we can no longer use human waste as fertilizer. However, back then, that is exactly what it was used for.

126
TO SEE OR NOT TO SEE, THAT IS THE QUESTION
December 23, 1998

Some would say "accidentally," but I say "the LORD." During a conversation a friend of mine began to ask questions about my vision and the possibility of having cataract surgery to restore some of it. My mother had just gone through the surgery and recovered all her vision.

After asking my permission, my friend went to her Pastoral Care Board to ask if they could do anything. She came back to me with a check for five hundred dollars. I went to two eye doctors and was told that there were no guarantees but, there was a good possibility that removing the cataract would greatly increase my vision.

I was also told that the surgery would cost about eight thousand dollars. I did not have any insurance since I had dropped it six years earlier. I had dropped it because it was costing me over five hundred dollars a year, had a seven-hundred-and-sixty-dollar deductible and, did not cover eye surgery.

Once the positive report came back from the doctor, my friend had several of her friends begin looking around for a solution. Her Deacon board agreed to pay for everything I could not but, they wanted to see if there were other means.

One of her friends told her that Medicaid supplement insurances did pay for that kind of surgery. At the time I dropped the insurance I had been told that the supplemental insurances cost two hundred and fifty dollars or more a month.

It turns out that the government has made agreements with many of the insurance providers to cover most of the costs for the disabled for the same forty-six dollars a month Medicaid was taking. I prayed about it and believed that the LORD would have me pursue this further so, I re-applied for Medicaid.

They lost my application and though I was on the phone with them several times a month, it took them three months to tell me that they lost it. By the time they told me, it was past the open enrollment period which meant I would have to pay much more per month and that I would not be covered for six months after they accepted my application.

I re-applied, agreeing to the higher cost and the instant they gave me the word that I had been reinstated, I called some of the insurance companies to apply with them. The first company I called told me that, except for the five dollar and ten-dollar co-pay per visit, the rest of the eight thousand dollars would be covered.

They took my information and scheduled a visit to my house with one of their reps. For two months later. I asked them if they could just send me the application and I would have someone help me fill it out and they said, "that is not how we usually did things."

The day of the visit came and went without a visit or a phone call. The day after I called the company and they apologized for the inconvenience. We scheduled another appointment for three weeks later. The day before I called to confirm but, once again the day came and passed.

I called again the next day and was told that the rep had quit and they did not have anyone else in my area. The lady asked if she could just send me the ap. to which I exclaimed, "that is what I asked them to do in the first place."

She said that once they got the ap back it would take up to two months to process it. I received the ap. And my wife filled it out for me. We sent it back the next day. I called two weeks later to make sure they got it and was told that they would not be able to cover me.

When I asked why, they told me that they were pulling out of New York state and could not take any more applications. I asked them how long they knew about this and she told me that they knew for a couple months. I then asked to speak with someone in charge and she assured me that she would have someone call me as soon as possible.

Though the Bible tells us to believe all things I did not believe her.

I was wrong, the manager called me back the next day. After recounting my story to him he said that he would try to get me in anyway.

He also said that, even if he did get me in, they would most likely be out of the state before I could have a surgery scheduled and that it would be better for me to try to go through another company. He gave me a list of names and numbers and I found another company.

I know now that the LORD was trying to teach me patience and I was not in the mood to learn. The other company gave me the same coverage the first one offered. I scheduled an appointment with the doctor to arrange and prepare for surgery.

Everything went smoothly from that moment on, thank you LORD. My mother wanted to take me to the hospital and stay with me but, they did not let you know the time of your surgery until the day before. My Mother works until three or four in the morning and they schedule appointments as early as six am.

Guess what time they scheduled me for, that is right, six am. I told my mother and she still wanted to do it so, when she got off work, she drove home to take care of her cats, came to my house at five-thirty am, took me to the hospital and waited.

After the surgery she drove me to my house and went home. She did not get to her house until about two pm and had to be to work at six pm so she did not bother to go to sleep.

Now for the surgery:

They told me that I would be awake through the whole thing. Since I am very muscular and lean, they thought I would need a little more anesthetic than the average person. What they did not take into account was the fact that I was a strict vegan.

Absolutely no animal products, not even Jello. No coffee, no soda, no junk food, except potato chips. Since my system was so pure the meds went right to where they needed to go without having to fight the pollution.

I had prayed about what to talk about during the operation and had committed to the LORD that, even if it meant losing my eye to an irate or upset surgeon, I was going to tell the O.R. crew that they were lost and had no hope unless they surrendered their lives to JESUS.

The LORD is so much wiser than we. I had such a peace about

the whole thing after committing it to HIS will that I did not even think about it again until the day of the surgery. When I arrived at the hospital, to my surprise, my pastor was waiting there for me.

I had thought about asking him to take me but it was so early in the morning I did not want to bother him. We prayed, I went into the changing room, got into one of their flimsy shirts/gowns, laid in the bed and submitted myself to the Chinese eye drop torture.

Every three minutes for a half hour a nurse would come in and put drops in my eye, many of them stung like bees. Then, when the drops were all over, they wheeled me down to the waiting area for the operating rooms.

They gave me a shot and, one minute later my doctor came over to speak with me. The anesthesiologist came over to speak with me and moments later they were wheeling me into the operating room. After saying a few words to each of the people that introduced themselves to me, I was gone.

I do not remember anything after that until I woke up in the recovery room. I had not eaten or drunk anything for the last sixteen hours which was a good thing because that was the worst case of nausea I have ever had.

The doctor came in to my room and removed the bandages. As he was doing so, he reminded me that I might not be able to see much for a few weeks. That was the only thing he was wrong about, the instant the bandages came off I could see that he needed a shave.

I could see my pastor and Mother as well. Usually, they bandage the eye and let it rest after the operation but, since this was my good eye, he just put a clear protective shield over it. On the way home I marveled at all the things I could see.

Without glasses I could now see better than I had been able to with glasses during the last seven years. When the doctor realized that I had a great deal more sight than he thought I might right after the operation, he remarked, it should improve over the next few weeks.

My reply was, "even if my sight does not clear up beyond what I have now, the LORD has blessed me." I could tell by the look on his face that he was not particularly happy with me giving all the glory to GOD, so, I thanked him too.

Between the nausea and the pain, I spent much of the next two days in bed. The day after the operation I was sitting in our living room next to the lamp. Elizabeth came over to sit on my lap and, for the first time, I was able to see her face.

I asked Joshua to sit with me as well and just stared at both of them for quite a while. Many people have told me over the years how beautiful my wife and children are but, since I could not see, it did not mean much to me.

I have always seen the beauty in the creation the LORD made in them. Now I was finally able to see what everyone else was talking about. I know that I am prejudiced but, I think I have the most beautiful wife and children in the world. Just think, that is how the LORD JESUS CHRIST thinks of you.

If he did not think he had the most beautiful bride in the world, he would not have suffered and died for her. Would you like to be so loved that someone would die for you? Just trust in what JESUS did for you and you too can experience that love.

Galatians 5:22-23 But the fruit of the Spirit is love, joy, peace, longsuffering, gentleness, goodness, faith. Meakness, temperance: against such there is no law.

Sadly, we have become such a lazy bunch that, reading the King James Bible is, "too hard." So, we choose lesser versions and, those versions change longsuffering to patience. What I went through was suffering and it was long.

Patience is more like waiting for your meal at a restaurant when it is taking longer than you think it should. Jesus told us that we would have suffering but we do not want to hear that. I know I did not want to hear it.

127
DOES PRAYER REALLY WORK?
FEBRUARY 24, 1999

It all started during a Bible study. We were discussing the effectiveness of prayer. It was the opinion of someone that we can actually change GOD's mind by prayer. It was my opinion that GOD is going to do what HE wants whether we pray or not but, HE allows us the privilege of participation.

We did not settle the question that night but, I decided that I needed to go through the Bible and find out what the LORD says about the subject.

Today I got up at 4:30 in order to be ready by 5:30. At that time my pastor would be here to drive me to the hospital for surgery on my left eye. The operation was to open a hole in the capsule and implant a lens. Since the capsule was very scarred and it had been twenty years since I had seen out of that eye, the doctor did not know what might need to be done.

Since I was so nauseous the first time, I decided that the next time I would make sure the anesthesiologist used less medication. We arrived at the hospital a few minutes before six. We parked in the wrong lot and so, we entered the building on the wrong side. We went in and walked around looking for an elevator. When we finally found them, one was waiting with the door open.

We stepped into it and pressed the button for the lobby. I took a tract out of my belly pack and straddled it over the hand rail. We stood there for a minute and the door did not close. Pastor pressed the lobby button again and we waited. After another minute went by, we decided that we should take another elevator. As soon as we got out, the door to the one we had been in, closed.

Pastor pressed the button for another elevator and the one to the left opened. We got on and I thought, 'The LORD made that happen so I could put a tract in each elevator.' I then took another one out of my pack and placed it on the hand rail of the second car as pastor pressed the lobby button on that elevator.

After a minute went by and the door to this car did not close, I told pastor Dave about a M*A*S*H* episode where they played practical jokes. I suggested that we might be on candid camera and that they had rigged the elevators to close only when they were empty. I said that as soon as we got off the elevator, the doors would close. He laughed and pressed the lobby button again. After another minute went by and the door was still open, we decided to test the theory by getting off and sure enough, the doors closed.

We walked around until we found another bank of elevators. While we were standing there someone passed by and we asked her how to get to ambulatory. When she told us, we realized that we were already in the lobby and that is why the doors would not close. We had been telling the car to go where it already was. We forgot to go back later and apologize to the elevators for confusing them like that.

We were standing a few feet from the intake desk and when pastor told the person my name, she said that we should have a seat in the waiting room. Less than five seconds after we sat down, she called us back to the desk to fill out the paper work.

On the drive to the hospital, I had reminded myself to have a talk with the anesthesiologist. Pastor had a teaching tape playing and, on the tape, Greg Lori said, "Just because a door opens does not mean that GOD was the one that opened it." After hearing that I thought perhaps I should not talk to the doctor about having received too much medicine last time.

I was in the O.R. waiting room minutes before they were to begin the operation when the anesthesiologist came up to me and asked his routine questions. As he was asking, I remembered that I wanted to ask him to use less medicine than they did last time. I recalled my thought in the car and then thought, 'If he asks me if I have any questions than that would be GOD opening the door." I forgot one thing, I forgot to pray.

He did ask me if I had any questions and so I told him what happened last time. When he suggested that being unconscious for the whole procedure was not a bad thing, I felt I should give up but, I pressed him a little further and he gave in. He agreed to use less and walked away.

They wheeled me in and began the I.V. knock out drops. Just before going under, they started with the injections into my eye. They said that, "This might sting a little," and, it did. At that moment I regretted not allowing the doctor to use as much medicine as he wanted.

As I began to wake up, I heard the surgeon repeating my name. After the third time I responded and he said, "You are moving around, you need to be still." I realized then that he still had my eye open and that I could really cause damage if I did not keep perfectly still. I tried to remain motionless but it was very difficult.

I was lying on a stretcher naked with my legs propped up by a pillow, I had a headache, my back was hurting, there was something sharp poking me in the top of my head, I was cold, uncomfortable and I needed to go to the bathroom. I tried to go back to sleep but, it was not possible. I began to pray for the LORD's strength because, I knew I could not hold out like this for very long.

I found out two things later. The first was that the capsule that they usually attach the lens to was too damaged to be used so, they had to implant it over the iris. That meant they had to make a larger incision and that the operation would take longer than expected and, that there was more risk involved.

Though cataract operations are routine compared to twenty years ago when I had my first eye operation, they are still difficult. They are even more difficult when you have to switch plans in the middle of the operation. And finally, they are further complicated by a patient coming out of a drug induced sleep who is moving around like he wants to dance.

The second thing that I found out after the procedure was what my pastor's wife went through. She told me later that evening that, around the same time I was waking up on the table, she was reading her Bible. She got the impression to pray for me and then, lost her vision. She started to pray and asked, "LORD, what should I pray?" The LORD told her to just intercede and, she did.

Toward the beginning of this story, I told you that someone at the Bible study said they believed prayer was more than I had claimed it was. In fact, that person suggested that we could change GOD's mind with our prayers. It may seem that way if you do not understand the dynamics of the relationships of those in the Bible that seemed as if they did change the LORD's mind.

What really goes on is, the LORD tells us of an impending disaster and already knows who will step up to the plate to intercede. When that person does, the awful thing does not happen and so, it looks like He changed His mind.

It was the LORD's intention for my surgery to come out well which is why He impressed upon my pastor's wife's heart to pray for me. He gave her the added incentive of temporary blindness so she could not be easily distracted and so that she would have a sign that I was the one to concentrate on. If she chose to ignore the LORD, He would have picked someone else.

Ephesians 1:9 Having made known unto us the mystery of his will, according to his good pleasure which he hath purposed in himself.

The mystery of His will concerning my operation was that He wanted to give me six more months of seeing my wife and children. The mystery of Su Sitterly going blind was so there would be no doubt as to whom the LORD wanted her to pray for.

128
WHOOPS, THAT'S NOT MY DAUGHTER
JUNE OF 1999

A year and a half earlier our church needed a new Leader. A missionary family was coming back to the USA after four years of service in China. Dave was not looking to become a pastor but, it was evident to his family and everyone in our church that it was the LORD's will for him to become our next Guide.

When it was time for them to go back to China, my family took his family and another friend, Cheryl, to dinner at a Chinese Restaurant. We all sat around a large round table. My daughter was six and my son was four. Being young and full of energy, they wanted to get down and move around.

The restaurant was not busy so the children started to chase each other around our table. In order to slow them down a bit, as they passed my chair I reached out and grabbed them. I would tickle them for a moment and then let them escape. It worked. They stopped running and started trying to sneak past my chair.

The adults were holding a conversation but, since I have always considered myself as more of a child than an adult, even now in my forties, I played with the children. They started getting better at sneaking past me, mostly by walking a little further behind my chair.

This caused me to have to reach further behind me to grab them. Elizabeth was getting so good at sneaking past me that I was determined to get her the next time around. As I heard her creeping up behind me, I prepared to catch her. I heard her accelerate and try to make it past me again.

I reached out behind me with my right hand and made contact. It wasn't my daughter though. It was the inner thigh of one of the waitresses. As with most Chinese restaurants, the majority of the workers in this one were Chinese. The waitress I had grabbed was of the afore mentioned nationality and did not speak much English other than what was on the menu.

From the way my wife reacted, I could tell that she was mortified. She jumped up and removed my hand from the waitress because I had not realized yet what had happened. She then tried to explain to the woman that I was blind and that I thought I was catching my daughter.

I am grateful that she was not upset enough to dump the tray of food she had in her hands onto my head. She stood there smiling while my wife tried to explain but, I do not think she understood any of what had just happened or my wife's explanation.

Since our pastor was there and did speak some Chinese, he tried his hand at explaining. It seemed as if she understood and then she left us to deliver her tray of food. Pastor Dave waited a few seconds after she left and then said to me, "I don't think she believed a word I said."

Needless to say, I have not played that game again with my children in a restaurant.

Proverbs 20:7 The just man walketh in his integrity: his children are blessed after him.

I tried to always be honest with everyone, especially my children. That meant that I had to apologize to them occasionally when I screwed up. Many people think that to admit to your child that you made a mistake is dangerous. I found that, when I did, in increased their love and respect for me because I was not pretending to be perfect.

129
MY MOST EMBARRASSING MOMENT
JULY OF 2000

Many of our friends from church were at the home of one of our members. They had an above ground pool and lots of back yard for games and socializing. I was in the pool with my children when I felt the need to use a bathroom. My daughter led me into the house and to one of the rest rooms.

Just as most seven-year-old children are, so was my daughter, not encumbered with details. She showed me where all the essentials were and then left me to do my business. While I was sitting on the throne a door burst open that I did not know was there. That door was one of the details that my daughter was oblivious to and so, it remained not locked.

The friends that we were visiting had three children. The oldest and youngest are girls and the middle one is a boy. The boy came into the bathroom and while completely ignoring me, proceeded to wash his hands. He then turned around and ran out. As he did, I tried to get him to close the door but, he was gone.

I sat there for a minute trying to think of what to do. I called for my wife. No answer. I called for my daughter. Again, no answer. I thought about standing up to try to find the door and close and lock it. Just at that moment their older daughter walked into the bathroom. She was about twelve.

Though I could not see her face, I knew from her sudden stop and complete silence that she was stunned to find me there. After a few seconds she turned and, figuring out what had happened, began to yell at her brother. After telling him that he should have closed the door she ran outside to tell the rest of the world what had just occurred, forgetting to close the door herself. My wife then came to my rescue, closing and locking the second door.

There have been many embarrassing moments in my life but I think this was the worst. I was part of the children's ministry in my church and was trying to develop a relationship with some of the pre-teen and teen agers. It was hard to get over the fact that this young lady had seen me with my bathing suit around my ankles sitting on her toilet.

Is it not interesting that the word embarrass has the word ass in it and, almost sounds like bare ass, which is what my state was at the time?

1 Corinthians 12:23 And those members of the body, which we think to be less honourable, upon these we bestow more abundant honour; and our uncomely parts have more abundant comeliness.

I know that a lot of people think that the King James Bible is too difficult to read. But, can you really say that you do not understand what this verse is saying? If your answer is yes, all it means is that our body parts that do not look as good as some other parts are honored by being covered by clothing.

I am so glad that, at the time my parts were not being covered by my suit, they were being hidden by a commode. I am also very relieved that I sat there thinking of what to do or I would have been standing up just as she walked in.

130
GO TO HELL AND FRY
MAY OF 2001

Marvin and Helen Frey became friends of ours while we were attending a church in Greenberg, New York. Marvin had written many classic Christian songs including "Kumbaya." Marvin had become a missionary to the inner-city youth of New York City. He and his wife ran a summer camp for the youth for decades.

Just in case you want to know, Marvin told me that, he was sitting by a fire in Africa on a missions trip. There were many men around the fire and they were singing a song that he had just written. Because of the language barrier and accents, his phrase, "Come by here, my LORD," came out "Kumbaya, my LORD."

Just a few years after we met him, the LORD took Marvin home. Thanks to the support of many people, Marvin's wife Helen was able to continue the mission. Several years later she decided to sell her home, pass the mission on to the care of others and move back to her home town in upstate New York.

Our church was celebrating its twentieth anniversary and Mrs. Frey was in attendance. I was speaking with someone who had heard of the camp and was interested in finding out more.

Just at that moment I heard Mrs. Frey talking with someone across the room to my right so, I said, "If you want to know more about the mission you can go to Helen Frey." My wife was standing to my side and saw the look on the face of the person I was talking with. It was not a good look. Her face became red and she looked shocked and offended. I heard the woman gasp but, having no other clues I could not figure out what had happened right away. The volume of conversation in the room did not lend itself to my picking up on what had just transpired either.

My wife had taken the woman by the arm and guided her over to Mrs. Frey for an introduction. After talking with Mrs. Frey for a while she came back over to me. I had gotten involved in other conversations and had forgotten all about the woman until she reintroduced herself and asked if she could speak with me.

After pulling me over to the side where she was confident that no one could overhear us, she told me that she thought I was insulting her by telling her to, "Go to Hell and fry." She said that she was greatly relieved when she was introduced to Mrs. Helen Frey and realized that I was merely pointing her in the correct direction to obtain the information she sought.

Mark 7:32 And they bring unto him one that was deaf, and had an impediment in his speech; and they beseech him to put his hand upon him.

I was blind, not deaf and though I did not have a speech impediment as such, it sure was an impediment to that woman for a few minutes. It taught me to listen better to what is coming out of my mouth.

131
I LOST JESUS
JULY 5, 2001

The first time I had ever heard that Jesus Christ was a person rather than a curse was just after my eighteenth birthday. I was a bicycle mechanic in Jersey City, New Jersey. After delivering a crib to a lady who seemed like she would have the baby while Joe and I were there.

I was helping Joe because his assistant called out sick. My boss asked me if I would help deliver the items that needed two people. Though my contract stipulated that my duties were only building and repairing bikes, I agreed.

My boss was a great guy, I was finished my work for the day and I hated just sitting around waiting for the clock to release me from work. After shlepping the crib to its new home on the second floor, we were about to leave when the woman asked us if we could assemble it for her.

She pleaded with us because she said that her husband didn't even know how to use a screw driver. Joe began to protest that assembly was not part of our job when I stopped him. I told him to go and deliver the items he could handle by himself and to pick me up for the rest when he was done.

As I was putting the crib together, she offered me a beer which I accepted since I was not driving. She then began to tell me about some guy named Jesus. I started to work faster because what she was saying sounded too weird to me.

I was walking toward the door to go wait on the front steps when she offered me another beer. I was going to refuse when I noticed the embossed debut album by Boston on their turn table. As I started drinking the other beer, she invited me back for dinner that evening to meet her husband.

I figured that, if they liked Boston and drank beer, they could not be too bad so, I accepted. When I rode my bike to their home that evening, he proceeded to tell me all about God, Jesus and the Holy Spirit. What he was telling me sounded great so, I accepted the LORD that evening.

When I told my mother, she went out and purchased a necklace with a fourteen-carat white man's representation of Jesus. I turned it into an earring and still wear it today.

Forward to July of 2001. Jovanna, our two children, our friend Mark and I were in a canoe on a body of water that we soon learned we were not supposed to be swimming in. Having been a life guard, I love being in the water.

I wanted my eight-year-old daughter Elizabeth and our six-year-old son Joshua to fall in love with the water as well. So, I would jump in and Jovanna would hand one of the children to me for a while. Then we would switch. When we were done, I would get back in the canoe.

When we were discovered in the water by some official, we were asked to leave. When I was sitting on the peer drying off to put on my clothing, I accidentally dropped my ear ring into the shallow water which was full of Lilly pads.

I wanted to cry. My friend Mark saw how devastated I was and sat there with a paddle for over thirty minutes looking for it. I did not think there was any chance he would find it when he reached into the water and pulled it from between two weeds.

There have been a few things in my life that were more wonderful than that moment, but very few. Getting saved, marrying Jovanna and having my children. Other than those things, I cannot think of anything that has given me as much joy as knowing that I did not lose Jesus after all.

John 10:28 And I give unto them eternal life; and they shall never perish, neither shall any man pluck them out of my hand.

Though many things have been plucked out of my hand, it is wonderful to know that I cannot be plucked out of His hand.

132
WHO WAS THAT OTHER WOMAN?
September of 2001

Over the years we have hosted students from Sweden, Brazil, Japan, China, Indonesia, Spain, Germany, Taiwan, France and other countries. We fell in love with our first student, Camilla. I started calling her vanilla because she was so sweet. Our family has kept up a relationship with her to this day. She has actually come back to visit with us twice.

During this visit my wife was recovering from a heart condition that she had and we asked Vanilla if she would take me to the post office. She, the children and I piled into the van and we drove there so I could mail off products to my customers. While we were there we ran into the new pastor of a church in our neighborhood.

I had met him before but my children had not so I introduced them. When I introduced him to Camilla, he did not hear what I said because he later asked me who that other woman was that I was with. I have to give him credit because he was trying to be subtle about holding me accountable because he thought I was having an affair.

I tried to explain it to him but it obviously did not work because a few days later he saw my children with Camilla. He walked up to them and said hello to the children and addressed Camilla as Mrs. Whitehead. Because of her accent I suppose, he was not able to understand her when she told him that she was not my wife.

For some reason he just could not get it out of his mind that Camilla was my wife. Then it dawned on me that he had not actually met my wife, he had just seen me with her from a distance. The next time I saw him I started from the beginning and explained the whole thing to him.

He finally understood. This was not the first time I had to explain to someone that the women they saw me with were just friends helping a blind man do his shopping and errands. There was actually a postal worker named Ray who would not believe my story. I finally had to bring my wife in and have her explain the situation to him. We showed him the matching wedding bands and our wedding picture to corroborate the story.

Sometimes it sure is fun being blind. Don't get me wrong, if there was a cure I would take it in a heartbeat but, I have learned to enjoy the weird things that happen to me.

1 Corinthians 5:12 For what have I to do to judge them also that are without? do not ye judge them that are within?

In the context of church or even better, a friend, that pastor was looking out for me and my family in trying to keep me straight. I am so glad to have people in my life that check up on me. As the next verse lets us know, God is the ultimate Judge.

In this verse though, the word judge does not mean condemn as too many people believe. It means to look at the evidence and make a decision. In his case, my pastor friend saw something that did not look right and, rather than go to someone else or start a rumor, he came to me with his concern.

Romans 14:12 So then every one of us shall give account of himself to God.

133
A WING OR A THIGH?
JUNE OF 2002

I was an elder in a small Christian Missionary Alliance church in Ossining, New York when this happened. The church was only about eight blocks from Sing Sing prison and there were only two elders and the pastor. We were holding a bible study in the home of the other elder's mother-in-law's home a few miles away in Croton-on-Hudson.

During the course of that study which lasted about two years, many people came and went. One of the attendees had brought her hair dresser and a friend. I believe there was at least one other new person there as well.

It was a very dynamic study and questions were encouraged. Often, we would go off on rabbit trails because the points of the topic being discussed would bring up a question in someone's mind that they just needed clarification on. Questions like, "Will there be animals in Heaven?" and "Is there life on other planets?"

In case you are wondering, yes, there will be animals in heaven, in fact, you, like Doctor Doolittle, will be able to talk with them. No, there is no life on any other planet in the Universe.

My wife and I usually arrived early for the studies as we did this particular evening. We sat in two folding chairs which were to the left of the door as you walked into the living room. Moments after sitting down, my wife got up for something. I was talking with someone and was not aware of that fact. Moments later, the study started.

Minutes into the discussion something was said and I turned to my wife which was to my right. I placed my right hand on her left thigh about a foot from her knee and leaned over to whisper a point to her about what was being said. Seconds later, someone grabbed my hand and removed it.

I immediately started to get attitudinal because I did not think anyone should have a problem with my hand on my wife's leg. I also thought, who the heck do they think they are, touching me without permission? Then I heard my wife's voice apologizing to the woman saying, "Sorry, he is blind and he thought you were me." She went on to explain that she had been sitting in that chair and that I did not know that she had moved.

Many people in the room laughed but the other woman did not. She offered to switch with my wife but she declined. I wish she had because I felt self-conscious for the rest of the study. If my memory serves, that lady did not return to the bible study, at least not for the duration of our stay in New York, which was only a few more weeks.

1 Timothy 5:22a Lay hands suddenly on no man.

I have tried to obey this verse, however, if I recounted all the times I have accidentally put my hand on a stranger, it could be a novella.

134
THE BLIND BURGLAR
MARCH OF 2003

If Murphy has anything to do with it, as soon as I type the next sentence, it will no longer be true. I have never locked myself out of my house, apartment or car and I have never lost my wallet or keys. I did leave my credit card with a restaurant in Canada once.

For some reason, wherever I have lived over the last nineteen years, my neighbors frequently lock themselves out of places. When I lived in Maryland, several of my neighbors locked themselves out of their apartments. I lived in a complex that had three buildings.

Each building had ten apartments in it. There were four on the third floor, four on the second floor and two on the first. As you reached the top floor landing there was an apartment directly to the left. That was Dave and Sandy. Then there was an apartment directly in front. That was Bill.

Then there was an apartment in front of you off to the right. That was mine. Then there was an apartment three steps to the right, that was Larry. Larry was the first to lock himself out and I offered to get in for him but, he was a little unstable and kicked the door in.

He then told the office that someone tried to break in and they came and fixed the damage. Sandy was next and took me up on my offer. I was able to get in without damaging anything. She was happy to get in but not happy that it was so easy, and for someone who could not see.

She had a security door knob put on. Bill was next. Since his apartment was in the back like mine, I was able to climb up the balcony poles and get in through his kitchen window. Bill's only worry was that I had put the screen back securely so that no bugs could get in.

Then Sandy locked herself out again. Well, her security door knob worked so well that I had to cut it off in order to get in. Even though she had just lost thirty-five dollars she was happy to know that it was no longer easy to break into her apartment.

There were many other people that had locked themselves out. Somehow the word had spread and they all came to me. After breaking up with my girlfriend I started to go to a non-denominational church. I had been going there for a few months and had gotten to know many of the people well.

We had been preparing for a Vacation Bible School. There was a supply closet that had only one key. Someone had gone into the closet to get some supplies and put the key on the shelf as they entered. They forgot to pick it up again on the way out.

I was walking by to go to the bathroom and heard a few people trying to do something by the closet door and asked if I could help. They told me what had happened and I suggested that I could have it opened very quickly. I got a thin bladed butter knife from the kitchen and, in three seconds had the door open.

One of the elders asked me what I did for a living before moving to New York. I told him that I was a break in artist. The rumor spread like wild fire and before I knew it, people were hiding their silver and jewelry whenever I went to their homes.

Just kidding but, there were quite a few questions and comments. Months after the incident a friend of ours from the church locked her keys in her car while the trunk was open. For some reason Lana thought that I might be able to help her. I cannot imagine where she got that idea.

It took some doing but, after lying in her trunk working on the back seat, I was able to put my arm through enough to unlock the back door. Just a few months before moving from New York to New Mexico, a very strange thing happened.

During my son's birthday party my neighbor from across the street rang the bell. She said that she had locked her keys in the house. Her husband's keys were inside as well. She wanted to borrow my phone to call a locksmith but, I told her I might be able to help.

I went across the street with Yvonne and in a few minutes, with the aid of a credit card, was able to open her door. She was delighted and shocked that I was able to do that without being able to see. The very next day, our next door neighbor to the right, Krishna, came over telling me that he had locked himself out of the house while going into his garage.

This one was even easier. I went over to his garage and in seconds had his door open. Now I know this is going to sound like fiction but, two days later, Raphael, my neighbor two doors to the left, locked himself out of the house having left his toddler inside.

He came to me in a panic but I assured him that we could get in very quickly. Just as my neighbor to the right had done, he locked himself out while going into the garage. On the way to his house, he pelted me with questions of technique.

I told him that I had done this for many neighbors and would be able to get him in with no trouble. He did not believe me until three seconds after arriving at his garage door and he was in the house. I attempted to bid him adieu but he asked me to wait a minute.

After checking to make sure his child was safe, he came out again and asked me to show him how to do what I did. Once I showed him, he was uneasy to find out how simple it was to break into people's homes. Hold on to your seat because there are two more.

Two weeks later one of my daughter's friends had locked herself out of her grandmother's house. We went over and a few minutes later I had the door open for her. I am sad to say that I was unable to get into the last one. The neighbor directly to my left, Sheri, had a teen-age daughter.

Tiffany had locked herself out so often that the mother gave us a spare key to let her in. The second to last time she locked herself out, she came over to get the key but, she never returned it. The last time she locked herself out, I was able to break into the screen door but, because of the weather stripping in the main door, I was unable to get in.

I am sure that I could have if I had destroyed the stripping but, I thought it would be better for her to wait a few hours until her mother got home. At least it would be less expensive than having to replace the stripping which had been professionally installed.

Now that I am in New Mexico, I wonder how long it is going to take before people start wanting me to break into their homes. Hopefully none of my neighbors will know it is me when they read this story.

Well, it only took fifteen months. Akiem, his wife, his mother-in-law and their two little children live only one block away. My wife befriended his wife and her mother, though her mother did not speak much English. One morning, Jovanna went outside and saw the grandmother walking past our house.

She looked distressed so my wife asked her what the problem was. She was able to figure out that the woman had been taking care of the nine-month-old little boy when she accidentally locked herself out of the home. She had also locked the boy inside.

She was on her way to her daughter's place of work with the bad news. Jovanna convinced her to wait a few minutes and she would drive her there. Then she remembered that I was a break in artist. I was in the shower when she gave me the news.

I cut my shower short, threw on my pants without underwear, shoes without socks and no shirt when she told me that the child was crying. I grabbed my wallet and Leatherman and we drove to the house because it would be thirty seconds quicker. When I got the door open in sixty seconds, the woman was shocked. I would have had it opened quicker but the seam was tight and I had to use a thinner card than my Amex.

My wife said that the stunned look on the grandmother's face would have been a great picture. Unfortunately, the look only lasted a second as she opened the door, grabbed the boy and came back out to profusely thank us. Maybe I should write a book called, "The Blind Burglar?"

Matthew 6:19 Lay not up for yourselves treasures upon earth, where moth and rust doth corrupt, and where thieves break through and steal:

Though the LORD has given me the talent to break into people's homes easily, I am glad that He has helped me use it to be a blessing to my neighbors and not a thief. Otherwise, I could have laid up a lot of treasure for myself.

135
LOOKING FOR A HAND OUT
OCTOBER 29, 2004

My family had been attending Calvary Chapel of Santa Fe for the last two years and had made many friends. One of those was like a friend in New York who could be a smart ass regarding my blindness.

Our church had three services at that time and I taught Sunday School for the first two and attended the service for the third. After a few worship songs, we were encouraged to greet the people around us. I did not think anyone was sitting around me because I did not hear anyone and no one passed me to sit further in the row.

I turned my head to the left, waited two seconds and, when no one said anything, I figured no one was there. I turned my head to the right and there was no one there either. Moments later, people began coming up to me to shake or hug and I knew them all.

The service went on and I went to the entrance area to see if I could get a ride home. Jovanna's heart was at its worst by this point and, I had to get forth and back with the help of friends many times. As I was listening for the voice of someone I could beg a ride from, one approached me in stitches.

When I asked him what was so funny, he began to tell me about a man who was angry with me. He said that the man was sitting in my row and, when it was time to greet your neighbors, he put out his hand and I looked right at him but refused to shake and turned away. He was further agitated because he saw me greet several other people.

When I asked if he could find the man so I could apologize and explain, he began to tell the man why I ignored him, I pulled out my cane and opened it.

They both had a good laugh and the new attendee went on his way.

Proverbs 17 9 He that covereth a transgression seeketh love; but he that repeateth a matter separateth very friends.

I used to watch the TV show, "The Odd Couple." In one episode, Tony Randall (Felix), was explaining to Jack Klugman (Oscar), that when you assume, "You make an ass out of you and me." I was grateful for that episode because I learned how to spell assume and to always confirm things.

136
WHY ISN'T HE DRIVING?
April 11, 2005

I have been a math professor, a legal consultant, homeschooled my two children, have taught from the pulpit of my church, taught Bible studies in my home and, to this day, I teach Sunday School. In all that teaching experience, I have encouraged those under my tutelage that there is no such thing as a dumb question.

I stick to that assertion because those are classroom type settings. However, in the real world, there are many stupid questions. This is the story of one such question. For the last two years before her heart surgery, my wife was mostly bed ridden.

Though it was difficult to see my wife suffer so, it was a great time of blessing for me and my children. We would walk a half mile to the grocery store with our two empty water jugs, five gallons each and my back pack.

I am sure we got a lot of strange looks from people but, I did not care much what they thought of me before I lost my sight and care even less now. My children were twelve and ten at the time of this occurrence and we would go to the store two or three times a week.

We would get some ice cream, crackers or chips and something to imbibe. We would then go to the fountain in the mall, sit, eat, drink and talk. We would then visit their favorite stores.

Starbucks, Baskin Robins, the toy store, the game store, the music store or Radio Shack. Once we were done with those, we would do our shopping, get our water, check out and figure out how to fit all our groceries in my back pack.

We would place my backpack on a bench, while loading it, then strap one five-gallon water jug to the top of my pack and the other to the bottom. They would then stand, one on each side of the pack, holding it steady so I could squat down and get into the shoulder straps.

If we were unable to get all the food into the pack, we would leave out the lightest or most fragile items and they would each carry a bag or share the carrying of the one bag. We would make up all kinds of word association games or math games on the way home.

Sometimes I would just listen to them tell me their desires. Other times we would play the license plate game. we would also make up a sentence word by word and whatever letter the first word we started with began with, the rest of the words had to begin with.

You could place your word anywhere in the sentence and believe me, some of the sentences were quite funny. On this particular day, I had to get to the store quickly so I needed a ride. My wife was not feeling up to taking me so, I asked one of our neighbors.

Rosemary agreed and, minutes later, we were pulling into the grocery store parking lot. That lot was usually full and, this day was no exception. We drove around circling the handicap parking spots several times waiting for a vacancy.

I told Rosemary that we did not have to park close to the store as I like to walk. She responded, "I do not like to walk so we will wait." Coming around the corner for the fifth time, there was a free spot. She began to pull in and, someone to our left tried to cut her off.

Now, neither one was able to get into the spot. Rosemary rolled down her window and, in a lady-like manner, shouted to the other woman that we were there first. The other woman shouted back, in not such a lady-like manner, my mother had a stroke and cannot walk very far.

My driver replied, as she grabbed my portable handicapped placard and waved it at the woman, "My friend is blind." Okay, here comes the funny part, with a serious expression, the other woman asked, "Then why isn't he driving?"

As anyone that knows me can tell you, I am almost never at a loss for words. That day, however, we were both speechless. Then we burst out in laughter at the same time. The other driver did not back off and, Rosemary did have a slightly better angle so, she began to inch forward.

The other driver finally gave up and backed up. I will not repeat the expletive she shot our way as she passed to the other side of our car. I am sure that the following will happen, though I am less sure that it will occur in my lifetime.

Since nineteen-ninety, I have heard that "they" are working on a car that is voice activated and fully automated. It has dozens of cameras linked to an on-board computer. The computer knows every road, traffic sign, speed limits and, because it is able to stream, it even knows the location of traffic difficulties.

Get in, turn it on, tell it where you want to go and, because it already knows where you are, you can take a nap until you arrive at your destination. Though this sounds great in some respects, I would have missed the above experience if that car had already been around.

Micah 6:8 He hath shewed thee, O man, what is good; and what doth the LORD require of thee, but to do justly, and to love mercy, and to walk humbly with thy God?

Though Rosemary was from Virginia, I think that some of my New York attitude must have rubbed off on her. I try to be humble and I do love mercy. As far as just, since I am completely blind and it would have been dangerous to get out of her car at this point, I had no choice.

I love children and old people and would have been happy to walk so a stroke victim could have a shorter distance to travel. Unfortunately, sometimes we are at the mercy of others.

137
BLOW ME DOWN
July 5, 2005

No, this is not a story about Popeye. It started when my family was eating at a restaurant in the Sanbusco Mall called El Tesoro. Joshua had finished his lunch and had too much energy to just sit and wait for the rest of us to conclude our meal. He asked if he could look around and we gave our permission with the stipulation that he not go outside.

Minutes later, he came running back with great enthusiasm for what he found. He wanted us to go back with him and, since we were almost finished, we went. What he found was a store called Science Toy Magic.

The owner had been a teacher before embarking on his new endeavor. By the time we last spoke with him in 2017, he spoke nine languages and was on his way to Ireland to hang out in a Kabutz for a month while brushing up on his Irish.

His store was full of games and toys that had a scientific lesson to learn. My birthday is July 4 and his is July 5. So, the day after my celebration, we went to see him with a lit candle in a cup cake. As we walked toward his store singing happy birthday, he asked us to stop and stay still.

My wife told me that he grabbed something from the store and jumped on his unicycle. She told me that he was riding away so I was now confused. Then he stopped, turned around and held something up. He then told me to hold the cupcake up in front of my face.

I heard a sound like someone dropping a phone book onto a desk from six inches above it. About two seconds after that sound, a wind hit me in the face after blowing out the candle. He then came riding back to tell me what had just taken place.

Through his laughter, he explained that he blew the candle out with an airzooka, a tube six inches in diameter and twelve inches long. It had a piece of rubber or plastic attached with bungee cords. He grabbed the knob attached to the bungee, pulled back about eight inches, aimed and let go before getting hot wax on my hand and messing up my hair.

From what I estimated afterward, it shot that bullet of air over thirty feet.

2 Chronicles 26:15 And he made in Jerusalem engines, invented by cunning men, to be on the towers and upon the bulwarks, to shoot arrows and great stones withal. And his name spread far abroad; for he was marvelously helped, till he was strong.

I do not know who invented the airzooka but, it was almost as good as water balloons and, unlike the weapons in the verse above, did no damage. If I had sight, I could invent dozens of games using that device.

138
SHE IS NOT THERE
MAY OF 2007

I love children of all ages. At each stage I have considered my children and thought that the present stage was the best. I think that's kind of cool because that means that when they get to be teen agers I will still think being their father is the greatest.

Though I do love new born babies, infants and toddlers, it was more beneficial to me when they were able to articulate their needs or desires. One of the less embarrassing things that happens to me happens when my wife is not present.

Many times we have been in a restaurant or other public place and I will begin to have a conversation with Jovanna. Rather, I will have a conversation with her chair until someone comes over and tells me that she is not there.

There have been times that I have talked to her chair for a minute, a minute and a half and even two minutes before someone has come over to let me know that my wife is not there. Now thankfully, my children are aware of the fact that my wife will get up from her chair and wander off somewhere.

If I begin to correspond with the furniture that had previously supported her lovely rear end, one of my children will interrupt me with, "Daddy, mommy is not there." Sometimes she will remember to tell me when she is departing temporarily but, sometimes she forgets or cannot.

I used to get angry, then I progressed to irritated, then to inconvenienced and finally I am used to it. The only problem is that someday my children will grow up, get married and move out of the home. Then how will I know if I am talking to my wife or her empty chair?

Philippians 4:14 Notwithstanding ye have well done, that ye did communicate with my affliction.

My children did very well in communicating my wife's absence.

139
WHAT IS THAT STICK ANYWAY?
SEPTEMBER OF 2009

I had been working for the Home Depot now for two years and three months. During that time, many associates came and went. As the new ones worked around me, they quickly got to know what I could do and what little I could not do. They got to know my patterns and usually knew when I was lost in the aisles.

They also knew how to get out of my way quickly. As you can imagine, most of our customers, especially the contractors, come to the store frequently. Those that come in weekly came to know me as well. They too learned to get out of my way.

I do not say this because I am rude, only because I walk as quickly as most sighted associates through the store. As the customers got used to me, they would stop me and ask for help either with their project or, more often to tell them where something was in the store.

It is such a wonderful feeling to be able to help the customers. It is equally wonderful to have people ask me where things are though they know I cannot see. Sometimes a customer will stop me to ask something and, when they finally realize what the white stick is in my hand, they start to back off.

I can usually gain their confidence and end up helping them as well. Of course, there are some that insist that I cannot help them and even some that sneak away not saying another word. Then there are those who do not get it. That is what this story is about.

I was walking from my office to the break room for lunch. I made it half way there when I came upon a traffic jam. I waited for the customers to scatter around me in their desired directions. I thought everything was clear so I began to walk the other half of the distance.

Two steps into the second half of my journey the tip of my cane hit the shoe of a man. you would be surprised how much information you can gather from the tap of a cane. I knew it was a shoe because of the sound and feel and I knew it was a man because he grunted when my cane hit his footwear.

I apologized, continued walking and arrived at the break room door with no further interruptions. I clocked out, had my lunch which took only half an hour, clocked back in and walked back to the door again. When I got there, one of our cashiers was there and asked me if I wanted her to walk me back to my office.

I said "yes, thank you" and she began to giggle. I asked her what was so funny and she asked me if I remembered hitting a man in the foot with my cane. I responded in the affirmative and she told me that he was mad because I had hit him and had not apologized.

I told her that I had and she said she knew that because she had been there and heard me say I was sorry. She said the man's question was, "What the hell is wrong with him? He hit me with that stick and did not even say he was sorry."

She said she then pointed to my cane and said to the man, "The reason he has that white stick is because he is blind." She said the man's eyes got very big and he sheepishly shrunk away.

Proverbs 3:30 Strive not with a man without cause, if he have done thee no harm.

Though it was an accident and though I did apologize, since he did not hear me or understand that I was blind, I wanted to find him, shake his hand and apologize to his face. I asked the girl to let me know if she saw him on the way back but, of course, she did not.

I did not want to strive with the man nor did I wish to make him feel bad. However, it would have been nice to apologize to his face and not as I was walking away from him. Though he was angry and expressed that anger to my co-worker, he did me no harm.

I have, however, been a little louder with my apologies when tapping people with my cane or bumping them. That way, if they do not understand what my white stick is for, maybe they will feel better having received my apology.

140
PAY ATTENTION, I AM BLIND!
November 23, 2010

You know how sometimes people just do not pay attention? Sometimes they do not hear you, sometimes they do not see you and, sometimes they do not do either. This was one of the times that the person did not do either.

It was time for me to take a break so, I put the phones overhead. Breaks are only supposed to last 15 minutes. Sometimes however, because so many people stop you in the isles, it can be thirty or forty minutes before you get back to your desk. We are told that customers come first and though I cannot make eye contact, I am pleased that so many of them stop me to ask questions.

For those that do not know what "overhead" means, it is when the phones ring on the overhead speakers and any of the 60 or 70 associates in the store at that time can answer the call. Everyone hates to hear the calls going overhead, especially the managers. Conversely, everyone loves to see me going back to my office because it means that the phones will soon not be their responsibility.

Most stores play the following game. Place everything in the same place for two or three years and, once most people know where the product is, switch the entire store around. The Home Depot is no exception. I had been working there for over three years when they decided to change some of the shelving units around, move others and even remove some others.

Naturally, they had to remove one of the shelves I used to get from my office to the break room. I figured out another route which, though less of a straight shot, got me where I needed to go. I used to go up isle three to the end, make a right and walk directly to the break room. Now, I have to go one third of the way up isle three, make a right, walk to isle two, make a left, go to the end of that isle, walk three steps into the main isle, make a right and go to the break room.

I admit, it is not longer but, if I am not walking straight, if I run into someone's basket or if I have to skirt product that has been off loaded in the middle isle, I can end up temporarily misplaced. That is the phrase my mother used to use for lost because, she never got lost.

Well, I was taking the new route when, upon turning left into isle two, I walked into a woman's basket. How do I know it was a woman's basket? Because the woman driving it let out an exclamation before driving around me. I began to walk down the aisle when I heard another woman calling me.

I figured she was going to ask me where something was. I would be able to give her an isle or at least a department and I would be on my way. I am sure you know that is not what happened. Instead, she asked, "Do you have any more of these?" So I asked her what the item was. You guessed it, she said, "These," as she pointed to something.

You have to know that, since I am allergic to all animals with fur or feathers, I do not have a seeing eye dog. When they train the first seeing eye Komodo dragons, I would love to get one but probably will not be able to afford one. So, I was using my white cane. I held it in front of me and said, "You will have to tell me the name of the product since I am blind."

She responded with, "Well, my eyes are bad too. If I give you the product number, can you help me look for another one?" I said, "Just a minute ma'am and I will get someone on the radio to come over and help you." She said, "You are already here, why can't you help me?"

I began to explain as one of my co-workers called out my name from half way down the aisle. When he got a few feet away, he asked how he could help. I told him that the lady was looking for a product and could not find any more. He said he would see if we had any left.

I bid the woman a good day. When I was a few feet away, she turned in my direction as she was saying, "I don't know why, oh," and that is as far as she got. I think she finally saw my cane and the fact that I was using it by hitting it against the metal shelf bottom.

She turned back to my fellow associate and said, "I didn't realize that he was blind." I was so glad that she had turned away from me because I started to laugh and would not have wanted to embarrass her.

Ecclesiastes 11:4 He that observeth the wind shall not sow; and he that regardeth the clouds shall not reap.

In other words, pay attention! If you want to throw your seed in the air to cover the ground but the wind is blowing, you will lose most of your seed. If you are ready to harvest but do not heed the clouds that will bring rain, you will lose your crop to mold, mildew and have a hard time to boot.

141
THE BLIND LEADING THE BLIND 3
JANUARY 27, 2011

Okay, I am very familiar with the phrase and know where it comes from, *Matthew 15:14 Let them alone: they be blind leaders of the blind. And if the blind lead the blind, both shall fall into the ditch* as well as *Luke 6:39 And he spake a parable unto them, Can the blind lead the blind? shall they not both fall into the ditch?*

So your question is, "Why did you have a blind mobility instructor?" I am sure you can figure out from the phrase what a mobility instructor is but, just in case you cannot, I will explain. Blind or visually impaired people need to be able to get from one place to another.

In many cases, family and friends can help. However, in some cases, because of the danger, difficulty or their unavailability, a trained instructor is best. This was one of those cases. I have been, at this point, working for the Home Depot for almost four years now.

My wife would drive me to and from work. Now that my daughter has her license, she sometimes takes me. When neither of them is available, co-workers will take me. I tried on my own a few times to walk home but, twice was stopped by someone who gave me a lift.

The other time, I got lost. Though I made it home before my family, which means they did not have the chance to worry, they were not very happy with me. That is when I decided to contact the New Mexico Commission for the Blind.

They arranged to have their instructor to be driven from Albuquerque to Santa Fe and spend a few hours with me figuring out the best route. The distance from my home to work is 1.5 miles from door to door.

We started from my home, walked to the main road a quarter of a mile away and walked the mile to the street my work is on. The trip, when I walk it with my wife or children, takes twenty-five to thirty minutes. This trip took us one hour and five minutes.

It took more than twice as long because the instructor had to point out landmarks, grade changes, poles and other obstacles. We decided to take a different route back to my home because most of the time we were only a foot or two from traffic.

The other concern is that most of the curbs have such a long-rounded corner it is hard to decide if you are walking straight to the other curb or possibly into traffic. Though the second trip was certainly les hazardous for the afore mentioned reasons, it had its problems as well.

Rather than a hundred cars passing you a minute, there were maybe two every sixty seconds. But there were a few blocks that were not paved, very rough and filled with their own obstacles. We arrived at a t and decided to go back to the main road.

We then walked one block to my street and turned onto it. My instructor was about 10 steps in front of me and I was about five minutes from home. This trip was taking about ten minutes longer than the first leg. The instructor was telling me that he was now on a driveway when, a 15-foot-long gate which was not secured swung open and hit me in the head.

It was extremely windy that day, with gusts of forty miles an hour, and, of course, neither one of us could see what was happening. I ended up with a bruise on my spinal cord, a concussion and PTSD. It took months for me to heal and, I was out of work while recovering.

Before you chastise me for two things, the first being that this is not a very funny story and that I should have known better than to have a blind person lead me, let me tell you some things. The instructor has been doing this for more than 20 years and nothing like this has happened before.

He did a great job of showing me the many dangers along both ways. The parable Jesus gave talked about the second blind man falling into a ditch. There were no ditches for me to fall into. That settles one question. As for the second, it certainly was funny in the strange sense.

A six feet high and fifteen feet long chain link gate has an awful lot of space that could have hit me and I would not have gotten seriously hurt. Also, it could have hit me in the shoulder, hand or arm and again, there would have been mild to no damage.

No, it had to be the very end of the gate which is only two and a half inches wide and is the fastest traveling part. I found out from the weather bureau that the wind was blowing at twenty-six MPH. Now, what about funny in the ha ha sense?

Well, you have to admit, there are many things that are initially painful but, later on you can laugh at. What about the Darwin awards? My children read them to me every year and, though most of the people die because of their foolishness, I laugh heartily.

Also, though this is not humorous, Romans 8:28 says, *And we know that all things work together for good to them that love God, to them who are the called according to his purpose.* I am called according to His purpose and, after all, if you cannot laugh at your own mistakes, you will probably end up with ulcers or high blood pressure from being too serious.

142
ARE THESE YOUR BULLETS, SIR?
April 30, 2011

Back in 1980, I had plans to attend college in order to get a degree in Special Education. During a tour of Bergen Community College, I met Robin Eckleberry.

After dating for a few months, we decided to marry. Unfortunately, we did not wait until marriage to become sexually active. As a result, Robin became pregnant. She did not tell me and I did not find out until my son, Anthony Frank Thomas Eckleberry was one-and-a-half-years-old.

I paid child support until he graduated high school. Every time I moved, I would send a letter to Anthony to make sure he knew where to reach me. I sent letters for his birthdays and at other times, and I sent a Christmas letter to him every year for over 15 years.

Because Robin had physical and emotional difficulties, Anthony was raised by his grandparents and his mother was more like an aunt or older sister to him.

Though I begged, pleaded and reasoned with his grandmother, Agnus, she would not allow me to have any contact with my son.

I never gave up hoping that Anthony would somehow seek me out. However, the hope began to wane after 2007. In early 1993, I had asked Agnus if she and his grandfather, Richard, had received all the letters I had sent to them. She said they did. I asked if they gave them to Anthony and she responded in the negative. She and Richard had decided that it was a good idea to pick my pockets and an equally good idea to disallow me any contact with my son.

Around January 17, 2013, Jovanna received a message on her Facebook page from someone named Jovi. Jovi was wondering if Jovanna's husband was the Raymond Whitehead that was born in New York City, lived in New Jersey a lot and had dated a Robin Eckleberry?

When my lovely bride responded in the affirmative, Jovi gave Jovanna their contact information. It turns out that Jovi is Anthony's wife and her name is Giovanna, the Italian version of Jovanna. Giovanna was called Jovanna during her formative years and now goes by Jovi. She does, however, allow me to call her by her given name.

I tried to call their home number but no one picked up and they had not engaged their answering machine. That evening, which also happened to be the day before Anthony's 32nd birthday, he and I spoke for the first time. After a few weeks, the four of us made arrangements to go out to New Jersey to meet my son, his wife and their almost six-year-old daughter, Alyssa.

I reserved two cottages in Holmes, Pennsylvania and we planned to be together for five days. The visit was wonderful. However, due to travel, lack of sleep and an imperfect balance of medications, I did not sleep well.

Pain, disorientation and rising at four a.m. contributed to ten 38-caliber hollow head bullets ending up in my carry-on. We were asked to step aside during the metal detection process at the airport. Initially we were told it would be about 30 minutes, we would sign some paperwork, they would confiscate the ammo and we would be on our way.

Without my permission or knowledge, they retrieved my checked bag, tore it in the process, spilled shampoo all over my jacket, removed my revolver and knives. You might ask why I had over $2,000 worth of knives in my checked bag. They were a sheath knife I have worn since 1971, a Leatherman, pocket and Swiss army knives that belonged to my son, my daughter and myself.

One of the Newark police officers must have thought that a completely blind man with no gun and only ten bullets was going to bring down the aircraft so, they questioned me, arrested me, cuffed me, questioned me some more and forced my wife to go back to New Mexico, leaving me by myself.

One of the questions was why I had so many knives. I responded by asking if I was still in the United States of America? Because in the

USA, you are innocent until proven guilty and do not have to explain the ownership of property that is legal. The cop said that I had an attitude and tried to get me to confess that I brought the bullets in my carryon luggage purposefully.

Jovanna had gotten a sandwich for me so, she put it in one of my bags for me to eat later. They made her take my other carry-on bag which had all my medication. The officer would not allow me to use my cane and would not allow me to be cuffed with my hands in front of me. As a result, my spinal injury was made worse and they set my recovery back several months.

The officer ran me into a door frame, chair, desk, another door frame, tripped me over a threshold and forgot to let me know about the steps.

All the while I was reminding him that I am blind. All he kept saying was, "Shut up and keep walking."

He placed me in a car, still with my hands cuffed behind me, and drove 20 minutes to the jail. Upon getting out of the car, they finally read my rights to me and I declined to speak to them without an attorney present.

They took me to a cell, finally took the cuffs off, took everything out of my pockets, took my sneakers and would not even let me have them without the laces. They kept me in that cell for two hours, did not allow me to have anything to eat and would not allow me to rest.

Remember the sandwich Jovanna packed for me? They either ate it themselves or threw it out. When I asked them for some food, they said they would have to order something for me. I told them about the sandwich and they ignored my request. They asked me what I would like, I told them a large salad would be fine and they never brought it.

Every time I would lay on the plastic covered two-inch-thick mattress which had no sheet or blanket, they would wait five minutes and then bang on the cell door. Then they would ask me something they had already asked me several times. Meanwhile, they were playing with my knives, cracking jokes and calling me Rambo.

After making me pay ten percent of the $15,000 bail and a $30 filing fee, they finally let me go. I was told that I had to return on June 7th. During processing they took my name, address and other identifying information. They also electronically fingerprinted me.

About three days before leaving for New Jersey, Jovanna started getting a rash on her stomach, right side and back. We thought it was a reaction to an allergy medication.

We left for New Jersey on June 4. By the next day, Jovanna was in so much pain and the rash had spread so much that we went to an urgent care facility. They charged us $170 to have the doctor look at my wife for two seconds and then spend five minutes telling us that, though the medicine he was going to prescribe would probably not work, he insisted she take it.

The drug store charged us $272 for 21 pills which did not help at all. Thank the LORD for ibuprofen because that is the only thing that helped Jovanna's pain. Instead of enjoying the extra time we planned to spend in New Jersey with family and the visits to friends in New York, we ended up staying in our room 95 percent of the time.

We showed up for court in the pouring rain. We had to go through metal detectors. We go into the court house and tell them we are there. After sitting in the hall for an hour, they tell us to go across the street to the other building and file the paperwork that will allow me to serve any jail or community service time in New Mexico.

We go through the rain, into the building, through the detectors, to the office for the paperwork only to be told that New Jersey does not have a treaty with New Mexico. I have to ask the question again, am I still in the United States of America? So, if I end up serving time or service, I will have to do it in New Jersey. Pardon me but, how stupid is that?

We go back through the rain, through the detector, back to the hall, let them know we are there and wait another half hour before they call me. When they do, I sign a paper after confirming that I am still me and am told we have to go across the street again to be processed.

We go through the rain and detector again and to the basement of the other building. I am asked to confirm my identity and address. I am fingerprinted again. I tell them that I did all this the day I was arrested. I get no response. I ask, "Do you not communicate with the other police department?" I am told, "No."

I am given a piece of paper and told to go across the street to the court to see the judge. We go through the still pouring rain, through the detector, into the elevator and to the judge's chamber.

She confirms that I am me and tells me that I have to come back in two weeks. I ask if I may ask a question. My request is granted. I ask if she can push the date out further because I live in New Mexico and airline tickets will cost too much to book in two weeks or less. She grants my petition and sets my return date for July 31. The entire exchange takes two minutes and 30 seconds and I am told that they could not do any of this without me present.

John 16:33 These things I have spoken unto you, that in me ye might have peace. In the world ye shall have tribulation: but be of good cheer; I have overcome the world.

The above verse reminds us that Jesus won. Unfortunately, God's adversary is acting like a spoiled brat and causing as much trouble as he can before he gets banished for one thousand years and then forever. Though horrible things will happen to those of us who belong to Christ, we should not lose our resolve to follow Him.

143
FLIPPED OUT
JUNE OF 2011

In 1973, My mother took me and my sisters Donna and Lisa to a place in Long Beach Island for vacation. We laid on the beach getting tanned, swam a lot, knocked down walls of sand to find lost treasures and flew kites. There was an ice cream place that would rival any you can find today and we went there every night. The only other thing we liked doing was at the trampoline farm.

The place had fifteen rectangular trampolines that were ground level. You paid for fifteen or thirty minutes at a time. My sisters and I were gymnasts and drew a crowd when we jumped. Because we had so much attention focused on us with our twists, flips and other moves, the owner allowed us to jump for free after our time ran out because we were bringing in business for him.

When others were around, he asked us to keep the tricks to a minimum. However, when no one was watching, he allowed us to jump between trampolines. As one of my sisters was doing a flip from one tramp to another, she landed with her head between the springs. She did not get hurt and only lost a few hairs that got stuck in the springs. Years after that happened, I reminded the sister it happened to and she insisted that the other one was to blame.

Unfortunately, the other sister lost a lot of her childhood memories. In either case, that was the only mishap we had in the few years we went to that place. The owner always remembered us and gave us the same deal each time. For me, year after year, it became more difficult to do the tricks as my vision was diminishing rapidly. I do not know if it was lack of fear or stupidity but, I kept doing the tricks anyway and never got hurt.

Decades later, June of 2006, my darling wife purchased a fifteen feet diameter trampoline for my birthday. It took three months to land my first forward flip. Since I was completely blind at the time, I have to admit, it was scary. I was then forty-six-years-old and had not performed a flip, accept in the water, since 1978. During the last week in August of 2011, I took my family to Aruba.

My mother and step-father had a time share there for over thirty years. We decided to go during the time that they would be there so they could show us all the best places to go and best restaurants to eat in. One of the places they took us to was a place where you could rent jet skis. Since my step-father did not like anything too dangerous, he stayed on the beach with me. That is, until my son Joshua was done with his ride.

I had asked him to come for me when he was finished so we could rent a double seater together. We went out on the ocean and got to fifty-two miles an hour. That gave me an idea. He slowed down so I could take the controls for a while. After driving for a while, I wanted to put my idea into play so, I handed back the controls. I told him to slowly gain speed until he maxed out.

I informed him that I was going to stand on the back of the seat and, once he reached maximum velocity, I would do a back flip off the back. He got up to about forty-two miles per hour when he yelled back to me that we were about to hit a wave made by a speed boat that had cut in front of us. I knew that I would not be able to stay on the seat when we hit the water speed bump so, I decided to do the flip as we hit the wave.

When I had given the instructions to my son earlier, I told him that the most important thing to remember was, "come back and get me!" As he came back toward me, he jumped off the jet ski into my arms and yelled, "Dad, that was so cool!"

Matthew 8:27 But the men marvelled, saying, What manner of man is this, that even the winds and the sea obey him!

Neither the wind nor the sea obeyed me that day. However, since GOD is in control of every atom of every molecule of everything we can see, hear, taste, touch or smell, He was in charge of the boat that caused the wave that made me jump earlier. That turned out to be a very good thing as, the next few days were very difficult with my brand-new brain injury. I cannot imagine how much more pain and confusion I would have been in if we had gotten the machine up to its sixty MPH stated maximum.

144
SURPRISE!
February of 2023

In January of 2023, Jovanna informed me that an artist she had been following was going to have an all day seminar, workshop, training thing. The end of the previous sentence tells you how much I know about art. Of course, I did study it in high school and college.

Also, the Metropolitan Museum of Art in New York City had a wonderful program. You could walk around the Museum with a guide and, if you were wearing gloves, which they provided, You could feel anything but the paintings. They also had a clean room where they would bring things that were behind glass for you to examine.

I actually got to hold a two-thousand-year-old Roman helmet, sword and chain mail. But, back to what my wife loves, painting. We decided to go to South Carolina for a week to have a mini vacation and for her to enjoy the art thing.

Her good friend Eneida and she began to tease me the week before the trip about what I would do for the day she would be gone. They suggested kite flying and fly fishing. Little did I know that there was a reason for the teasing other than pulling my chain. As you will see, it was supposed to be a distraction.

It worked! We arrived at our Air B and B. Just a side note, why are they called B and B when there is no breakfast and what is the air about? Anyway, back to the story. It was dinner time so, we walked around the neighborhood and found a restaurant. We had pizza.

After our meal, we found a mom and pop store and purchased a few supplies. We had a wonderful following day walking around Charleston and, when we arrived back at our abode, my wife helped me prepare for the lonely next day. Well, the next morning, just before leaving for her artistic day, there was a knock on the door.

Jovanna went to answer it though I offered. When she opened it, I thought I would hear a conversation. However, what I heard were two sets of footsteps heading my way. Someone stopped in front of me and said hello. My brain said, "That sounds just like my baby sister, Terri."

When I did not respond, and after a little giggle from the intruder, I heard, "Hello Ray Ray." Another side story. When I was ten-years-old, a song came on the radio which my father and step-mother decided they wanted to dance to. So, Ray Senior picked up Margie and Mary took Dan and they began to dance.

I had no one to shake it with and, my disappointment must have shown on my face because, Mary said, "You can have the next one to dance with." Mary was very pregnant with Terri at the time and, I could not wait for, "my dance partner." That is one of the reasons she has always been my special baby sister.

When Margie and Dan were very small, they could not say Raymond so, it came out Ray Ray. When Terri was able to try saying my name, it also came out Ray Ray. However, by that time, I thing she had been pre-programmed to say my name that way. to this day, my sisters still call me Ray Ray but, my brother no longer stutters.

So, when I heard my sister's name for me, I freaked. It was not a stranger standing in front of me but, my baby. Moments later, her husband Micky came in. Since they have a house in Myrtle Beach, I was naïve enough to believe that they had just driven over for the day.

A few more moments and, Rose and her husband Marvelous Marvin came in followed by my brother and his girlfriend Tina. Now I finally got it. My wife had collaborated with my family to come down from Maryland to spend the day with me. So now, I was waiting for my sister Margie and her husband David to walk in.

When they did not, I asked about them. I was told that they would arrive tomorrow and, we could all spend the day together, including my wonderful bride. That was one of the most fantastic surprises I have ever received and yet another reason that I say, "My wife is the most beautiful woman in the world!"

Proverbs 31:10 Who can find a virtuous woman? for her price is far above rubies. 12 She will do him good and not evil all the days of her life.

28 Her children arise up, and call her blessed; her husband also, and he praiseth her. 30 Favour is deceitful, and beauty is vain: but a woman that feareth the LORD, she shall be praised.

Verses ten through thirty-one of Proverbs 31 are all descriptive of yo bonita esposa. I chose the previous four as to not make this story twice as long. I know that I used verse ten before but, since it was the second verse in the story, "The Mayfair", and since this story took place forty-eight years later and, since there are three verses to buttress this one, I thought I could get away with using it again.

From the age of fourteen until I reached thirty-one, I spent a lot of energy trying to find a good wife. I failed miserably. It was not until I gave my life to Jesus and allowed Him to find a wife for me that I had success. As of the writing of this story, we have shared thirty-two years of marriage.

Verse 12 states that one of the virtues of a good wife is that, "she will do him good." That is certainly true for me. Verse 28 lets us know that, if she is this kind of wife and mother, her children and husband will let her and others know about it.

Verse 30 lets us know where her focus should be and, as I have said many times, "I am so glad to know that my wife loves Jesus more than she loves me." If she loved me more, I would screw things up as Adam did with Eve.

This last story is by a friend of mine. When I told her that I was writing a book about my experiences, she told me this story. I asked if I could put it in my book and she agreed. I hope you enjoy it as much as I did.

145
DADDY'S LITTLE GARDENER
BY
TONIA VALLETTA TRAPP

My family moved to Manassas, Virginia when I was five years old and I spent much of my childhood there. My parents have owned two different houses in Virginia and are about to buy their third as of the time I was writing this. My favorite house was the first one.

The first house we lived in was the best for several reasons. One of my favorite things about that house was that, to my child's mind, the front and back yards were gigantic. Also, there were woods behind our back yard, just beyond our fence, which seemed to stretch on and on indefinitely.

What fun I had playing outside and dreaming of what lay beyond the fences and gates at the perimeters. I remember one occasion in particular when I was playing in the front yard. I stumbled upon a peculiar thing I had never seen before. I was perhaps seven or eight years old at the time.

I was traipsing about on the side of our very long driveway where the strip of grass running the length of the driveway was much narrower than on the other side. On that side of our property was a wooden fence with horizontal planks spaced a few inches apart, and on the other side of the fence was a drop off of at least five feet at its highest point. Our house overlooked the yard of our next door neighbor. I liked to walk alongside the fence and discover what interesting plants might be growing there.

On this particular occasion, I encountered a new kind of weed. It consisted of several long stalks growing straight up from the ground, with no flowers on the tops. Not only were they flowerless but, the ugly stalks had nasty little thorns all over them which were sharp. I did not like the looks of this at all. I thought to myself, in my seven-year-old mind, "It is bad for these thorny, ugly weedy things to be growing in my yard. Why would anyone want to have things like this around? Something must be done about this."

So, I made up my mind to do what needed to be done: I would destroy the nasty weeds. I went about the task methodically and without mercy, removing the thorns from the stalks, pulling the stalks from the ground, breaking them into smaller pieces, and putting all the refuse into a neat little pile. I remember being proud of myself for doing a good thing, for helping my daddy keep such ugly things out of his pretty yard.

Daddy loved working in the yard and adding things to it to make it look good. He often enlisted the help of his children in the yard projects, my younger brother and me at first, and later my sister.

Finally, my task was complete, and there lay before me a neat little heap of debris from the weeds I had so thoroughly destroyed. Now, I don't remember exactly what happened next. Either I went looking for my daddy to tell him about what I had done, or Daddy came and found me. Either way, the conversation that ensued went something like this.

After looking at the pile of refuse I had made he asked, "Tonia, what is this here? What have you been doing?" So I explained to him about the thorny weeds I had found with no flowers on them. I told him that I had pulled them up and had gotten rid of them because I thought they were not supposed to be in our yard.

Daddy then quietly, and with kindness in his voice, explained to me that the weeds I had pulled up were something called roses, and that Daddy himself had planted these in our yard. He told me that, given time to grow, the thorny stalks would have blossomed with beautiful flowers, and that was why Daddy had planted them.

I remember feeling sad and disappointed in myself because I had destroyed something Daddy had wanted to grow. I had done what I thought was best, but it turned out that I had made a terrible mistake. But I got over it, as one must do when such things happen. I had many more outdoor adventures, less destructive ones I assure you.

What I recall most vividly about my pulling of the roses is the way that my dad reacted when he learned of my mistake. He reacted with kindness and gentleness, sentiments that are not borne of anger, but are borne of forgiveness. I cannot know what thoughts and emotions my dad felt when I told him what I had done. But whatever those were, Daddy forgave me for my mistake.

I wonder how many times my heavenly Father has planted a beautiful flower in the garden of someone's life, only to have an impetuous little child like me summarily pluck up what He has planted because in its early growth it looks like a weed. I know that He has planted His roses in my own garden, beginning as stems of situation with sharp thorns of circumstance. And like the real roses that we buy in dozens, God's roses are beautiful if we have the patience to let them grow and flower.

Patience is something that I wish I possessed in much greater quantity. But in the meantime, while the roses grow, I am so glad that my heavenly Father is a God of forgiveness. Heaven knows that with little children like me helping Him with the gardening, God would have to be abundantly patient and forgiving.

IN CONCLUSION
March of 2024

At the time I finished writing this book, I had experienced the following: Five years of my sixty-four in the hospital three days to three weeks at a time with one stint that lasted exactly one year, thirty-five broken bones, being shot, being hit by twenty-seven automobiles as a pedestrian, the victim of seven car accidents of which I was never the driver. Three motorcycle accidents of which I was at fault twice, overcoming eight years of cancer with no radiation or chemo and enjoying my wife, family and friends despite living with twenty-three medical conditions.

In my introduction, I stated three reasons for this book. If you do not remember the first two, turn back to the beginning and read the introduction again. If you cannot remember the third and most important reason, I will restate it here:

Do you have difficulties in your life? I know that the answer to that question is yes. The answer to your difficulties is Jesus. That is the most important message I hope you walk away with after reading this book. Though I do believe in healing, there is not much of it happening today.

Why? Because, the main reason for the forty-seven recorded miracles of our LORD was to prove who He is. Maybe He will not heal whatever ails you today. However, the miracle He will provide, if you choose to follow Him, is to help you live within your limitations as a productive and joy-filled child of His.

Raymond Joseph Whitehead

www.ingramcontent.com/pod-product-compliance
Lightning Source LLC
Chambersburg PA
CBHW011754220426
43672CB00018B/2952